CAMBRIDGE LIBRARY COLLECTION

Books of enduring scholarly value

Religion

For centuries, scripture and theology were the focus of prodigious amounts of scholarship and publishing, dominated in the English-speaking world by the work of Protestant Christians. Enlightenment philosophy and science, anthropology, ethnology and the colonial experience all brought new perspectives, lively debates and heated controversies to the study of religion and its role in the world, many of which continue to this day. This series explores the editing and interpretation of religious texts, the history of religious ideas and institutions, and not least the encounter between religion and science.

Fragments of Philo Judaeus

The scholar and philosopher Philo Judaeus, born around 25 BCE in Alexandria, blended his knowledge of Jewish law and scripture with his command of Greek philosophy in his influential works, ensuring that he became a subject of intellectual enquiry in his own right. However, James Rendel Harris (1852–1941), a biblical scholar, palaeographer and Fellow of Clare College, Cambridge, thought Philo too 'slenderly prized' in Britain. Harris intended this collection, published in 1886, to bring together surviving fragments of Philo's work. In a detailed introduction, he explains the complicated tasks involved in identifying and classifying these ancient texts, and also points out that this volume is intended to provide a basis for future research on Philo. The fragments are presented in their original Greek, most of them accompanied by a Latin translation. Harris provides notes throughout, and the book continues to offer a valuable resource for biblical and philosophical scholarship.

Fragments of
Philo Judaeus

EDITED BY J. RENDEL HARRIS

CAMBRIDGE
UNIVERSITY PRESS

CAMBRIDGE UNIVERSITY PRESS

Cambridge, New York, Melbourne, Madrid, Cape Town,
Singapore, São Paolo, Delhi, Tokyo, Mexico City

Published in the United States of America by Cambridge University Press, New York

www.cambridge.org
Information on this title: www.cambridge.org/9781108039673

© in this compilation Cambridge University Press 2012

This edition first published 1886
This digitally printed version 2012

ISBN 978-1-108-03967-3 Paperback

FRAGMENTS

OF

PHILO JUDÆUS.

London: C. J. CLAY & SONS,
CAMBRIDGE UNIVERSITY PRESS WAREHOUSE,
AVE MARIA LANE.

Cambridge: DEIGHTON, BELL AND CO.
Leipzig: F. A. BROCKHAUS.

FRAGMENTS

OF

PHILO JUDÆUS

NEWLY EDITED BY

J. RENDEL HARRIS, M.A.

FELLOW OF CLARE COLLEGE, CAMBRIDGE,
PROFESSOR OF BIBLICAL LANGUAGES IN HAVERFORD COLLEGE, PENNSYLVANIA.

WITH TWO FACSIMILES.

EDITED FOR THE SYNDICS OF THE UNIVERSITY PRESS.

CAMBRIDGE:
AT THE UNIVERSITY PRESS.
1886

CAMBRIDGE:

PRINTED BY C. J. CLAY, M.A. AND SONS,

AT THE UNIVERSITY PRESS.

PREFACE.

THIS little book may perhaps be described most succinctly as scaffolding for the next edition of Philo. It has often been a regret to me that, especially in England, this great writer has been so slenderly prized, and I well remember the indignation with which I first read the sentences in Liddon's *Bampton Lectures* in which he is described as "only a thoughtful, not insincere, but half-heathenized believer in the Revelation of Sinai, groping in a twilight which he has made darker by his Hellenic tastes." Nor was the feeling diminished when one found that in depreciating so great a writer the theologian too often had as companions the philosopher and the historian, and that no one has in recent times arisen to illustrate towards the indifferent or superficial student the Philonean maxim that the wise man is the ransom of the foolish. Perhaps we may yet find that we have carried bricks for some such master-builder.

With regard to the book itself, it will be noticed that it is published at the expense of the Syndics of the University Press and with the excellence of mechanical workmanship which characterises that famous establishment. But for the assistance thus rendered it is doubtful whether the book would ever have seen the light.

Its dimensions have been carefully limited by avoiding the useless insertion of various readings in the texts employed which promised faithfully to lead nowhere, and by the removal of some matters which would have been interesting if they could have been compressed within a reasonable space. For example, my first intention was to combine the fragments of Josephus with my Philo Collection, and I had also done some work upon the problem (not wholly an unimportant one) of the genealogical relations of the various MSS. and Collections of Parallels. Upon second thoughts all of this has been removed.

Finally, whatever of excellence or accuracy is to be found in the following pages is largely due to the co-operative criticism of friends whose sympathy and encouragement I highly prize, though I have been ashamed to carve their scholarly names upon so slight a sapling.

J. R. H.

CLARE COLLEGE,
June, 1886.

INTRODUCTION.

ON COD. REG. 923 OF THE NATIONAL LIBRARY AT PARIS.

THE manuscript described in the following pages drew my attention *The MS. is a volume of "Parallels"* in the summer of 1884 when I was occupied in the examination of some of the treasures of the National Library at Paris. It was exposed to view in one of the upright cases (armoire XVII.) of the Galerie Mazarine, adjacent, if I remember rightly, to the celebrated Codex Ephraemi Syri, the Codex Claromontanus of S. Paul and the Coislin Octateuch. The ticket attached to it intimated that it was a volume of "Sentences des Saints Pères." As the book was in uncial Greek characters of the ninth century, and adorned with interesting marginal pictures, and was apparently unpublished, I determined to examine it carefully. The first *somewhat like the Codex Rupefucaldi to which Tischendorf and Lequien refer,* impression upon my mind was that this was the Codex Rupefucaldinus of the Parallela Sacra of S. John Damascene, a manuscript of which Tischendorf had given a notice in the preface to the eighth edition of his New Testament, citing it under the form Dam. par. cod. If this were the case the manuscript would have been interesting not only on account of its rich collection of biblical and patristic excerpts, but as being of such antiquity that, as Scrivener remarks in his *Introduction to the Criticism of the New Testament* (p. 420), it could be referred to the same century as the father whose work it contains. An examination however of the text of S. John Damascene's Parallels, as edited by Lequien, shewed that this supposition could not be verified[1]. Lequien's text (which has been reproduced in Migne *Patrologia Græca* XCV. XCVI.) is based upon a MS. in the Vatican Library, to which he has appended a few readings and foot-notes from the Codex Rupefucaldinus. Finding the diversity between these two texts to be remarkable, he reprinted a portion of the additional Patristic matter of the latter MS. under the title Parallela Rupefucaldina. What was interesting *and even more like*

---

[1] It will be shewn later on that it must, however, be the MS. of which Tischendorf speaks, though he has confounded it with the Cod. Rup. which is a totally different book. Scrivener's note must also be corrected, as far as relates to that Codex.

the MS. which formed the basis of Lequien's text.

Such MSS. often contain valuable extracts from lost or important texts,

and there are many of them yet unexamined.

in the examination of Lequien's text by the side of the Paris manuscript was the obvious diversity of the latter from either of Lequien's copies. It approached however more nearly to the Vatican copy than to the other.

I determined therefore to read the MS. through with the printed text, and especially to note any additional matter that might be found in it. Some of the results of this collation, especially as regards the text of Philo, are contained in the following pages. An exact edition of S. John Damascene's Parallels is however not a matter of such request as to make it worth while to print variants collected from nearly 800 pages of uncial Greek; still it seems to me that although the general interest in Patristic texts is but slight in the present century, the extracts which the volume contains of sub-apostolic writings and a few of the biblical variants might be acceptable to those who are engaged in editing the Septuagint, the New Testament, and the Ante-Nicene Fathers.

It is proper to state that Lequien seems to have been perfectly aware of the existence of other copies, since he notes in the preface "In Bibliotheca etiam Medicea perinde exstat Parallelorum codex ordine alphabetico digestus, *Vaticano non in totum absimilis;* sed in quo Patrum sententiæ media parte truncatæ, non integræ nec ad longum referuntur. Adduntur insuper hinc inde e scriptoribus profanis symbolæ, contra quam sibi Ioannes Damascenus proposuerat[1]." This MS. is fully described and the most important conclusions deduced from it with regard to early gnomologies in Curt Wachsmuth's *Griechische Florilegien*.

Lequien also notes that readings from a MS. of Parallels preserved at Venice were communicated to him by Banduri, and that this MS. was older than his own Vatican copy. This MS. must be the one described by Montfaucon in his Italian Diary (p. 36 Eng. Trans.). "We spent the afternoon in viewing the Grecian Archbishop of Philadelphia's MSS. I took notice among his MSS. . . . a vellum book of an excellent character and the eleventh century, St John Damascene's Parallels and other pieces of his." I suppose this copy now to be in the Nanian Library. And there must be many copies of this collection of quotations in the different European libraries, which would repay an examination[2].

---

[1] Migne 95, col. 1037.

[2] E.g. in M. Omont's Catalogue des Manuscrits Grecs de Bruxelles, p. 15:

"32 (11836) S. Joannis Damasceni Sententiæ . . . . XIIIᵉ siècle Bombycin, 171 feuillets, 165 sur 112 millim. . . . (Jacobins de St Honoré, de Paris)."

Several other copies will be found described in the following pages.

In the same connexion it should be added that in Cod. Coislin. 20 there are at the beginning two leaves written in sloping uncials of the ninth century which evidently belonged at one time to a Volume of Parallels. My attention was drawn to these by Dr Hort. They seem to have been first noticed by Dr Burgon, who however described them wrongly as fragments of the Septuagint. (His note is 'Bound up with it (Coislin. 20) are some leaves of the LXX. of about the VIIIth century.' *Last Twelve Verses* p. 229 n.)

The question arises here as to what has become of the Codex Rupefucaldinus to which Tischendorf and Lequien refer[1]. Its name indicates that it once belonged to Cardinal Rochefoucauld; and Lequien affirms that the copy was presented by him to the library of the Jesuit fathers in Paris. It must then have disappeared at the dispersion of that library, which brought many MSS. into English collections; after some labour and enquiry, in which I had the invaluable assistance of the ever-courteous M. Omont of the National Library, I received information that the book had passed into Sir Thomas Phillips' library at Middle-Hill and was now to be found in the possession of his son-in-law, Mr Fenwick of Cheltenham. The number of this MS. in the Phillips Collection is 1450 = Meerman 94; a charge of one pound per diem is made to all persons who collate in this library, and this renders prolonged or careful study impossible for the majority of scholars; one can hardly say that it makes the books accessible to any.

The Codex Rupefucaldinus is now at Cheltenham.

This identification being made, we must remove the confusion which arises from a statement made by Pitra to the effect that the MS. was to be found at Oxford. For this MS. is the Codex Claromontanus from which Halloix edited a long passage from Justin *De Resurrectione* in his life of Justin, and a collection of fragments of Irenæus in his life of that father. Lequien expressly states, p. 730, that Halloix edited these fragments "quæ cum ejusdem S. Martyris operibus edita non sunt, sed seorsim a Petro Halloixio, cum hæc accepisset ex *eodem Codice Rupefucaldino*[2]": while Grabe, on the other hand, *Spicilegium* II. 167, refers the passages to Cod. Claromontanus. It is, therefore, unfortunate that Pitra should speak in *Anal. Sac.* ii. XXI. as if the Codex were at Oxford "Visus est (sc. Cod. Coislin. 276)

---

[1] There seems to be a general opinion that it is lost: for example, in a recent number of the *Theologische Literaturzeitung* (Oct. 31, 1885, col. 534), Neumann remarks (reviewing Zahn's *Supplementum Clementinum*) "Den wich-tigsten cod. Rupef. der *Sacr. Parall.* auf dessen Bedeutung de Lagarde mehrfach hingewiesen, hat leider auch Zahn nicht wieder aufspüren können."

[2] Cf. Halloix. *Script. Eccles. Or.* ii. 299.

eadem continere quam Damasceni Parallela ex codice Claromontano, *nunc* Oxoniensi, pervulgata."

The following is the description given of Cod. Rupef. in the Catal. Cod. MSS. Coll. Claromontani:

"No. 150. Codex membranaceus in fol. majori constans foliis 300, XI circiter seculo exaratus quo continentur S. Ioannis Damasceni Eclogæ seu Parallelorum excerptiones cum earum indice quæ non occurrunt in editione Michaelis le Quien (circa medium hujus codicis octo insunt folia chartacea in quibus manu recenti supplentur quæ in eo desiderabantur)."

The identity of the Claromontane and Rupefucald Parallels is suspected by Lightfoot in his recent edition of the Ignatian Letters, vol. I. p. 210 "Claromontanus, a MS. which seems closely to resemble the Rupefucaldinus."

So much having been premised with regard to the different copies, a few remarks must be made with regard to the general subject of Parallels.

These "Parallels" are commonly referred to John of Damascus but with little show of reason.

We may I think dismiss the idea from our minds that these collections are due solely to S. John Damascene.

If no other evidence were forthcoming, the extreme unlikeliness of our finding so many early copies (some of which themselves shew traces of being taken from earlier manuscripts) of the work of an eighth century father, would be noted at once. But there is other testimony: Lequien draws attention to the Scholia in the text of the Codex Rup., which fix the date of digestion of the book in the reign of the Emperor Heraclius[1]. There is one for instance (ed. Leq. p. 749) which comments on a passage in Ezekiel in the following manner:

Σχόλιον· τοῦτο καὶ ἡμῖν ἐκ τῶν ἡμετέρων συμβέβηκεν ἁμαρτημάτων. Καύχημα γὰρ καὶ δόξασμα παντὸς γένους χριστιανῶν ὁ σωτήριος σταυρὸς καὶ ἡ ζωηφόρος ἀνάστασις ὑπῆρχον ἅτινα διὰ τὸ μεμιαμμένον

Βενετοπράσινον ὄνομα ὃ ἐπεθήκαμεν ἑαυτοῖς καὶ ἐβδελύχθημεν ὑπὸ χριστοῦ τοῦ ἁγιάσαντος ἡμᾶς τῷ θείῳ αὐτοῦ ὀνόματι, εἰς χεῖρας μεμιαμμένων παρεδόθησαν καὶ ἐμιάνθησαν.

The writer is evidently alluding to the carrying off of the Cross of Helena into Persia by Chosroes, and he writes before the time when the sacred symbol had been recovered by the successful wars of Heraclius (that is, more than a century before the time of John of Damascus); reference is

[1] Hilgenfeld seems to assume that the MS. was actually written at this time: "Cod. Rupefucaldinus vel Claromontanus imperante Heraclio I. (610—641) conscriptus." *Ev. sec. Hebræos*, etc. p. 63.

also made to the blue and green factions which were then disturbing the John of Damascus may however have re-arranged an earlier collection. peace and undermining the stability of the empire (Βενετοπράσινος). It is clear, then, that the origin of the Sacra Parallela is to be sought at least as far back as the third decade of the seventh century: and if this be so, the most we can infer from the preface attributed to John Damascene in Codd. Vat. and Rup. is that as far as regards the Scriptural or Patristic matter he rearranged or augmented an earlier collection, and any profane quotations may have been absorbed from existing gnomologies. If we may hazard a conjecture we should say that the original matter was arranged alphabetically under different titles, so as to include all proper subjects in an order proceeding from the creation of man to the day of death; the title of the first series of extracts being

A. περὶ τῆς τοῦ ἀνθρώπου πλάσεως καὶ κατασκευῆς.

and the last being

Ω. περὶ ὥρας καὶ ἡμέρας θανάτου κτέ.

and this must have been altered by John Damascene, something on the principle of Dogberry,

"Write God first: for God forbid but that God should go before such villains"; so that the book begins with the doctrine of the Trinity.

A. περὶ ἀϊδίου θεότητος τῆς ἁγίας καὶ ὁμοουσίου Τριάδος.

The question then arises as to whether any traces of John Damascene are found in our book.

The margins of the book are filled with medallion portraits of persons An acquaintance with John Damascene is found in our Codex. of ecclesiastical manner and habit; these are meant to represent the different writers from whom quotations are made; and M. Bordier in his description of the Ornaments of Greek MSS. in the National Library alludes to the portrait of John Damascene as found in the volume. I have not however been able to verify his statement.

M. Bordier's observation runs as follows:

"Pour Moïse, ayant besoin d'un saint personnage investi du caractère sacerdotal, il peint un homme à barbe noire, portant sur la poitrine une étole blanchée ornée de deux croix rouges: pour un homme qui fut une partie de sa vie illustre dans le monde, Jean Damascène, il est en laïque, vêtu d'une toge et la tête ceinte d'un bandeau de perles, &c."

But whether M. Bordier is right or wrong in this identification, it should

be noticed that there is a single passage in which he is quoted. On f. 146 we find

Ιω Μουνζούρ ἐκ τοῦ ν΄ κεφ. Ἀδύνατον εὑρεθῆναι δύο τινα μὴ [δι]αφέροντα ἀλλήλων κατά τι.

Now this John Munzur is the celebrated John of Damascus. Cf. Suidas: Ἰωάννης ὁ Δαμασκηνὸς ὁ ἐπικληθεὶς Μανσούρ and a number of other references collected by Leo Allatius in the Prolegomena prefixed to Lequien's edition of John of Damascus. The name itself is said by some to be the name of his father and by others to be an insulting cognomen attached to him by the Emperor[1]. For a discussion of this point see the Prolegomena referred to. Especial attention should be paid to a quotation from Cedrenus in which he calls him Ἰωάννης μοναχὸς καὶ πρεσβύτερος ὁ χρυσορρόας ὁ τοῦ Μανσοὺρ, for this quotation seems to shew that he is also spoken of as Monk and Presbyter. For this reason one would incline to believe that a connexion exists between John of Damascus and any florilegium bearing the name of John Monachus, John Presbyter or a compound of the two. (The cases in which such a title is added by a later hand are of course more doubtful.)

The same conclusion as to the existence of Collections of Sacred Parallels earlier than John of Damascus is drawn in a somewhat different manner in a note at the beginning of the book by some former possessor or librarian. "Codex membr. litteris uncialibus nono ad minimum saec. scriptus quo continentur Parallela e variis Scripturae veterumque Ecclesiae doctorum locis collectis nempe Ignatii, Clementis Romani et Alexandrini, Dyonisii Alexandrini, Philonis, Josephi, Eusebii, Athanasii, Basilii, Gregorii, Chrysostomi, Nili, Evagrii et Maximi qui cum saec. VI vixerit saec. octavi revocandus videtur horumce Parallelorum scriptor, antiquior quippe Joanne Damasceno cui uberiora Parallela vulgandi noster hic auctor materiam praebuit."

A superior limit of time may of course be found in the latest author quoted: but it is doubtful whether Maximus does belong to the period assigned above, and I believe that he is rather regarded by some as a contemporary of John Damascene.

Cod. Reg. 923 quotes the following non-biblical authors.

The following is a more extended list of the authors quoted:

Apostoli Sancti (= Ap. Const.).	Basil.
Athanasius.	Cassian (Abbas).
Athenodorus (Frater Gregorii).	Chrysostom.

---

[1] Cf. Langen, *Johannes von Damaskus*, p. 20.

Clemens Rom. (= Clem. Hom.).

Clemens Alex.

Cyril.

Democritus (Philos.).

Diadochus.

Didymus.

Dionysius Areop.

Dionysius Alex.

Doctrina Petri.

Epiphanius.

Ephraim.

Eusebius.

Eustathius.

Evagrius.

Greg. Thaum.

Greg. Naz.

Greg. Nyss.

Hippolytus.

Hesychius.

Ignatius.

Irenæus.

Isidore Pelus.

John Climacus.

Josephus.

Justin.

Marcus Diadochus.

Maximus.

Methodius.

Moses (Abbas).

Μουνζούρ ('Ιωάννης).

Nilus.

Philo Jud.

Pythagoras.

Sancti Senes.

Serapion.

Sextus Rom. (generally given as Sextrus).

Synesius.

Theotimus Scythes.

Theophilus Ant.

Theophilus Episc.

We shall probably be safe in regarding John of Damascus as the latest of the writers referred to: only one passage has been inserted from his writings and that of a very trivial character. There is no necessity, however, on account of this quotation, to regard the MS. as a collection of Damascene Parallels.

We shall see presently that an important collection of Parallels in the Vatican Library bears the names of Leontius and John: and it is interesting to note that in Cod. Coislin. 294, which is a collection of Parallels, both the writers Leontius Damascenus and Joannes Mansur are quoted. It is probable, therefore, that Damascus is the real home of the Collection of Parallels from which successive editions and arrangements by different hands have been derived.

After I had finished my examination of the Paris MS., I discovered that M. l'Abbé Martin had just published an account of it in his *Description Technique des Manuscrits grecs relatifs au Nouveau Testament conservés dans les Bibliothèques de Paris.* (Maisonneuve 1884.) In this he also printed a few N. T. variants selected principally from the first 32 leaves of the Manu- *Attention had previously been drawn to this book by l'Abbé Martin.*

script[1], and to the book itself he attached the name Codex Martinianus and the critical letter Ω[2], thus placing it among the Uncial texts of the New Testament. I see no objection to this as the book undoubtedly contains large portions of Scripture copied directly from early Uncials; but on the other hand it should be noted that Dr Hort in his Introduction to N. T. thinks it best to class collections of parallels with Patristic authorities. If we adopt the suggestion of my friend l'Abbé Martin, we may have to add at the same time several other MSS. of Parallels to the table of Uncial texts of the N.T., a process which would require a good many alterations or expansions to be made in the notation of Tischendorf's critical apparatus.

Two fragments of Justin were extracted from Cod. Reg. by the Benedictine editor of Justin, (Fragg. x, xv of Otto). The note on these passages (p. 396) added by the editor contains the important information that the MS. was brought (? in the eighteenth century) from Constantinople. "Reperitur etiam (fragmentum) in antiquissimo Codice Regio 923, paucis abhinc annis Constantinopoli allato, quo continentur Parallela, ex quibus non pauca S. Joannes Damascenus transtulit in sua."

Nor should we omit to notice that an important fragment wrongly ascribed to Clem. Rom., but in reality from the Clem. Hom., is pointed out by Nolte as existing in Cod. Reg.[3]

Brief description of the MS. Now let us proceed in order to the description of our MS, and the results derived from it in the New Testament and in Patristic literature. The MS. is a folio, with its text arranged, as will be seen from the attached facsimiles, in double columns, in lines about 36 to the column, and each line containing 13—15 letters. The size of the pages 14 inches by $9\frac{1}{2}$[4]. The character is a sloping uncial of a period at least as early as the ninth century, although in some cases the script has been coarsely retraced, as in some lines of the first photograph, and deficient pages added by the hand of a later and more ignorant scribe.

---

[1] But what did the Abbé mean by citing the following as curious variants χαρρὰν καὶ ἑξῆς (Acts vii. 1), κατοικεῖ καὶ τὰ ἑξῆς (Acts xvii. 24)? We can quite understand that "De ces variantes il y en a peu qui aient pour elles l'appui des anciens manuscrits."

[2] I have quoted the MS. uniformly as Cod. Reg.: I should have preferred to write it Cod. Parisiensis; but it has to be quoted in a manner similar to the copies of Lequien (Par. Vat. and Par. Rup.): now we cannot very well write Par. Par.

[3] Nolte's note will be found in *Theolog. Quartalschrift* xli. p. 276 (1859). "Fragment vi. welches sich auch in cod. reg. Paris 923. f. 368 vers. sec. col. jedoch mit mannigfachen Abweichungen findet, ist aus Homil. Clem. iv. c. 11. entlehnt." Correct Nolte's reference to f. 309, and cf. Lightfoot, *Clement of Rome* p. 217 and *Appendix* p. 460.

[4] More closely according to M. Bordier, 0,356 cm. × 0,265 cm.

In many places there are instances of missing leaves either in Cod. Reg. or its ancestry. For instance the title given in Lequien 507 as ε 13 breaks off in Reg. at the close of the quotation from Eccli. xxvii. 29 at the bottom of f. 156 b. The MS. resumes again in ε 21 (Leq. 520) in a quotation from Clement ἀν|άγκην. Reference to the order of titles in Reg. shews that the following subjects have been omitted:

θ΄. περὶ ἐνεδρεύοντος ἐπιβουλὴν τοῦ πλησίον· ὅτι αὐτὸς ἐμπεσεῖται
(the last extract only being lost);

ι΄. περὶ ἐμπορίας· καὶ ὅτι αἱ περὶ τὰ βιωτικὰ ἐνδελεχεῖς ἀσχολίαι συγχέουσιν
    ἡμῶν τὴν ζωὴν καὶ ἀποστεροῦσι τῶν αἰωνίων ἀγαθῶν

ια΄. περὶ ἐνυπνίων καὶ μαντείων

ιβ΄. περὶ ἑκουσίων καὶ ἀκουσίων ἁμαρτημάτων

as far as the point indicated above in the quotation from Clement.

The quaternions being numbered in the right-hand bottom corner of the first leaf, we have f. 151 marked with ιθ΄ and f. 158 with κ΄, we should be inclined to infer that a single leaf was missing in this quaternion; it is not, however, safe to draw a conclusion hastily in a MS. where the matter is so much displaced as in Reg., nor without measuring the compass of the omitted matter in Cod. Rup.

It will be observed in the photographs that the writing is placed over the lines ruled by the scribe, a custom which accords with the date deduced from other considerations.

Accents and breathings are inserted with much irregularity, apparently by the first hand; the accent in a diphthong is usually placed on the first letter. The scribe amongst other eccentricities often places a circumflex on the antepenultimate. When a preposition immediately precedes a noun, a single accent is sometimes placed upon the two words.

Itacisms occur frequently of every kind. No MS. that I know affords a better opportunity for their study: I have generally contented myself with tacitly correcting them, as well as the accents.

The abbreviations are those common to Biblical uncial MSS. of the period. Sometimes as many as three letters are built into a common symbol, e.g. the syllable ΝΗΝ on f. 339 is made of two Ν's with a cross-bar between. A few tachygraphic signs such as that for την, may be found. An apostrophus is sometimes found at the end of a proper name, as in the Codex Sinaiticus and other early documents. Thus on fol. 2 we have ⲁⲇⲁⲙ, and in our photograph (248 a. 2. 1) 'ⲁⲃⲣⲁⲁⲙ.

The letters are remarkable for the fineness of the cross strokes, which makes many passages difficult to read rapidly: and a similar statement might perhaps have been made with regard to the exemplar from which the MS. was copied, seeing that there are frequent errors on the part of the copyist exactly similar to those into which his readers are likely to fall. The letters are well formed, the oval letters, ⲉ ⲑ ⲟ ⲥ, being much contracted horizontally, and as usual in MSS. of this class, ⲑ ⲇ with pronounced hooks. ⲍ has its form made by two strokes of the pen, but on the first facsimile we notice that an omitted ⲍ has been restored in the common form made by a single ductus.

The punctuation marks are chiefly the high and low point, accompanied by a final colon at the end of passages. ⲓ and ⲩ have the double diacritical point. And I think that a case of interrogation mark may be found in the MS. (on fol. 15 b for instance). No cases as far as I know occur of iota subscript or ascript.

The arrangement of the matter according to the index and where the disarranged portions of the book are readjusted, is first alphabetical, the various subjects being arranged under heads according to the leading word in a sentence : thus the first title is Περὶ ἀνθρώπου πλάσεως, and begins the letter ⲁ. Each title is then illustrated first by extracts from the Old Testament, next from the New Testament, then from the leading Church fathers, and finally from Philo and Josephus. Occasionally sentences and gnomic sayings are introduced from the philosophers.

Thus on the photograph of fol. 248 a, the extract on the left (line 10) begins with a statement written on a gold ground that the passage which follows is from a discourse τοῦ ἁγίου Βασιλείου κατὰ πλεονεκτούντων (sic). This is followed by a new title on gold,

περὶ παραχωρητικῶν καὶ εὐείκτων ὅτι εἰρηνικὸν καὶ ψυχοφελὲς τοῦτο.

And the first extract under the new title is indicated by the word Γενέσεως, and so on throughout the book, with few variations.

The illuminations are the most striking feature of the whole book. The facsimile of fol. 248 a shews us first an ordinary ecclesiastical portrait hundreds of which occur, and which serve to represent the fathers quoted. This one, accordingly, must be Basil.

The picture on the margin of the right-hand column represents the battle between the herdsmen of Lot and Abraham, with plenty of sheep in the foreground. This is followed by a picture representing the conference between Abraham and Lot, and another shewing Abraham in the act of intercession for Sodom.

The book must have been written first and illuminated after, for in our other facsimile over against a passage from S. John's Gospel concerning the true Vine, the artist has by oversight introduced an illustration of a totally different passage, namely the one in which the gardener appeals to his master to spare the unfruitful fig-tree yet another year. Unless indeed it should be that the tree represented is really a vine, in which case the scribe has fused the passages together in his mind. The attitude of the petitioning gardener is very pathetic!

The whole series of illustrations is interesting, and some require no small skill in the interpretation.

At the beginning of the book is a leaf of cursive writing of a considerably later date: it is written in two columns of 30 lines each, and bears something of the appearance of having been copied from an early bicolumnar uncial text[1]. The two columns of the verso are subjoined:

ἔργων· ὡς δηλοῖ
καὶ ἡ τοῦ σαββά-
του προσηγορί-
α κατάπαυσιν
ἑβραικῶς σημαί-
νουσα· εἰ δέ τις
καὶ ὑψηλότερος πε-
ρὶ ταῦτα λόγος
ἄλλοι φιλοσοφεί-
τωσαν. ἡ τιμὴ
δὲ αὐτοῖς οὐκ ἐ-
ν ἡμέραις μόνον
ἀλλὰ καὶ εἰς ἐνιαυ-
τοὺς φθάνουσα.
ἡ μὲν οὖν τῶν ἡ-
μετέρων τὸ σάβ-   (l. ἡμερῶν)
βατον· τοῦτο δὴ
τὸ συνεχῶς πα-
ρ' αὐτοῖς τιμώμε-
νον. καθ' ὃ καὶ ἡ

καὶ ἔτεσιν· αἱ μὲν
οὖν τῶν ἡμερῶν
ἑβδομάδες γεν-
νῶσι τὴν πεντηκο-
στήν, κλήτην [ἁγί-]   [l. κλητὴν]
αν παρ' αὐτοῖς ἡ-
μέραν· αἱ δὲ τῶν
ἐτῶν τὸν ἰωβελαῖ-
ον παρ' αὐτοῖς ὀ-
νομαζόμενον,
ὁμοίως γῆς τε ἄ-
φεσιν ἔχοντα καὶ
δουλῶν ἐλευθερί-   [l. δούλων]
αν καὶ κτήσεων
ὠνητῶν ἀναχώ-
ρησιν· καθιεροῦ-
σι γὰρ, οὐ γενημά-
των μόνον οὐδὲ
πρωτοτόκων ἀλ-
λ' ἤδη καὶ ἡμερῶν

[1] Dr Hort identifies this passage as coming from Greg. Naz. *Orat.* XLI. § 2 in Pentecosten.

τῆς ζύμης ἄρσις
ἰσάριθμος· ἡ δὲ
τῶν ἐτῶν ἑβδο-   (l. ἐτῶν ὁ)
ματικὸς ἐνιαυτὸς
τῆς ἀφέσεως.
καὶ οὐκ ἐν ἑβδομά-
σι μόνον ἀλλὰ καὶ
ἐν ἑβδομάσιν ἑ-
βδομάδων, ὁμοί-
ως ἔν τε ἡμέραις

καὶ ἐτῶν ἀπαρχὰς
τῷ θεῷ τοῦτο τὸ γέ-
νος· οὕτως ὁ ἑ-
πτὰ τιμώμενος
ἀριθμὸς τὴν τι-
μὴν τῆς πεντηκο-
στῆς συνήγαγεν·
ὁ γὰρ ἑπτὰ ἐπὶ ἑ-
αυτὸν συντιθέμενος
γεννᾷ τὸν πεντήκοντα.

Tischendorf's use of "Parallels." We have already alluded to the readings which Tischendorf extracted from the Parallela Sacra. He seems to have seen the importance of these quotations in the seventh edition of the New Testament (1859).

In the prolegomena to this text (p. xxiii) he remarks as follows:

"Item Johannis Damasceni perlustravi plura, maxime commentarios in Pauli epistulas et quae in parallelis sacris ad easdem spectant." And on p. cclxv. in referring to patristic authorities of the eighth century, he observes:

"Prae multis vero eminet Johannes Damascenus, cuius commentarium in epp. Pauli pertractavimus in ed. Mich. Lequien; item permulta ex sacris eius parallelis adscripsimus."

These quotations in the seventh edition are usually cited without a reference, as they could easily be found in a continuous exposition, but the passages from the parallels have references given.

Thus on Heb. xi. 13 we have as follows:

λαβοντες c. DEKL al longe pl Thdrt Dam (et par 371) al.

where the authority of John Damascene is twice appealed to, first in the ordinary text and commentary of the Hebrews, the latter of which is sometimes distinguished as Dam^{com} as in Heb. i. 3, and secondly in a passage found on the 371st page of Lequien's edition of the Parallels. These references to the Parallels are not however very complete. The seventh edition refers only to three passages for the text of the Hebrews, viz. to p. 371 of Lequien, where Heb. xi. 13—16, 32, 33 are quoted,

To p. 673 Heb. xii. 5—11,

And to p. 358 Heb. xiii. 17.

From these passages Tisch. extracts six variants, but it must not be supposed that these references imply anything like an exhaustive treatment.

In the eighth edition much more use is made of the collection, which is cited as Dam^par. and Dam^par. cod. as intimated above[1], and I do not think it need be pointed out that a very large further use may be made, by future New Testament collators, of Parallels to be found in the large European libraries.

An important question arises with regard to the MS. from which Mangey published fragments of Philo under the name of Johannes Monachus Ineditus. He obtained these extracts, I believe, from Thomas Carte, and writes concerning them as follows: A collection of Parallels is also used by Mangey, the editor of Philo

'Sunt haec fragmenta ex Cod. MS. Collegii Ludovici Magni Soc. Jes. Qui cod. sic inscribitur Ἰωάννου πρεσβυτέρου καὶ μοναχοῦ τοῦ Δαμασκηνοῦ ἐκλογῶν βιβλίον Α′ καὶ Β′. Titulorum vero discrepantia tum inversa ordinis ratio liquido sunt argumento excerptorem hunc alium esse a Damasceno illo Sacrorum Parallelorum auctore. Cui sententiae suffragatur Michael le Quien, Johannis Damasceni operum praeclarus editor, qui docet codicem istum noni esse saeculi.'

What has become of this Codex? At first sight the description seems not unlike Coislin. 276, described by Montfaucon as of the tenth century, diverse from the edited Parallels, and its title being *Joannis Monachi et Presbyteri Eclogae*. But the order of titles given by Montfaucon does not seem to agree with Mangey's description. Is it possible that in editing fragments from John Monachus Mangey is really going over the ground again with the Codex Rupefucaldinus? For certainly the title printed by Lequien from this MS. agrees precisely with that given by Mangey. And does not this supposition also explain why Lequien is quoted as an authority for the date of the Codex (though I cannot verify the passage referred to)? I believe that this supposition is the correct one, and will be verified by an examination of the MS. at Cheltenham. which seems the same as Cod. Rup.

We must also draw attention to the following important copies of Parallels, of which use has been made by collectors.

Mai in his *Scriptorum Veterum Nova Collectio*, Vol. I. et VII. has pointed out and used the Cod. Vat. 1553 (olim Cryptoferratensis) which bears the title *Res Sacrae Leontii et Joannis*.

Pitra in *Analecta Sacra*, II. xxi. and elsewhere has quoted largely from Cod. Coislin. 276, already referred to, and wonders that so little attention has been paid to it. "Codicem Parisiensem, quem miror a nemine, ni

---

[1] But see further on this point on p. xx.

fallor, collatum, comminisci juvat. Coislinianus est sub num. 276[1], olim fortasse neglectus vel a Maurinis quia visus est eadem continere quam Damasceni Parallela."

And many other copies yet uncollated might easily be pointed out.

From a similar collection, as I suppose, in the Library of the Patriarch of Alexandria at Cairo, Tischendorf extracted in 1853 a number of valuable passages, which he printed at the end of his *Philonea*.

FURTHER REMARKS ON THE CODEX RUPEFUCALDI.

The whole of the preceding and almost all of the succeeding matter was written out for the press before I was able to undertake the expedition necessary to the verification of the suppositions thus made with regard to Cod. Rup., and even now a complete study of the recovered codex remains to be made, four days being all the time that I have been able to bestow upon it. The results thus arrived at are as follows:

The Codex Rupefucaldi is a magnificently written volume of 285 leaves (in addition a few blank leaves at the beginning and end), the numbered leaves being 284, and one number repeated (= f. 218 bis). To my surprise, it is not an uncial MS. at all, but an early cursive with a few rubricated uncials at the beginning, middle and end; and dating, as near as I can judge, and in accordance with the tradition of the library, from the eleventh century.

The rubricated uncials at the beginning are as follows:

Ἰωάννου πρεσβυτέρου καὶ μοναχοῦ τοῦ δαμασκηνοῦ τῶν ἐκλογῶν βιβλίον αʹ καὶ βʹ.

And in the middle, f. 177 b, at the close of στοιχεῖον ε, where perhaps from weariness the scribe was constrained to obtrude his personality more definitely upon his work, are the abbreviated words,

χριστὲ ὁ Θεός, σῶσόν με

At the end stands the subscription,

τέλος τῶν ἐκλογῶν τοῦ ὁσίου π̅ρ̅ς̅ ἡμῶν μοναχοῦ καὶ πρεσβυτέρου Ἰωάννου τοῦ Δαμασκηνοῦ + δόξα σοι, χριστέ, ὁ θεὸς ἡμῶν πάντων ἕνεκεν.

---

[1] Wrongly given by Pitra as 279.

The preface and titles to the Parallels are written in a bicolumnar form with about 40 lines to the column: the rest of the MS. is written in the ordinary manner, the initials and titles and authors' names being rubricated subsequently to the writing of the rest of the matter, but with such care that I have thus far only detected a single dropped initial, and the whole book is a marvel of exact calligraphy.

On f. 1 stands the superscription:

"Collegii Claromontani Parisiensis Societat. Jesu ex dono eminentiss. Cardinal. Rupifucaldi."

Between ff. 161 and 162 are eight leaves on paper in a modern hand, in which an attempt has been made to restore a missing quaternion or quaternions from the printed Vatican Parallels (beginning Par. Vat. 432 D ἐὰν ὀμνύῃς and ending with Par. Vat. 462 B σπηλαῖον | λῃστῶν.

The identity of the MS. with the missing book is evident not only from the headings and subscription but from a comparison with the Par. Rup. of Lequien, the John Monachus of Mangey, and the extracts from it in Halloix and other patristic writers. So valuable and complete (with the exception noted) is this MS. that if it had crossed my path earlier I should have made it the basis of almost all the subsequent work, and printed from it the greater part of the Philonea collected by Mai, Pitra, and Tischendorf, as well as those quotations which are current in the Melissa of Antony.

As it is, I have contented myself with noting the references and a few readings, and reserve a fuller account of the Patristic excerpts for a future tract on Ante-Nicene Patristic Fragments. But now, what are we to say about Tischendorf's description of this MS.? The prolegomena to the VIIIth edition of the New Testament, or rather the fragmentary notice which stands in the place of prolegomena, says (p. xvi):

Dam [par. cod] i.e. Joh. Damasceni parallela sacra ex Cod. Rupefuc. Saeculi fere 8.

It is needless to say that by no reasoning can we identify this book with Cod. Rup. Tischendorf is evidently quoting from an uncial MS. Can it be that after all he is referring to Cod. Reg., and has made the hasty identification to which our own first thoughts were led under his influence? Let us see some of the readings which he quotes from the book.

In general, as intimated previously, the references are given as follows: Matt. xxii. 8 ἐστιν Dam[par. 382] om.; Mark xii. 44 περισσευοντος αυτοις (et Or. Dam[par. cod.]); UΓΔ et mu Dam[par. ed.] περισσευματος αυτων. In the last passage the references clearly refer to the printed parallels and to the edited text of Lequien. If we turn, however, to the critical apparatus of the Epistle to the Hebrews, we are astonished to find a new notation: e.g. Heb. xii. 1 Dam^{paris} τρεχομεν Heb. xii. 3 ὑμων Dam^{paris} om. xii. 4 Dam^{paris} αντεκατεστητε, &c., all of which readings may be found in Reg. f. 341 b. While on xii. 7 we have εἰς παιδειαν supported by Dam. ad h. l. et ^{parall 673} (et ^{paris}). The first of these references is, of course, to the commentary on the Pauline Epistles; the second to the printed text of parallels; while the third is from f. 260 of Cod. Reg. We have no doubt then that Tischendorf is really referring in these readings to our Paris MS., seeing that there is no other to which we can attach the mark of place (Parisiensis) nor of date (viii. sæc. fere) so as to agree both with his descriptions and citations.

FURTHER REMARKS ON COD. COISLIN. 20.

We have alluded to the uncial fragments of a MS. of parallels which are found at the beginning of Cod. Coislin. 20. A few more notes are added with regard to them in order to shew the close connection that subsists between them and the Cod. Reg.

The MS. from which they are taken is bicolumnar, and contained (as a little restoration of the damaged parts will shew) 36 lines to the column and about 16 letters to the line. The first leaf contains as follows: after four lines of a sentence whose beginning is wanting, μηδὲ γογγύσῃς ὡς ὀλίγον βραδύνων ἵνα μηδὲ ὀλίγον τοῦ ὅλου ζημίαν ὑπομείνῃς, the text follows as in Lequien 621, in the middle of a passage attributed to Chrysostom, ὅσον γὰρ νηστεία κτέ...ἔπιεν. It then continues with the fragment of the same homily (Lequien 622) beginning νηστεία καὶ δέησις...μόνον πρὸς μόνῳ. It then adds from Basil περὶ νηστείας the fragment on 622, as far as ἀντλεῖς: and so concludes the titles under N at the foot of the first column of the verso. In all this it is strictly following the order in Cod. Reg., with the single exception that it has avoided the transposition of the passage from Basil over the last of the extracts attributed to Chrysostom.

Letter ξ then begins, precisely as in Cod. Reg., as follows:

Cτοιχειον Ξ.

π ξένων καὶ φιλοξενίας καὶ ὅτι
ἀπαρρησίαστος ὁ ξένος πάντοτε.

The extracts then follow the order in Cod. Reg., viz. :

Gen. Ἀναβλέψας Ἀβραὰμ κτέ. followed by a *Scholium* which is given completely in Reg., but only indicated by an abbreviation in Coislin, the bottom of the leaf where it probably was written being cut away.

Exod. Προσήλυτον κτέ.
Levit. ἐάν τις προσέλθῃ κτέ.

with which the first leaf ends.

The second leaf begins with οὐκ οἶδας ἄρτι κτέ. from the Gospel of John c. xiii.

This is followed by Matt. xiv. 6, 7

and a sentence τοῦ ἁγίου βασιλείου ἐκ τῶν εἰς τὸν α΄ ψαλμόν Μὴ ἐναπομείνῃς τοῖς κακῶς βουλευθεῖσιν.

These passages belong under the title, περὶ ὅρκου.
Then comes

περὶ ὀρφανῶν καὶ χηρῶν

The passages are given in the order, Exodus xxii., Proverbs xxiii., Prov. i., Sirach iv., Sirach xxxv., i Tim. v. 5, i Tim. v. 11, i Cor., Jac. i., Philo, Tob., Ps. xciii., Zacharias. It will be seen that this order is confused; but the matter contained is almost exactly the same as that in Cod. Reg.

The next title is

περὶ οἴνου καὶ χρήσεως αὐτοῦ

the extracts being from Psalm ciii. and Proverbs as in Reg., and so the leaf ends.

On the whole it will be found that there is a much closer agreement between Coislin and Reg. than between Coislin and Vat. or Coislin and Rup. : the latter codex for instance has three additional titles thrust in between περὶ ὅρκων and περὶ ὀρφανῶν. The Coislin fragment is, therefore, though not a part of the Cod. Reg., so like to it that there is either a relationship between them or they both are derived without much change from the primitive collection of parallels.

ON THE EDITED AND UNEDITED FRAGMENTS OF
PHILO JUDÆUS.

SO much having been said with regard to the subject of Parallels, we proceed to the practical use of the special manuscript to which we have drawn attention. It has been already intimated that there seems very little prospect of publishing the text in full, or, which is nearly the same thing, of re-editing the Parallels of Lequien. We are accordingly obliged to make what use we can of the extracts (i) for the recension of the text of the Old and New Testaments, (ii) for the text of the earlier Fathers. Reserving the former for another opportunity, we have concluded that the most useful thing would be to select a new series of passages from the oldest Greek Fathers and identify and classify them as far as possible. And since Philo is one of the writers most frequently quoted, and one for whose text in late days least has been done, we have devoted the remainder of the present book to this writer alone. For it soon becomes evident that it is of little use merely to reprint the extracts from Philo contained in the Codex, unless a complete study be made at the same time of the fragments already edited, and rightly or wrongly ascribed to him. In other words we have done many months' hewing of wood and drawing of water for the next editor of Philo, who may bless us if he finds the work done well, but cannot altogether curse us when he finds references given to sources from which he can with greater fulness and certainty draw for himself.

A further reason why we have taken this in hand, besides the need of a re-edited and expanded text of Philo, lies in the fact that we have a profound reverence amounting almost to a cultus for the Alexandrian sage; to us his fragments are no mere chaff and draff, but such blessed brokenness of truth just dawning on the world that one would almost imagine him to be holding out to us what had previously passed through the hands of the

Master himself. I do not mean to imply by this that the portions of his writings selected by the earlier Christian Parallelists are the most beautiful of his sayings: as far as I know, none of them seeks to employ his doctrine of the Logos in direct illustration and defence of the Christian Faith: I have never anywhere found quoted the magnificent passage in the *De Somniis* II. § 37, καὶ ψυχῇ δ' εὐδαίμονι τὸ ἱερώτατον ἔκπωμα προτεινούσῃ, τὸν ἑαυτῆς λογισμόν, τίς ἐπιχεῖ τοὺς ἱεροὺς κυάθους τῆς πρὸς ἀλήθειαν εὐφροσύνης ὅτι μὴ οἰνοχόος τοῦ θεοῦ καὶ συμποσίαρχος λόγος; and the general supposition amongst Ecclesiastical writers that Christian attention was drawn to Philo by his monastic works is not verified by our quotations. For example there is only one extract from *De Vita Contemplativa* and only one from *Quod Omnis Probus*. Nor have I, which is more surprising, found any consciousness on the part of those making the extracts, of the close parallelism between Philonian terms and the language of the New Testament. But this does not prevent us from feeling that a certain worth attaches to even the least quotations from so great a writer, and that unless the fragments are gathered up, something will be lost.

In the case in question an additional interest arises from the fact that the lost writings of Philo are many, and of many of those which are preserved the Greek has disappeared.

Philo himself often alludes to works which he has written (and almost all his books form an ordered series of expositions) which are not now to be found amongst his collected writings. For example he opens his treatise *De Ebrietate* with the remark that in the previous treatise he had discussed the opinions of other philosophers on the subject of drunkenness. It appears therefore that our present treatise is the second of two on the same subject, of which the former is lost, unless we take the words to refer to the *De Plantatione*, and what confirms us in this belief is the fact that we often find passages referred to *De Ebrietate* in Parallels which do not seem to occur in the published treatise.

The treatise "Who is the Heir of Divine Things" opens with the statement that the previous book had been περὶ μισθῶν. It is possible that this may be a reference to the *De Migratione Abrahami* and the promise discussed in it "Surely blessing I will bless thee," but I do not feel sure of the point.

The book which preceded the *De Somniis* I. was a discourse on visions, which also seems to be lost. The treatise *Quod Omnis Probus Liber* was preceded by another to which Eusebius and Jerome are said to refer, the title of which seems to have been complementary to this one, περὶ τοῦ πάντα δοῦλον εἶναι φαῦλον.

The opening of the treatise against Flaccus seems to me to bear the mark of incompleteness, and we are confirmed in this belief by a number of unrecognized fragments referred thereto. The same must be said of the treatise against Gaius, at the close of which the writer breaks off with the remark λεκτέον δὲ καὶ τὴν παλινῳδίαν πρὸς Γάιον. In another passage *De Mut. Nom.* § 6 (I. 586), he refers to treatises on Covenants which he has written, and it is perhaps to these that Jerome refers when he includes a treatise *De Testamentis* amongst the writings of Philo[1].

Further, the quotations which Eusebius makes from Philo are often taken from books which have disappeared either in Greek, or altogether, such as the Questions on Genesis, Exodus, &c., the book *De Providentia* and the *Hypothetica*, which was a sort of hortatory treatise on ethics, and indirectly was an apology for the Jewish people.

A great step was taken in the direction of restoring Philo when Aucher published with a number of other tracts an Armenian and Latin edition of the *De Providentia* and of the greater part of the Questions on the Pentateuch. By the aid of this book we have been enabled to restore more than a hundred fragments of the Questions to their proper places. The treatise has an especial value; with the exception of one or two glosses it is, I believe, pure Philo; and it is, as pointed out by Mai and Aucher, the basis of many of Ambrose's expositions on the book of Genesis.

A single instance of this may be taken from the beginning of Ambrose's treatise on Cain and Abel.

Ambrose, *Cain et Abel* I. c. 1 § 2.	Questions on Genesis I. 58 (Aucher II. 41).
Adam autem cognovit Evam mulierem suam, quae concepit et peperit Cain et dixit; Acquisivi hominem per Deum. Quae acquirimus, ex quo, et a quo et per quid acquirimus, considerari solet: ex quo, tamquam ex materia: a quo, quis auctor; per quid, tamquam per aliquid instrumentum. Numquid hic sic dicit: *Acquisivi hominem per Deum:* ut Deum intelligas instrumentum? Non utique: &c.	*An recte dictum fuerit de Cain: Acquisivi hominem per Deum?* Distinguitur esse ab aliquo et ex aliquo et per aliquid; ex aliquo sicut ex materia; ab aliquo ut a causa; et per aliquid, ut per instrumentum. Atqui pater et creator universorum non est instrumentum, sed causa, &c.

---

[1] Cf. *De SS. Abelis et Caini*, § 12 ad fin.

Let us now enumerate briefly the sources from which the principal collections of fragments of Philo have come.

Mangey edited his fragments in the following order:

a'. The fragments from lost books quoted by Eusebius.

β'. The fragments which he could not identify ascribed to Philo in the printed text of Damascene's Parallels (ed. Lequien). N.B. Those which he did identify may be compared with a number of texts of the same passages especially in the Cod. Reg. 923, but I have not, for want of space, gone over the ground again at length in order to add a few variants.

γ'. The fragments from Cod. Rupef. also printed by Lequien.

δ'. The fragments from John Monachus, which, as we have shewn, is only another name for the part of Cod. Rupef. neglected by Lequien.

ε'. A number of extracts from the Melissa of Antony.

ς'. Some unidentified extracts from an Oxford Florilegium Cod. Barocc. No. 143.

ζ'. A French Catena (Cod. Reg. 1825) brought to light a number more.

To the foregoing we may make additions as follows:

η'. The *Res Sacræ* of Leontius and John as edited by Mai: vide supra.

θ'. A large collection made by Pitra *Anal. Sac.* II. from Cod. Coislin. 276, and from certain codices in the Vatican Library.

ι'. A collection made by Tischendorf and published in his *Philonea*, one passage from Cod. Vat. 746, the rest from a Florilegium at Cairo.

ια'. The Cod. Reg. 923 described above.

ιβ'. Some passages given by Cramer, in his *Anecd. Oxon.* IV. and in his Catena on the New Testament.

ιγ'. The whole of the fragments referred to Philo in the *Loci Communes* of Maximus and his literary follower Antony (Melissa) need to be re-examined; and as will be seen below I have made a large number of fresh identifications.

ιδ'. The great Leipsic (printed) Catena (Lips. 1771) of Nicephorus is full of fragments of Philo. It was made from two private MSS. in Constantinople, see Zahn *Suppl. Clem.* p. 5. I have gone through the book, and, I believe, identified them all, but the result was disappointing, as there seemed to be indications that the text had been artificially conformed to the printed edition of Mangey. At all events, it often differs little from it.

ιε΄. Closely connected with this beautiful Catena is the British Museum Catena (Cod. Burney 34) which with Cod. Reg. 1825, and one or two other Catenas, is probably derived from the same original as the Leipsic Catena. I have worked through the Burney Catena and identified almost every passage.

ιϚ΄. Somewhat different from the preceding, but often agreeing with it in quotations, is the (Latin) Catena of Zephyrus the Florentine (Colon. 1572) which contains many extracts from Philo. Zephyrus says that his translation was made from a "Codex vetustus" (? Florentinus). I have gone through this Catena and identified nearly all the passages referred to.

ιζ΄. A Latin Catena on Genesis published at Paris in 1546 by Aloysius Lippomanus, and followed by a second volume in 1550 containing a Catena on Exodus. I have examined and verified, I believe, all the passages quoted from Philo in this Catena.

ιη΄. Attention should also be given to Cordier's (Latin) Catena on Luke, published at Antwerp in 1628 from a MS. in the Library of S. Mark at Venice. A similar Catena exists, according to Cordier, in the library at Vienna. (? Cod. Vind. theol. gr. 71.) Zahn points out (*Suppl. Clem.* 7) that this Catena is only a part of a great four-vol. Cat. of Nicetas on Luke. I have identified all the passages of Philo translated by Cordier. In particular it will be found that on Luke xxii. 1 he quotes almost the whole of the treatise *De Septenario*.

ιθ΄. A number of passages are also given in the Florilegium of Georgis (? Georgides, Georgidios) Monachus, published in Migne *Patr. Gr.* 117. In this Catena the passages are arranged alphabetically, in the order of their initial letters. Zahn points out the importance for the text of a Florentine MS. plut. ix. cod. 15 from fol. 25 a—103 a.

κ΄. The commentary of Procopius on the Pentateuch is full of passages and abridgments from Philo.

These are the principal sources for Philonea: and no doubt the list might be largely increased. Our space does not permit us to print at length all the extracts referred to nor the variants occurring therein; even in passages referred to, our remarks are of necessity brief. Indeed, until the matter is gone into, one has little idea of the enormous extent to which Philo is quoted by Christian writers.

We may now proceed to arrange in order the results of our investigations, beginning with those fragments which can with any show of truth be ascribed to special lost books, and in particular devoting especial attention to the lost books of the *Quæstiones in Genesim, Exodum et Leviticum*, by which means we shall remove from the collections in Mangey and other writers the greater part of their accumulated fragments.

Our first collection is from the lost book styled the fourth of the Allegories of the Sacred Laws. At present there are only three such books; but the extracts published by Mai shew that the numeration of books of Allegories ran beyond these three, and that this numeration after a certain point became double; so that the treatise *Quod Det. Pot.* is almost always cited as VII. and VIII. of the Allegories[1]. And we may remark here that these ancient titles are much to be trusted. They often conserve ancient names of books, which have given place to others in later copies. For instance, our Cod. Reg. often speaks of the books ζητημάτων εἰς τὴν ἐξαγωγήν, which last word is employed by Philo instead of ἔξοδος, just as he often uses ἐπίνομις in place of δευτερονόμιον.

Fragments of Philo from the lost fourth book of the Allegories of the Sacred Laws.

[πάντων μέν, εἰ δεῖ τὸ ἀληθὲς εἰπεῖν, ἄκυρον ἄνθρωπος, οὐδενὸς ἐνειλημμένος, οὐχ ὅτι τῶν ἄλλων, ἀλλ᾽ οὐδὲ τῶν περὶ αὐτὸν βεβαίως, οὐχ ὑγείας, οὐκ εὐαισθησίας, οὐκ ἀρτιότητος τῆς περὶ τὰ ἄλλα τοῦ σώματος, οὐχὶ φωνῆς, οὐκ ἀγχινοίας. Τὰ γὰρ κατὰ πλοῦτον ἢ δόξαν ἢ φίλους ἢ ἀρχὰς ἢ ὅσα ἄλλα τυχηρά, τίς οὐκ οἶδεν, ὡς ἐστὶν ἀβέβαια; Ὥστε ἀνάγκη ὁμολογεῖν, ὅτι περὶ ἕνα τὸ κῦρος τῶν ἀπάντων ἐστί, τὸν ὄντα ὄντως κίριον.]

Dam. Par. 326, but in Cod. Reg. 923 (fol. 55) it is referred to ἐκ τοῦ τῆς νόμων ἱερῶν ἀλληγορίας. On the other hand this title may more properly belong to the immediately preceding extract only, which I identify as coming from the treatise *Quod Det. Pot.* § 37, for this treatise is often described as VII. and VIII. *Alleg. Sac. Leg.* Hence we enclose the preceding in brackets.

[1] This double numeration may have arisen from counting the treatise *De Mundi Opificio* as the first book of the Allegories: and on f. 23 of Cod. Rup. a passage from I. *Leg. Alleg.* is quoted as ἐκ τοῦ δευτέρου τῆς νόμων ἱερῶν ἀλληγορίας.

ἀμήχανον συνυπάρχειν τὴν πρὸς κόσμον ἀγάπην τῇ πρὸς τὸν θεὸν ἀγάπῃ, ὡς ἀμήχανον συνυπάρχειν ἀλλήλοις φῶς καὶ σκότος.

Lequien prints this passage with a note of suspicion on account of the
apparently Christian sentiment which it contains; but we remark that it
occurs twice in the printed parallels, p. 370 and p. 382, each time with
a reference to Philo, that Cod. Reg. 923 in the latter case prefixes ἐκ τῆς
νόμων ἀλληγορίας, while Mai (*Script. Vet. Coll.* Vol. VII. p. 95) gives the
same passage from Cod. Vat. 1553 with the preface ἐκ τοῦ δ' τῆς νόμων
ἀλληγορίας.

τῶν πολιτικῶν ἐὰν τὰς ὕλας ἀφέλῃς, κενὸν τῦφον εὑρήσεις νοῦν οὐκ ἔχοντα. Μέχρι μὲν γὰρ ἡ τῶν ἐκτὸς πρόσεστιν ἀφθονία,	σύνεσις ἐπακολουθεῖν δοκεῖ καὶ ἀγχίνοια· ὅταν δὲ περιαιρεθῇ, συμπεριαιρεῖ καὶ τὸ δοκεῖν ἔτι φρονεῖν.

Printed by Mangey (II. 661) from the Parallels of John Monachus
(= Rup. f. 29 b), where the heading is expressly ἐκ τῆς δ' τῶν νόμων ἱερῶν
ἀλληγορίας; also found in Maximus (ed. Combefis. II. 623). The first
sentence is also found twice in Anton Melissa col. 1033 and 1184, in both
cases reading τάφον.

εἰκότως μελέτην μὲν θανάτου, σκιὰν δὲ καὶ ὑπόγραμμον τῆς αὖθις ἐπομένης ἀνα-βιώσεως τὸν ὕπνον οἱ τὰ ἀληθῆ πεφρονη-	κότες ἀπεφήναντο· ἑκατέρων γὰρ ἐναργεῖς φέρει τὰς εἰκόνας· μεθιστᾷ γὰρ καὶ παριστᾷ τὸν αὐτὸν ἐξ ὁλοκλήρου. Plat. *Phædo* 81 A.

Mangey (II. 667) from John Monachus (= Rup. f. 265); also in Maximus
(II. 615), and in Cod. Reg. 923 (f. 342 b), where it is referred to the
Allegories of the Law.

φασί τινες, ὅτι ὕστατον ἀποδύεται τὸν τῆς κενοδοξίας χιτῶνα ὁ σοφός· καὶ ἂν γὰρ τῶν ἄλλων τις παθῶν περικρατήσῃ, ἀλλὰ τῆς	δόξης καὶ τοῦ παρὰ τοῖς πολλοῖς ἐπαίνου πέφυκεν ἡττᾶσθαι.

Mangey (II. 668). From John Monachus (= Cod. Rup. f. 267), with the
heading ἐκ τοῦ α' τῆς νόμων ἱερῶν ἀλληγορίας, where we should probably
read δ' for α', owing to the confusion common amongst uncial characters.

Also in Anton Melissa col. 1184 reading ἀποδύσεται, περικρατήσει, and
omitting ἂν and τις.

The next passage is from Mai (*Script. Vet. Coll.* VII. p. 95) and is found
in the Parallels of Leontius and John (Cod. Vat. 1553), from which a part of
it is quoted by Turrianus, *de epist. pont.* IV. 296 b.

ἐκ τοῦ δ' τῆς νόμων ἱερῶν ἀλληγορίας.
ἰδοὺ δέδωκά φησιν πρὸ προσώπου σου
τὰ μαχόμενα, τὴν ζωὴν καὶ τὸν θάνατον,
τὸ ἀγαθὸν καὶ τὸ κακόν· ἔκλεξαι τὴν ζωὴν
ἵνα ζήσῃ· μακάριον χρῆμα, προθέντος ἀμ-
φότερα τοῦ δημιουργοῦ, τὸ ἄμεινον ἰσχύειν
λαβεῖν τὴν ψυχήν· μακαριώτερον δὲ τὸ μὴ
αὐτὴν ἑλέσθαι, τὸν δὲ δημιουργὸν προσά-
γεσθαι καὶ βελτιῶσαι· οὐδὲ γὰρ κυρίως
ἀνθρώπινος νοῦς αἱρεῖται δι' ἑαυτοῦ τὸ
ἀγαθόν, ἀλλὰ κατ' ἐπιφροσύνην θεοῦ δωρου-
μένου τοῖς ἀξίοις τὰ κάλλιστα· δυοῖν γὰρ
ὄντων κεφαλαίων παρὰ τῷ νομοθέτῃ, τοῦ
μὲν ὅτι οὐχ ὡς ἄνθρωπος ἡνιοχεῖ τὰ πάντα
ὁ θεός, τοῦ δὲ ὅτι ὡς ἄνθρωπος παιδεύει
καὶ σωφρονίζει, ὅτ' ἂν μὲν τὸ δεύτερον
κατασκευάζῃ, τὸ ὡς ἄνθρωπος καὶ τὸ ἐφ'
ἡμῖν εἰσάγῃ, ὡς ἱκανὸς καὶ γνῶναί τι καὶ

βούλεσθαι καὶ ἑλέσθαι καὶ φυγεῖν· ὅτ' ἂν
δὲ τὸ πρῶτον καὶ ἄμεινον, ὅτι οὐχ ὡς ἄνθρωπος τὰς πάντων δυνάμεις καὶ αἰτίας
ἀνάψῃ θεῷ μηδὲν ὑπολειπόμενος ἔργον τῷ
γενομένῳ ἀλλὰ δείξας ἄπρακτον αὐτὸ καὶ
πάσχον, δηλοῖ δὲ ὅτ' ἂν φῇ δι' ἑτέρων
ὅτι ἔγνω ὁ θεὸς τοὺς ὄντας αὐτοῦ καὶ τοὺς
ἁγίους αὐτοῦ προσηγάγετο· εἰ δὲ ἐκλογαί τε Num. xvi.
καὶ ἀπεκλογαὶ κυρίως ὑπὸ τοῦ ἑνὸς αἰτίου [5.]
γίνονται, τί μοι παραινεῖς ὦ νομοθέτα τὴν
ζωὴν καὶ τὸν θάνατον αἱρεῖσθαι ὡς τῆς
αἱρέσεως αὐτοκράτορι; ἀλλ' εἴποι ἄν, τῶν
τοιούτων εἰσαγωγικώτερον ἄκουε· λέγεται
γὰρ ταῦτα τοῖς μήπω τὰ μεγάλα μεμυη-
μένοις μυστήρια περί τε ἀρχῆς καὶ ἐξουσίας
τοῦ ἀγενήτου καὶ περὶ ἄγαν οὐδενείας τοῦ
γενητοῦ.

The next passage is from the same source as the preceding (Mai, *Script. Vet. Coll.* VII. p. 107).

ἐκ τοῦ δ' τῶν νόμων ἱερῶν ἀλληγορίας.
προσήκει τὸν πολιτικὸν μὴ ἁπλῶς ὁμιλεῖν,
ἀλλ' ἔχειν διττὸν λόγον, τὸν μὲν ἀληθείας
καὶ τοῦ συμφέροντος, τὸν δὲ δόξης καὶ τοῦ
ἡδέος· ἀνάγκη γὰρ τῷ πολιτικῷ μὴ ὅσα
φρονεῖν συμφέροντα ἡγεῖται, καὶ λέγειν
ἄντικρυς, ἀλλ' ἔνια ἀποκρύπτεσθαι διὰ τὸ
πολλάκις τὸν ἀκροατὴν ἀλλοτρίως διακεί-
μενον εἶναι πρὸς τὸ ἀκολάκευτον καὶ εὐθὺς
τοῦ ἀληθοῦς ἀφηνιάζειν, ὡς μηδὲν ἔτι τῶν
εἰς ἐπανόρθωσιν προΐεσθαι· ἀεὶ δέ γε τοῖς

σοφοῖς ἐοικέναι τῶν ἰατρῶν, οἳ καίειν τε
καὶ τέμνειν ἢ κενοῦν μέλλοντες, ἤ τι τῶν
οὐκ ἡδέων μὲν λυσιτελῶν δὲ τοῖς κάμνουσι
ποιεῖν, οὐ προλέγουσι τὰς θεραπείας, ἀλλ'
ἔστιν ὅτε καὶ πυνθανομένων ἀρνοῦνται· εἶτ'
ἐξαίφνης οὐδὲν ἐλπισάντων τοιούτων ἀλλὰ
καὶ τἀναντία προσδοκησάντων, τὴν θεραπείαν μάλα εὐτόνως ἐπιφέρουσι, τὸ ψεύ-
σασθαι μετὰ τοῦ συμφέροντος κρεῖττον
ἀληθείας ἀλυσιτελοῦς ὑπολαμβάνοντες.

Mai reads ἀκολάστευτον.

τῆς εὐδαιμονίας ἐστὶ τὸ πέρας θεοῦ βοήθεια· οὐ γὰρ ἐνδεῖν ἔτι δύναται βοηθοῦντος
θεοῦ.

Mangey (II. 668) from John Monachus (= Rup. f. 120), with the heading
ἐκ τοῦ δ' τῆς νόμων ἱερῶν ἀλληγορίας.

Fragments of Philo from the lost portion of the book
περὶ γιγάντων.

ἀδύνατον οἶμαι μηδὲν ῥυπωθῆναι τῆς αὐτῆς καὶ ἂν ὡς ἐν ἀνθρώποις τέλειος ψυχῆς, μηδὲ τὰ τελευταῖα καὶ κατωτάτω εἶναι δοκῇ.

John Monach. (Mang. II. 662) = Rup. f. 67 b, reading δοκεῖ and headed ἐκ τοῦ περὶ γιγάντων: Pitra, *Anal. Sac.* II. 309 (Cod. Coislin. 276, f. 47) (l. ῥυπισθῆναι), τοῦ αὐτοῦ περὶ τῶν γιγάντων.

ἀνδρείας ἐστὶ τὸ δύσπληκτον εἶναι ὑπὸ καλῶς ἢ αἰσχρῶς σωθῆναι, καὶ τὸ νίκης φόβων τῶν περὶ θάνατον, καὶ τὸ εὐθαρσῆ αἴτιον εἶναι. παρέπεται δὲ τῇ ἀνδρείᾳ ἡ ἐν τοῖς δεινοῖς καὶ τὸ εὔτολμον ἐν τοῖς κιν- εὐτολμία καὶ εὐψυχία καὶ τὸ θάρσος. δύνοις καὶ τὸ μᾶλλον αἱρεῖσθαι τεθνάναι

John Monach. (Mang. II. 665) ἐκ τοῦ περὶ γιγάντων = Cod. Rup. f. 185.

πέφυκε τοῖς μεγάλοις ἀκολουθεῖν φθόνος.

John Monach. (Mang. II. 668) without heading.
Cod. Reg. 923, f. 354 b περὶ γιγάντων.
It should be noticed that the sentiment is found also in the *De Sampsone*, edited by Aucher from the Armenian (II. 560), "Quoniam, ut dicitur, solet magnum virum sequi invidia."

τῆς ψυχῆς τὸ εἶδος οὐκ ἐκ τῶν αὐτῶν μόνην γὰρ αὐτὴν ὁ γεννήσας πατὴρ ἐλευ- στοιχείων ἐξ ὧν τὰ ἄλλα ἀπετελεῖτο διε- θερίας ἠξίωσε καὶ τὰ τῆς ἀνάγκης ἀνεὶς πλάσθη, καθαρωτέρας τε καὶ ἀμείνονος ἔλαχε δεσμὰ ἄφετον εἴασε, δωρησάμενος αὐτῇ τῆς οὐσίας, ἐξ ἧς καὶ αἱ θεῖαι φύσεις ἐδη- τοῦ πρεπωδεστάτου καὶ οἰκειοτάτου κτή- μιουργοῦντο· παρ' ὃ καὶ μόνον τῶν ἐν ματος αὐτῷ, τοῦ ἑκουσίου μοῖραν, ἣν ἠδύ- ἡμῖν εἰκότως ἄφθαρτον ἔδοξεν εἶναι διάνοια· νατο δέξασθαι.

In Cod. Reg. f. 377 this is headed περὶ γιγάντων.
The passage is, however, found in *De Mundo* § 3 (Mang. II. 607), a treatise which is largely made up out of previous writings of Philo.

τῷ ἄριστα νομοθετήσοντι τέλος ἐν προ- Cod. Rup. f. 113 ἐκ τοῦ περὶ τῶν γιγάν- κεῖσθαι δεῖ· πάντας ὠφελεῖσθαι τοὺς ἐν- των. τυγχάνοντας.

H.   2

From the lost part of the treatise of Philo against Flaccus.

οὐκ ἔστι παρὰ θεῷ, οὔτε πονηρὸν ὄντα ἀπολέσαι τὸν ἀγαθὸν μισθὸν περὶ ἑνὸς ἀγαθοῦ μετὰ πλειόνων κακῶν πεπραγμένου, οὔτε πάλιν ἀγαθὸν ὄντα ἀπολέσαι τὴν κόλασιν καὶ μὴ λαβεῖν αὐτήν, εἰ μετὰ πλειόνων ἀγαθῶν ἕν τι γένηται πονηρεύων· ἀνάγκη γὰρ ζυγῷ καὶ σταθμῷ πάντα ἀποδιδόναι τὸν θεόν.

Dam. Par. 349 (reading ἕν τινι γένηται);
Tischendorf, *Philonea*, p. 154 e cod. Cahirino;
Maximus (ed. Combefis. II. 642) (reading ἐάν τι γένηται).
Cod. Reg. 923, fol. 68 b, reading θεοῦ, ἀπωλέσαι, ἕν τινι γένηται πονηρὸν, &c., and expressly referring the passage to a treatise *contra Flaccum*. The same ascription is also given in Pitra, *Anal. Sac.* II. p. 310 e cod. Coislin. 276, f. 111.

αἰσχροὶ καὶ εἰκαῖοι οἱ ἐν τοῖς ματαίοις εὐφυΐαν ἀνεπιδεικνύντες, βραδεῖς μὲν ὄντες τὰ καλὰ παιδευθῆναι, τὰ δὲ ἐναντία μανθάνειν ὀξύτατοι καὶ προχειρότατοι.

Dam. Par. 379. Also Cod. Reg. 923, fol. 23, with distinct reference to *In Flaccum* and Cod. Rup. f. 45 (Φίλωνος).

Fragments from the lost book of Philo περὶ εὐσεβείας.

τοῦ μὴ προθύμως ὠφελεῖν ἄμεινον τὸ μηδὲ ὅλως ὑπισχνεῖσθαι. τῷ μὲν γὰρ οὐδεμία μέμψις ἕπεται, τῷ δὲ παρὰ μὲν τῶν ἀσθενεστέρων ἄχθος, παρὰ δὲ τῶν δυνατωτέρων μέγα μῖσος καὶ κόλασις αἰώνιος.

So printed from John Monachus in Mangey (II. 667), but in Cod. Reg. fol. 344 the word δυνατωτέρων is accidentally omitted, and the rest of the sentence reads μετὰ μίσους καὶ κόλασις παραίτιος, which seems nearer to the original text. And further the passage is referred to the treatise περὶ εὐσεβείας.

The same codex on fol. 265 b introduces another quotation as ἐκ τοῦ περὶ εὐσεβείας,

ὡς ἂν ἔχουσιν οἱ θύοντες (fol. 266) αὐτοῖς τὸν μισθὸν ὁ μείζονός (Cod. μιζονος) ἐστι· a passage which I confess I do not understand.

The next is from Pitra, *Anal. Sac.* II. 310, from Cod. Coislin. 276, fol. 169.

ἐκ τοῦ περὶ εὐσεβείας κεφαλαίου. τίνας γὰρ μᾶλλον εἰκὸς εὐθυμίας ἄγειν καὶ χάριτας ἢ τοὺς προσιόντας ἀγαθῷ καὶ ὠφέλειαν ἐλπίζοντας ἀγαθῶν· ἔστιν δὲ ὁ θεὸς τὸ πρεσβύτατον, ἄρδων, καθάπερ ἐκ πηγῆς τῆς

ἑαυτοῦ φύσεως, ἀνθρώπων γένει τὰ σωτήρια. συγγενὲς γὰρ οὐδὲν ἄλλο, ὡς ἐλπὶς εὐχῇ· καὶ γὰρ τὰ ἀμείνω προσδοκῶντες, εὐχόμεθα· καὶ εὐξάμενοι, χρηστὰ πάντως ἐλπίζομεν.

Fragments from the lost treatise of Philo De Animalibus *with the Latin of Aucher.*

(Aucher I. 125.)

§ 6...

Τὸ ζητεῖν καὶ πυνθάνεσθαι πρὸς διδασκαλίαν ἀνυσιμώτατον.

Dam. Par. 613 ⎫ without heading except Φί-
Cod. Reg. 923, f. 230 ⎭ λωνος.

§ 6...

Quaerere enim interrogareque multum favet expeditque doctrinae.

(Aucher I. 125.)

§ 7. Διδάσκουσι μὲν οἱ τὰς ἰδίας τέχνας μυοῦντες ἑτέρους, ἑρμηνεύουσι δὲ οἱ ἀλλοτρίαν ἀκοὴν εὐστοχίᾳ μνήμης ἀπαγγέλλοντες.

Mai, *Script. Vet.* VII. 99 (Cod. Vat. 1553), Φίλωνος· ἐκ τοῦ περὶ τῶν ἀλόγων ζώων.

§ 7.........Docent enim ii, qui propriam sententiam edocent alios. Exponunt autem illi, qui ab aliis auditu percepta exacte memoriae referunt.
....

(Aucher I. 172.)

§ 100...

Τὸ νέμειν ἴσα τοῖς ἀνίσοις τῆς μεγίστης ἐστὶν ἀδικίας.

Dam. Par. 556 ⎫ Φίλωνος.
Cod. Reg. 923, f. 208 ⎭

§ 100...

Indignis distribuere aequalia summa est iniuria.
....

Our next collection consists of the surviving fragments of the *Quæstiones in Genesim et Exodum*, accompanied by the corresponding Latin Version made by Aucher from those parts of the Quæstiones which are preserved in the Armenian

Codices to which he refers for his text. First we give the passages which are certainly identified; afterwards those which are ascribed to these books, but either not identified, wrongly referred, or else belonging to those parts of the lost books which are not extant in the Armenian.

Quæstiones in Genesim.

LIB. I.

Gen. ii. 18.

§ 17. Φίλους ἡγητέον τοὺς βοηθεῖν καὶ ἀντωφελεῖν ἐθέλοντας καὶ ἂν μὴ δύνωνται. Φιλία γὰρ ἐν τῷ χρειώδει μᾶλλον ἢ κράσει καὶ συμφωνίᾳ βεβαίῳ τῶν ἠθῶν, ὡς ἕκαστον τῶν συνελθόντων εἰς φιλικὴν κοινωνίαν τὸ Πυθαγόρειον ῥῆμα ἐπιφθέγξασθαι, ὅτι " ἆρά ἐστι φίλος ἕτερον ὡς ἐγώ."

From Dam. Par. 788 (Cod. Rupef. f. 275) with reference ἐκ τοῦ αʹ τῶν ἐν γενέσει ζητημάτων. The first sentence (with change to the singular number) in Maximus (II. 548) and Anton Melissa, col. 849. We should add οὐκ before ἐν τῷ χρειώδει. Cf. Clem. Al. *Strom.* II. 9. 41; Plutarch, *de Amic. mult.* 2.

Gen. ii. 19.

§ 20. ....

Ἀνδρὸς δὲ ἐπιστημονικωτάτου καὶ φρονήσει διαφέροντος οἰκειότατον τοῦτο τὸ ἔργον· οὐ σοφῷ μόνον, ἀλλὰ καὶ τῷ πρώτῳ γηγενεῖ τῶν ὀνομάτων ἡ θέσις· ἔδει γὰρ ἡγεμόνα μὲν τοῦ ἀνθρωπείου, βασιλέα δὲ τῶν γηγενῶν πάντων καὶ τοῦτο λαχεῖν γέρας ἐξαίρετον, ἵνα, ὥσπερ πρῶτος ᾔδει τὰ ζῷα καὶ πρῶτος ἀξιωθῇ τῆς ἐπὶ πᾶσιν ἀρχῆς, καὶ

Gen. ii. 18.

Cur dicit: "Non est bonum esse hominem solum; faciamus ei adiutorem secundum ipsum"?

§ 17. His designat communitatem habendam esse non cum omnibus, sed cum iis qui adiuvari et prodesse volunt, etsi vix possint; quoniam amor non magis in utilitate quam in concordia harmonica stabilis moris consistit; ita ut unusquisque convenientium in communitatem amoris Pythagoream valeat vocem edere: *Utique amicus est alter ego.*

Gen. ii. 19.

§ 20. ....

[Namque apte singulis naturalis accedit nomenclatio quum homo sapiens scientiaque praestantior interveniat.] Et profecto propria est menti sapientis solius,[1] immo primo terrigenae positio nominum; quoniam oportebat principem humani generis regemque universorum terrigenarum hanc quoque sortiri dignitatem.

[1] The negative has here dropped from the Greek text of the Armenian translator?

πρῶτος εἰσηγητὴς καὶ εὑρετὴς γένηται τῶν ἐπωνυμιῶν. Ἄτοπον γὰρ ἦν, ἀνώνυμα αὐτὰ καταλειφθέντα ὑπό τινος νεωτέρου προσονομασθῆναι, ἐπὶ καταλύσει τῆς τοῦ πρεσβυτέρου τιμῆς τε καὶ εὐκλείας.

....

From Dam. Par. 748 = Cod.Rup. f. 21 b, with reference to the questions on Genesis and reading εὐγενεῖ where the Latin shews γηγενεῖ to be the correct reading.

Qui nempe primus vidit animantia et ipse primus dignus fuit qui praeesset cunctis sicut princeps, decuit ut esset etiam primus nomenclator et inventor nominum. Siquidem abs re fuisset et insanum anonyma ea relinquendo praetermittere, vel a iuniore quopiam nomina accipere in contemptum dissolutionemque honoris ac laudis senioris.

....

Gen. ii. 19.

"Ἤγαγεν ὁ θεὸς τὰ ζῶα πρὸς τὸν Ἀδάμ, ἰδεῖν τί καλέσει αὐτά."

§ 21. Οὐ γὰρ ἐνδυάζει θεός· ἀλλ᾽ ἐπειδὴ νοῦν ἔδωκε τῷ ἀνθρώπῳ τῷ πρωτογενεῖ καὶ σπουδαίῳ, καθ᾽ ὃ ἐπιστημονικὸς ὢν πέφυκε λογίζεσθαι, καθάπερ ὑφηγητὴς γνώριμον κινεῖ πρὸς ἐπίδειξιν οἰκείαν καὶ ἀφορᾷ τὰ ἄριστα αὐτοῦ τῆς ψυχῆς ἔγγονα. Φανερῶς δὲ πάλιν καὶ διὰ τούτου πᾶν τὸ ἑκούσιον καὶ ἐφ᾽ ἡμῖν διατυποῖ, τοὺς πάντα κατ᾽ ἀνάγκην εἶναι λέγοντας δυσωπῶν. Ἢ ἐπεὶ ἔμελλον οἱ ἄνθρωποι χρῆσθαι, διὰ τοῦτο ἄνθρωπον αὐτὰ θέσθαι προσέταττεν.

From Dam. Par. p. 748 (Cod. Rupef. f. 21 b), ἐκ τῶν ἐν γενέσει ζητουμένων.

Gen. ii. 19.

Cur dicit: "Adduxit animalia ad Adam, ut videret quid vocaret ea," quandoquidem non dubitat deus?

§ 21. Vere alienum est a divina virtute dubitare......Sed quoniam intellectum dedit homini, maxime primo terrigenae atque virtutis studioso, quatenus sapiens est effectus, ita ut ex ipsa natura praeditus fuerit, ut perpenderet sicut dux [et princeps familiaris], dedit ei ut moveretur demonstraretque officium proprium; atque vidit reapse animi eius partum optimum. Adhaec evidenter per hoc omne voluntarium in nobis quoque imprimit, illos confutans, qui omnia ex necessitate fieri dictitant. Vel etiam quia hominum erat uti animantibus, ideo homini dedit, ut nomina illis poneret.

Gen. ii. 21.

§ 24. ....
Ὁ ὕπνος κατὰ τὸν προφήτην ἔκστασίς ἐστιν, οὐχὶ κατὰ μανίαν, ἀλλὰ κατὰ τὴν τῶν αἰσθήσεων ὕφεσιν καὶ τὴν ἀναχώρησιν τοῦ λογισμοῦ. Τότε γὰρ αἱ μὲν αἰσθήσεις ἐξίστανται τῶν αἰσθητῶν[1], ὁ δὲ οὐκέτι νευρο-

[1] The words καὶ ὁ λογισμὸς ἀναχωρεῖ ἐκ τῶν αἰσθήσεων appear to have stood here.

Gen. ii. 21.

§ 24. ....
Explanavit propheta noster. Somnus enim in se proprie ecstasis est, non ea, quae propior est amentiae, sed secundum sensuum solutionem absentiamque consilii. Tunc enim sensus recedunt a sensibilibus [et intellectus abest a sensibus,] non roborans nervos eorum neque

σπαστῶν οὐδὲ παρέχων κίνησιν αὐταῖς
ἠρεμεῖ, αἱ δὲ τὰς ἐνεργείας ἀποτετμημέναι
τῷ διεζεῦχθαι τῶν αἰσθητῶν ἀκίνητοι καὶ
ἀργαὶ ὑπεκλέλυνται.

From Joh. Monachus (Mangey II.
667 = Rup. f. 265) and Cod. Reg. 923
fol. 342 b, reading ἀλλ' ἡ κατὰ τῶν (where
the τὴν is accidentally omitted) and veri-
fying Mangey's conjecture νευροσπαστῶν.

praestans motum illis quoque, qui usum
operationis sortiti sint, abductis a sensibilibus.

Gen. ii. 23.

§ 28. ....

Ὡς προφήτης φησίν, οὔτε γεγονέναι ἐκ συνο-
μιλίας, οὔτε ἐκ γυναικός, ὡς οἱ μετέπειτα,
ἀλλά τινα φύσιν ἐν μεθορίῳ, καθάπερ ἀπὸ
ἀμπέλου κλήματιδος ἀφαιρεθείσης εἰς ἑτέρας ἀμπέλου γένεσιν.

From Dam. Par. 748 (e Cod. Rupef.
f. 21 b) ἐκ τῶν ἐν γενέσει ζητουμένων.

Gen. ii. 23.

§ 28. ....

Ut propheta dicit, quia de viro facta
fuit, non ex terra, quemadmodum ille,
neque ex semine, ut caeteri post illum,
sed natura quadam mediocri, atque sicut
ex vite ramus eductus ad alterius vitis
generationem.

Gen. ii. 24.

Διό φησιν· "῞Ενεκεν τούτου καταλείψει
ἄνθρωπος τὸν πατέρα καὶ τὴν μητέρα αὐτοῦ
καὶ προσκολληθήσεται πρὸς τὴν γυναῖκα
αὐτοῦ· καὶ ἔσονται δύο εἰς σάρκα μίαν";

§ 29. ....τὸ εὐαφέστατον
καὶ αἰσθητικώτατον, ἐν ᾧ καὶ τὸ ἀλγεῖν καὶ
τὸ ἤδεσθαι.

From Dam. Par. 748, Mang. II. 654
(e cod. Rup. f. 21 b) ἐκ τῶν ἐν γενέσει
ζητουμένων.

Gen. ii. 24.

Cur dicit: "Propterea relinquet homo
patrem suum et matrem, et adhaerebit
uxori suae; et erunt duo in carne una"?

§ 29. ....

Indicat nimium tangibilem ac sensi-
bilem esse, in qua dolore affici et volup-
tate frui consistit.

Gen. iii. 19.

Τί ἐστιν "ἕως τοῦ ἐπιστρέψαι σε εἰς τὴν
γῆν ἐξ ἧς ἐλήφθης"; οὐ γὰρ ἐκ γῆς διεπλάσθη μόνον ὁ ἄνθρωπος ἀλλὰ καὶ θείου
πνεύματος.

§ 51. Ἐπειδὴ δὲ οὐ διέμεινεν ἀδιάστρο-
φος, προστάξεως θείας ἠλόγηκε καὶ τοῦ

Gen. iii. 19.

Quid est, "Donec revertaris in terram,
de qua sumptus es"? non enim de terra
sola creatus fuit homo, verum etiam ex
divino spiritu.

§ 51. [Primum terrigenam terra caelo-
que compactum fuisse constat.] Verum

κρείττονος μέρους ἀποτεμνόμενος οὐρανομί-
μητον πολιτείαν ὅλον αὐτὸν προσένειμε τῇ
γῇ. Εἰ μὲν γὰρ ἀρετῆς, ἥτις ἀθανατίζει,
ἐραστὴς ἐγένετο, πάντως ἂν ἐλάμβανε κλῆρον τὸν οὐρανόν· ἐπειδὴ δὲ ἡδονὴν ἐζήτησε,
δι' ἧς ψυχικὸς θάνατος ἐπιγίνεται, τῇ γῇ
προσενεμήθη.

....

From Dam. Par. p. 748 (e cod. Rupef.
f. 20 b) with reference ἐκ τῶν ἐν γενέσει
ζητουμένων.

quia non constitit incorruptus, sed mandatum dei despexit, ex optima parte effu-
giens, caelo, totum se mancipium terrae
dedit, crassiori ac graviori elemento.
Deinde si quis virtutis desiderio arsit,
quae immortalem facit animam, omnino
adeptus est sortem caelestem. Quia
vero voluptatis aemulus fuit, qua mors
acquiritur spiritualis, terrae se rursum
tradidit.

....

Gen. iii. 22.

§ 55. ....

Οὔτε ἐνδυασμὸς οὔτε φθόνος περὶ θεόν·
χρῆται δὲ πολλάκις ὀνόμασιν ἐνδυαστικοῖς
ἢ διανοητικοῖς κατ' ἀναφορὰν ἐπὶ τὸ "ὡς
ἄνθρωπος" κεφάλαιον. Διττὰ γάρ, ὡς πολλάκις ἔφην, ἐστὶν τὰ ἀνωτάτω κεφάλαια·
τὸ μὲν "οὐχ ὡς ἄνθρωπος ὁ θεός," τὸ δὲ
"ὡς ἄνθρωπος παιδεύει τὸν υἱόν." Τὸ μὲν
πρότερον ἐξουσίας τὸ δὲ δεύτερον παιδείας
καὶ εἰσαγωγῆς ἐστιν.

From the Parallels of John Monachus
(Mang. II. 669) = Cod. Rup. with heading ἐκ τῶν αὐτῶν = ἐκ τοῦ β′ τῶν ἐν γενέσει
ζητημάτων. Also with some modifications
in Procopius (Mai, *Auct. Class.* VI. 208).

Gen. iii. 22.

§ 55. ....

[Verum est] nec dubitare nec invidere
divinitatem: utitur tamen plerumque
rebus nominibusque dubiis, annuens fere
caput illud: *ut homo.* Duplex enim est,
ut dixi, superius caput: aliquando, *non
ut homo deus:* et aliquando: *sicut homo
instruit filium, sic dominus moneat te.*
Primum itaque principatus est, secundum vero disciplinae.

....

Gen. iv. 4.

§ 62. [πρό γε μὴν "τὸ προσφέρειν δῶρα
καὶ θυσίας."] Ζητῶν τίνι διαφέρει δῶρον
θυσίας, εὑρίσκω ὅτι ὁ μὲν θύων ἐπιδιαιρεῖ,
τὸ μὲν αἷμα τῷ βωμῷ προχέων, τὰ δὲ κρέα
οἴκαδε κομίζων· ὁ δὲ δωρούμενος ὅλον ἔοικε
παραχωρεῖν τῷ λαμβάνοντι· ὁ μὲν οὖν φίλαυτος διανομεὺς οἷος ὁ Κάϊν, ὁ δὲ φιλόθεος
δωρῆται οἷον ὁ Ἄβελ.

Cramer, *Catena in Heb.* p. 580, e cod.
Paris. 238. Also in Procopius (Mai, *Auct.*

Gen. iv. 4.

§ 62. Quam distinctionem habet munus a sacrificio?

Ille, qui mactat sacrificium divisione
facta, sanguinem circa aram fundit et
carnem ducit domum. Qui vero instar
muneris offert totum, ut visum est,
offert acceptanti. Sui itaque ipsius
amator distributor est, sicut Cain;
amator vero dei munerator est, sicut
Abel.

Class. VI. 220) as far as λαμβάνοντι, and
adding remarks on the difference between
the φίλαυτος and the φιλόθεος, the διανομεὺς and the δωρητικός. We may therefore correct the impossible reading of
Cramer to δωρητικὸς οἷος.

Gen. iv. 7.

§ 64. ....
Τὸ εὐχαριστεῖν θεῷ καθ' ἑαυτό, ὀρθῶς ἔχον
ἐστί· τὸ δὲ μήτε πρῶτον, μήτε ἐκ τῶν πρώτων ἀπαρχόμενον, ψεκτόν. Οὐ γὰρ δεῖ τὰ
μὲν πρεσβεῖα ἐν τῇ γενέσει τιθέναι, τὰ δὲ
δεύτερα τῷ δωρησαμένῳ θεῷ προσφέρειν.
Ἥδε ἐστὶν ἐπίληπτος διαίρεσις, ἀταξίαν
τινὰ τάξεως εἰσηγουμένη.

From Joh. Monach. (Mang. II. 668) =
Rup. f. 269 b. Also worked over by
Procopius (Mai, *Auct. Class.* VI. 221), from
whose text and the Latin we see that
ἑαυτῷ must be supplied before τιθέναι.

Gen. iv. 10.

§ 65. ....
Τὸ μὴ ἁμαρτάνειν μηδὲν τὸ παράπαν μέγιστον ἀγαθόν· τὸ ἁμαρτάνοντα ἐντραπῆναι
συγγενὲς ἐκείνου, νεώτερον, ὡς ἄν τις εἴποι,
παρὰ πρεσβύτερον. Εἰσὶ γὰρ οἱ ἐπὶ ἁμαρτα-
νομένοις ὡς ἐπὶ κατορθώμασιν ἀγαλλόμενοι
δυσίατον, μᾶλλον δὲ ἀνίατον νόσον ἔχοντες.

From Dam. Par. 751 = Rup. f. 46 b,
with reference ἐκ τῶν ἐν γενέσει ζητουμένων. Cf. for the first sentence, Procopius *in loc.*

Gen. iv. 23.

§ 77. ....
Ὁ μὲν Κάϊν, ἐπειδὴ τὸ μέγεθος τοῦ ἄγους
ἠγνόησε, τοῦ μηδέποτε περιπεσεῖν θανάτῳ,
τιμωρίας δίδωσιν ἁπλουστέρας. Ὁ δὲ μι-
μητὴς ἐκείνου, μὴ δυνάμενος εἰς τὴν αὐτὴν

Gen. iv. 7.

§ 64. ....
Praeterea gratias referre deo in se ipso
seorsim rectum est; non autem primum
auctorem, neque ex primitiis novella
munera recipere eum (nostra negli-
gentia) improbandum. Quoniam non
oportet priora, quae dantur in creatis,
sibi, secunda vero sapientissimo (crea-
tori) offerre: quae est divisio vitupe-
randa et improbanda, praeposterum
referens ordinem.

Gen. iv. 10.

§ 65. ....
Quoniam nihil omnino peccare maxi-
mum est bonum; qui vero peccat et
erubescens pudore afficitur, cognatus est
eius, iunior, ut ita dixerim, maioris.
Sunt enim, qui de peccatis tamquam de
rectitudine exsultantes, difficili sanatu,
imo insanabili morbo laborant.

Gen. iv. 23.

§ 77. ....
Propterea et Cain [auctor existens homi-
cidii], quum ignoravit gravitatem inqui-
namenti, eo quod antea nunquam occur-
rerat mors, poenam luit simpliciorem,

ἀπολογίαν τῆς ἀγνοίας συμφυγεῖν, δεκαπλᾶς
εἰκότως ὑπομένει δίκας....Διὰ τοῦτο "ἐκ δὲ
Λάμεχ ἑβδομηκοντάκις ἑπτά"· διὰ τὴν εἰρη-
μένην αἰτίαν, καθ᾽ ἣν ὁ δεύτερος ἁμαρτὼν
καὶ μὴ σωφρονισθεὶς τῇ τοῦ προηδικηκότος
τιμωρίᾳ τήν τε ἐκείνου παντελῶς ἀναδέχεται
ἁπλουστέραν οὖσαν, καθάπερ ἐν ἀριθμοῖς
αἱ μονάδες ἔχουσι, καὶ πολυπλασιωτέραν,
ὁμοιουμένην ταῖς ἐν ἀρίθμοις δεκάσιν. ἣν
γνωσιμαχῶν Λάμεχ καθ᾽ ἑαυτοῦ.

From Dam. Par. (Cod. Rupef.) p. 776.
It is found in fact twice, f. 128 b, and f.
271, as far as πολυπλασιωτέραν, also in
Cod. Reg. 923, fol. 356 b with the following variants.

Κάϊν—add ἴσως Reg.
αὐτὴν ἀπολογ. om. αὐτὴν Rup.
συμφυγεῖν· καταφυγεῖν Rup.
δεκαπλᾶς· διπλᾶς Rup.
ἐκ δὲ Λάμεχ· omit δὲ Reg.
τιμωρίᾳ κτέ. read τιμωρίᾳ οὐ μόνον τῇ
ἐκείνου παντελῶς ἀναδέχεσθαι ἀλλὰ καὶ
πόλυ πλειοτέραν Reg.

Gen. iv. 26.

§ 79. ....
Ἐλπίς ἐστι προπάθειά τις, χαρὰ πρὸ χαρᾶς,
ἀγαθῶν οὖσα προσδοκία.
From Anton Melissa (*Patr. Gr.* 136,
col. 789). For τις, χαρὰ read τις χαρᾶς.

Gen. v. 24.

§ 85. ....
Ibid. Ἤδη τινὲς ἀψίκοροι γευσάμενοι καλοκἀγαθίας καὶ ἐλπίδα παρασχόντες ὑγιείας εἰς
τὴν αὐτὴν ἐπανέστρεψαν νόσον.
From Dam. Par. 784 (Cod. Rupef.) apparently as ἐκ τῶν ἐν ἐξόδῳ ζητημάτων,
an easy confusion.
H.

[septuplum in unitatis ordine.] Imitator
autem eius quum haud possit ad eandem
apologiam ignorantiae confugere, duplicem debet sustinere poenam......ex La-
mech vero septuagesies septem praedictis
de causis: eo quod secundus iste peccans,
nec doctus poena primi delinquentis et
eiusdem omnino percipit supplicium,
quod simplicius est, ut in numeris unum,
et multiplicem poenam aequalem denario
inter numeros.

The last sentence in the Greek appears
to be a gloss.

Gen. iv. 26.

§ 79. ....
Spes autem praesagium quoddam gaudii
est; ante vero gaudium exspectatio bonorum est.
Exprimit Gr. vocem προπάθεια vel
προπάθημα (Aucher).

Gen. v. 24.

§ 85. ....
Ecce enim nonnulli citius expleri videntur gustata probitate, atque spe data
sanitatis denuo in eundem recidunt
morbum.
Ecce (the Armenian translator read
ἴδε).

3

Gen. vi. 1.

§ 89. Ἀεὶ φθάνουσι τὴν δίκην αἱ τοῦ θεοῦ χάριτες. Ἔργον γὰρ αὐτῷ προηγούμενον τὸ εὐεργετεῖν, τὸ δὲ κολάζειν ἑπόμενον. Φιλεῖ δέ, ὅταν μέλλῃ μεγάλα συνίστασθαι κακά, μεγάλων καὶ πολλῶν ἀγαθῶν ἀφθονία προγενέσθαι.

....

From Joh. Monach. (Mangey II. 670) ἐκ τῶν ἐν ἐξόδῳ ζητουμένων.

Gen. vi. 1.

§ 89. Semper divinae gratiae praecedunt iudicium, quoniam opus dei prius est benefacere, deperdere vero postmodum sequitur. Ipse tamen amat et solet, quando mala sunt futura gravia, ut producatur antea maiorum multorumque bonorum copia.

....

Gen. vi. 4.

§ 92. ....

Πνευματικαὶ τῶν ἀγγέλων οὐσίαι· εἰκάζονται δὲ πολλάκις ἀνθρώπων ἰδέαις, πρὸς τὰς ὑποκειμένας χρείας μεταμορφούμενοι.

Dam. Par. 309. It occurs again in Dam. Par. 772 (Cod. Rupef.) with slight variations and an ascription ἐκ τοῦ α΄ τῶν ἐν γενέσει ζητουμένων.

Gen. vi. 4.

§ 92. ....

Enim vero spiritalis est angelorum substantia, passim tamen occurrit, ut hominum imitantes speciem pro rebus usurpandis sese commutent.

Gen. vi. 6.

§ 93. Ἔνιοι νομίζουσι μεταμέλειαν ἐμφαίνεσθαι περὶ τὸ θεῖον διὰ τῶν ὀνομάτων· οὐκ εὖ δὲ ὑπονοοῦσι. Χωρὶς γὰρ τοῦ μὴ τρέπεσθαι τὸ θεῖον, οὔτε τὸ "ἐνεθυμήθη" οὔτε τὸ "ἐνενόησεν" δηλωτικὰ μεταμελείας ἐστίν— τὸ δὲ θεῖον ἄτρεπτον—ἀλλ' ἀκραιφνοῦς λογισμοῦ περιεσκεμμένου τὴν αἰτίαν, ἧς ἕνεκα ἐποίησεν τὸν ἄνθρωπον ἐπὶ τῆς γῆς.

From Joh. Monach. (Mang. II. 669) ἐκ τοῦ β΄ τῶν ἐν γενέσει ζητημάτων.

Gen. vi. 6.

§ 93. Quidam putant poenitere divinitatem videri his verbis : verum haud recte putant, quoniam immutabilis est divinitas, nec [illud] curare cogitando neque agitare in mente indicia poenitentiae sunt, sed lucidi certique consilii, quo curam prae se fert agitans in mente causam, propter quam fecit hominem super terram.

Gen. vi. 7.

Διὰ τί ἄνθρωπον ἀπειλῶν ἀπαλεῖψαι καὶ τὰ ἄλογα προσδιαφθείρει;

§ 94. Διότι οὐ προηγουμένως δι' ἑαυτὰ γέγονε τὰ ἄλογα ἀλλὰ χάριν ἀνθρώπων καὶ τῆς τούτων ὑπηρεσίας, ὧν διαφθειρομένων

Gen. vi. 7.

Cur minatus hominem delere, iumenta quoque cum illo corrumpere ait ?

§ 94. Quod non necessarie ac primarie propter se ipsa facta sunt animalia, sed propter homines et pro servitio illorum

εἰκότως καὶ ἐκεῖνα συνδιαφθείρεται, μηκέτι ὄντων δι' οὓς γέγονε.

From Catena Inedita Cod. Reg. 1825 (Mang. ΙΙ. 675), also in Catena Mus. Britt. (Cod. Burney 34) f. 35, (φίλωνος ἑβραίου) transposing ἄνθρωπον and ἀπειλῶν and omitting καὶ before ἐκεῖνα; also in the Leipsic Catena Ι. col. 141, where it is attributed to Procopius. It is followed in Cod. Burney by the following passage, which is evidently not Philo but a gloss of Procopius: ὁ μὲν ἁπλούστερός φησι ὅτι Νῶε οὐκ ἦν ἐπὶ τῆς γῆς καὶ οἱ σὺν αὐτῷ· ἐπὶ ξύλου γὰρ ἦσαν ὀχούμενοι· ὁ δὲ βλέπεται ὅτι ὅπου θησαυρὸς ἐκεῖ καὶ ἡ καρδία αὐτοῦ κτέ. Cf. Mai (*Auct. Class.* VI. pp. 255, 262.)

Gen. vi. 13.

§ 100. ....

'Ο καιρὸς παρὰ τοῖς φαυλοτέροις νομίζεται εἶναι θεὸς τὸν ὄντα ὄντως παρακαλυπτόμένοις...καὶ θεοπλαστούντων καὶ ἐξ ἐναντίας τιθέντων τῷ ἀληθεῖ θεῷ τὸ λέγειν τὸν καιρὸν αἴτιον τῶν ἐν τῷ βίῳ πραγμάτων εἶναι. τοῖς γὰρ εὐσεβέσι οὐ καιρὸν ἀλλὰ θεὸν παρ' οὗ καὶ οἱ καιροὶ καὶ οἱ χρόνοι· πλὴν αἴτιον οὐ πάντων ἀλλὰ μόνων ἀγαθῶν καὶ τῶν κατ' ἀρετήν· ὡς γὰρ ἀμέτοχος κακίας, οὕτω καὶ ἀναίτιος.

From Cod. Rup. f. 193 (Φίλωνος· περὶ κοσμοποιίας); the last sentence also in Pitra (*Anal. Sacr.* II. 307), from Cod. Coislin. 276, f. 238, and again in Rup. 222 b.

quibus corruptis iure meritoque et illa cum istis corrumpuntur, quum non amplius sint illi, in quorum gratiam facta fuere.

Gen. vi. 13.

§ 100. ....

Secundo *tempus* (ut Cronus s. Chronus) ab hominum pessimis putatur deus, volentibus Ens essentiale abscondere, quapropter dixit: *Tempus cuiuscumque hominis venit contra me*, quod nimirum humanum tempus deum creant (ethnici), et opponunt vero (deo). [Attamen iam intimatum est caeteris quoque locis (scripturae s.), ita se habentibus: *Longe abscessit ab illis tempus, dominus autem in nobis est.* Ac si diceret: Pravis hominibus] tempus putatur causa rerum mundi, sapientibus vero et optimis non tempus, sed deus, a quo tempora et tempestates. Causa sane non omnium, sed bonorum tantum eorumque qui secundum virtutem sint: sicut enim expers est malitiae, ita etiam nec causa.

Quæstiones in Genesim.

Lib. II.

Gen. vi. 14.

§ 5. ....

Δυνατὸν ἐν τριακοστῷ ἔτει αὐτὸν ἄνθρωπον πάππον γενέσθαι· ἡβᾶν μὲν περὶ τὴν τεσσερεσκαιδεκάτην ἡλικίαν, ἐν ᾗ σπείρει, τὸ δὲ σπαρὲν ἐντὸς ἐνιαυτοῦ γενόμενον, πάλιν πεντεκαιδεκάτῳ ἔτει τὸ ὅμοιον ἑαυτῷ γεννᾶν.

Dam. Par. 314.

Gen. vi. 14.

§ 5. ....

Ex homine in tricennio potest avus haberi, quoniam pubertatem attingit quarto decimo aetatis anno, quo seminare potest; semen autem eius inter annum confectum, iterum post annos quindecim generat similem sibi.

Gen. vi. 17.

§ 9. ....

Διότι οὐ προηγουμένως δι' ἑαυτὰ γέγονε τὰ ἄλογα, ἀλλὰ χάριν ἀνθρώπων καὶ τῆς τούτων ὑπηρεσίας, ὧν διαφθειρομένων εἰκότως καὶ ἐκεῖνα συνδιαφθείρεται, μηκέτι ὄντων δι' οὓς γέγονε.

I have repeated the above Greek passage from 1 Quaest. in Gen. § 94, not as being the proper counterpart to the Latin, but very similar to it.

Gen. vi. 17.

§ 9. ....

Tertio animalia facta sunt non propter se, ut a sapientibus dictum est, sed propter hominum servitium opusque decusque : iure itaque sublatis iis, propter quos fuere, illa quoque contigit vita privari.

Cf. the following passage from Catena Lippomani in Gen. vi. f. 129 b.

Philo Hebraeus :

"Et ego corrumpo eos cum terra." Deus etiam animalia corrupit et internecioni dedit quia non propter se sed propter hominem condita fuerant, quo sublato, ipsa quoque e medio tolluntur.

Gen. vii. 2.

§ 12. ....

Ἡ ἐν τῷ φαύλῳ κακία διδυμοτοκεῖ. Διχόνους γὰρ [καὶ] ἐπαμφοτερὴς ὁ ἄφρων, τὰ ἄμικτα μιγνύς, καὶ φύρων καὶ συγχέων τὰ διακρίνεσθαι δυνάμενα, τοιαῦτα ἐν ψυχῇ χρώματα ἐπιφέρων, οἷάπερ ὁ λεπρὸς ἐν τῷ σώματι, μιαίνων καὶ τοὺς ὑγιεῖς λογισμοὺς ἀπὸ τῶν θανατούντων ἅμα καὶ φονώντων.

From John Monachus (Mang. II. 663) = Rup. f. 125 and again on f. 138 b. Mangey's emendation φονώντων for πο-

Gen. vii. 2.

§ 12. ....

At in improbo malitia gemella exsistit, quoniam anceps et dubius est iniquus ut haesitabundus, immixta commiscens inficiensque, confundendo ea quae facile disiungi possunt. Tales sunt, qui colorem indunt animae, velut variegatus ac leprosus in corpore, infecto et inquinato sano consilio a mortifero exitiosoque.

νούντων is confirmed by the Latin text and by the alternative passage in the Codex.

Gen. vii. 4.

Τί ἐστι ἐξαλείψω πᾶσαν τὴν ἐξανάστασιν ἣν ἐποίησα ἀπὸ προσώπου τῆς γῆς;

§ 15. Τί φασι οὐκ "ἀπὸ τῆς γῆς" ἀλλ᾽ "ἀπὸ τοῦ προσώπου τῆς γῆς"; τουτέστι τῆς ἐπιφανείας ἵνα ἐν τῷ βάθει ἡ ζωτικὴ δύναμις τῶν σπερμάτων ὅλων οὖσα φυλάττηται σῶα καὶ ἀπαθὴς παντὸς τοῦ βλάπτειν δυναμένου· τῆς γὰρ ἰδίας προθέσεως οὐκ ἐπιλέλησται ὁ ποιητής· ἀλλὰ τὰ μὲν ἄνω καὶ κατ᾽ αὐτὴν τὴν ἐπιφάνειαν κινούμενα φθείρει, τὰς δὲ ῥίζας βυθίους ἐᾷ πρὸς γένεσιν ἄλλων.

From Cat. Burney fol. 35 b, and Cat. Lipsiensis I. col. 144, with the heading Φίλωνος ἐπισκόπου, the Leipsic catena reading βυθίας. Cod. Burney also adds a long gloss beginning οὐκ ἐπειδὴ τῷ δημιουργῷ τὰ μὲν καθαρὰ τὰ δὲ ἀκάθαρτα κτέ.

[Καὶ ἐξήλειψε πᾶν τὸ ἀνάστημα ὃ ἦν ἐπὶ προσώπου τῆς γῆς.]

Θεοπρεπῶς τὸ ἐξαλείψω ὥσπερ τῶν ἀπαλειφομένων τὰ μὲν γράμματα ἀπαλείφονται, αἱ δέλτοι δὲ διαμένουσιν· ἡ μὲν γὰρ ἀσεβὴς γενεὰ ἐξήλειπται, τὸ δὲ κατὰ διαδοχὴν τῆς οὐσίας γένος διετηρήθη, ὡς δίκαιον.

Pitra (*Anal. Sac.* II. 313) from Cod. Vat. 748, f. 23 and Cod. Vat. 1657, f. 23.

Gen. vii. 4.

Quid est "Delebo omnem suscitationem (naturae) vigentem, quam feci, a facie terrae"?

§ 15. [Nonne ergo demirati resilitis, haec audientes, ob pulchritudinem sententiae?] Non enim dixit: *de terra* delere sed "*de facie terrae*", videlicet ex superficie: quod nempe in profunditate vitalis virtus seminum omnium incolumis servetur et immunis ab omni malo quod potest damnum ferre. Quoniam propositionis suae non est oblitus creator, sed illos, qui obiter et secundum solam superficiem moventur, corrumpit; radices tamen in profunditate relinquit ad generationem aliarum causarum. Verum divinitus sane et illud *Delebo* scriptum est; evenit enim, ut delendis deletis litteris pinax litterarum permaneat idem. Quo probat, quod inconstantem generationem propter impietatem delebit litterarum instar; conversationem autem et essentiam humani generis perpetuo servabit pro futurorum semine.

A portion of the same passage is also found in Catena Lippomani on Gen. vii. p. 136, as follows.

Philo Episcopus.

Delebo a facie terrae quia radices ac semina eorum quae super terram diluvio corrupta sunt, sub terra universorum opifex ad reparationem servari voluit. Ac quemadmodum literae quidem delentur, tabella tamen manet, ita impiorum quidem genus deletum est, successio tamen secundum essentiam manet.

Gen. vii. 11.

§ 17. ....

Κατὰ τὸν τῆς ἰσημερίας καιρὸν ἐπισκήπτει ὁ κατακλυσμὸς ἐν ᾗ καὶ τὸν τοῦ γένους ἀρχηγέτην διαπεπλάσθαι φασίν· ὁ δὲ ἕβδομος μὴν λέγεται καὶ πρῶτος καθ᾽ ἑτέραν καὶ ἑτέραν ἐπιβολήν· διὸ καὶ ἡ τοῦ Νῶε πρόσοδος ἐξομοιοῦται τῷ πρώτῳ γηγενεῖ ὡς ἀρχὴ συστάσεως δευτέρου κόσμου.

The above passage from Cod. Burney fol. 36 a (φίλωνος) and Cat. Lipsiensis I. col. 149 seems to be based on parts of the parallel passage in the Quaestiones: but it must be admitted, in view of the frequent repetition of the same ideas and expressions in Philo, that the identification is somewhat uncertain. The text in Cod. Burney is a little confused, reading καθ᾽ ἑτέρας καὶ ἑτέρας καὶ ἑτέραν ἐπιβολήν.

Gen. vii. 11.

§ 17. ....

Quod si autumnali aequinoctio factum fuisset diluvium, [quum nihil esset in terra, sed omnia collecta in congeriem propriam, nullatenus veluti supplicium crederetur, sed potius beneficium, aqua purgante campos et montes.] Quum tamen et primus terrigena eadem tempestate creatus fuerit, [quem oracula divina Adam vocant—quia nimirum omnimodo decebat, ut etiam humani generis proavus vel protoparens sive pater, aut quoquo modo oporteat nominare maiorem illum, crearetur tempore verni aequinoctii, quum cuncta terrena fructibus plena essent... Vernum autem aequinoctium fit] mense septimo, qui et primus dicitur sub vario conceptu. Quoniam itaque et a Noë post corruptionem a diluvio factam primum generationis exordium fit, iterum seminatis hominibus, similis (ideo) noscitur primo terrigenae, quantum fieri potest.

Gen. viii. 6.

§ 34. ....

Αἱ αἰσθήσεις θυρίσιν ἐοίκασι. Διὰ γὰρ τούτων ὡσανεὶ θυρίδων ἐπεισέρχεται τῷ νῷ ἡ κατάληψις τῶν αἰσθητῶν· καὶ πάλιν ὁ νοῦς ἐκκύπτει δι᾽ αὐτῶν. Μέρος δέ ἐστι τῶν θυρίδων, λέγω δὴ τῶν αἰσθήσεων, ἡ ὅρασις, ἐπεὶ καὶ ψυχῆς μάλιστα συγγενής, ὅτιπερ καὶ τῷ καλλίστῳ τῶν ὄντων, φωτί, οἰκεία, καὶ ὑπηρέτης τῶν θείων. Ἥτις καὶ τὴν εἰς φιλοσοφίαν ὁδὸν ἔτεμε τὴν πρώτην. Θεασάμενος γὰρ ἡλίου κίνησιν καὶ σελήνης, καὶ τὰς τῶν ἀστέρων περιόδους, καὶ τὴν ἀπλανῆ περιφορὰν τοῦ σύμπαντος οὐρανοῦ,

Gen. viii. 6.

§ 34. ....

Corporis fenestras imitatae sunt singulae partes sensuum, quoniam per istos tamquam per fenestras intrat in intellectum comprehensio sensibilium, et rursus intellectus quasi porrectus attendit per istos. Pars autem fenestrarum, sensuum inquam, (nobilior) est visus : quippe qui et animae maxime affinis est, et pulcherrimae entium lucis familiaris atque minister sacrorum, quique viam ad philosophiam primus paravit. Videns enim solis motum, ac lunae caeterorumque

καὶ τὴν παντὸς τοῦ λόγου κρείττονα τάξιν τε καὶ ἁρμονίαν, καὶ τὸν τοῦ κόσμου μόνον ἀψευδέστατον κοσμοποιόν, διήγγελλε τῷ ἡγεμόνι λογισμῷ ἃ εἶδεν. Ὁ δὲ ἐν ὄμματι ὀξυδερκεστέρῳ θεασάμενος καὶ ταῦτα καὶ παραδείγματι καὶ εἴδει διὰ τούτων ἀνωτέρω καὶ τὸν ἁπάντων αἴτιον, εὐθὺς εἰς ἔννοιαν ἦλθε θεοῦ καὶ γενέσεως καὶ προνοίας, λογισάμενος, ὅτι ὅλη φύσις οὐκ αὐτοματισθεῖσα γέγονεν, ἀλλ' ἀνάγκη ποιητὴν εἶναι καὶ πατέρα, κυβερνήτην τε καὶ ἡνίοχον, ὃς καὶ πεποίηκε καὶ ποιήματα αὐτοῦ σώζει.

From John Monachus (Mangey II. 665) = Cod. Rup. f. 221. With heading ἐκ τοῦ περὶ κοσμοποιΐας. Mangey conjectures παραδειγματικὰ εἴδη τούτων, which seems to be right as far as the first two words are concerned. We must however retain διὰ before τούτων for *per ista* of the Latin.

planetarum vagationes, et infallibilem circumlationem totius caeli, atque superiorem omni ratione ordinem harmoniamque, sicut et unicum mundi verum opificem, retulit solus uni principi consiliorum, quidquid vidit. Ille vero (intellectus) acuto oculo cernens cum ista, tum per ista superiores ideas demonstrativas universorumque causam, illico statim intellexit deum, una cum conceptu generationis ac providentiae; quod nempe visibilis haec natura non [per se facta est. Nam fieri nequibat, ut talis harmonia, ordo, ratio, analogia constantissima, et talis ac tanta concordia, atque vera prosperitas felicissima] suapte (vi) exsisteret, sed necesse est aliquem esse creatorem ac patrem sicut gubernatorem atque aurigam, qui haec generavit et generata ipsa salva et sana servat.

Gen. viii. 21.

§ 54. Ἡ πρότασις ἐμφαίνει μεταμέλειαν, ἀνοίκειον πάθος θείας δυνάμεως. Ἀνθρώποις μὲν γὰρ ἀσθενεῖς αἱ γνῶμαι καὶ ἀβέβαιοι, ὡς τὰ πράγματα πολλῆς γέμοντα ἀδηλότητος. Θεῷ δὲ οὐδὲν ἄδηλον, οὐδὲν ἀκατάληπτον· ἰσχυρογνωμονέστατος γὰρ καὶ βεβαιότατος. Πῶς οὖν τῆς αὐτῆς ὑπούσης αἰτίας, ἐπιστάμενος ἐξ ἀρχῆς ὅτι ἔγκειται ἡ διάνοια τοῦ ἀνθρώπου ἐπιμελῶς ἐπὶ τὰ πονηρὰ ἐκ νεότητος, πρῶτον μὲν ἔφθειρεν τὸ γένος κατακλυσμῷ, μετὰ δὲ ταῦτα φησὶν μηκέτι διαφθείρειν, καίτοι διαμενούσης ἐν τῇ ψυχῇ τῆς αὐτῆς κακίας; Λεκτέον οὖν ὅτι πᾶσα ἡ τοιάδε τῶν λόγων ἰδέα περιέχεται ἐν τοῖς νόμοις πρὸς μάθησιν καὶ ὠφέλειαν διδασκαλίας, μᾶλλον ἢ πρὸς τὴν φύσιν τῆς ἀληθείας. Διττῶν γὰρ ὄντων κεφαλαίων

Gen. viii. 21.

§ 54. Rationes allatae indicare videntur poenitentiam, quae non est affectio familiaris divinae virtuti. Nam hominum ingenia fragilia sunt atque inconstantia, ita ut (s. sicut et) res apud illos incertae omnino sint; deo vero nihil incertum, nihil imperceptibile, validissimi enim consilii est ac constantissimi. Quomodo ergo quum eaedem rationes adsint, quod nimirum ab initio conscius erat mentem humanam iacere diligenter in malis a iuventute, praevenerit corrumpere genus humanum per diluvium, posthac autem dicit non ultra corrumpere velle, dum tamen restant in animo eadem mala? Verum dicendum est, quod cuncta huiusmodi verborum genera com-

ἃ κεῖται διὰ πάσης τῆς νομοθεσίας· ἑνὸς μὲν
καθ᾽ ὃ λέγεται, "οὐχ ὡς ἄνθρωπος ὁ θεός"·
ἑτέρου δὲ καθ᾽ ὃ "ὡς ἄνθρωπος" παιδεύειν
λέγεται υἱόν· τὸ μὲν πρότερον τῆς ἀληθείας
ἐστίν· ὄντως γὰρ ὁ θεός, οὐχ ὡς ἄνθρωπος
ἀλλ᾽ οὐδὲ ὡς ἥλιος, οὐδὲ ὡς οὐρανὸς οὐδὲ ὡς
κόσμος αἰσθητὸς ἢ νοητὸς ἀλλ᾽ ὡς θεὸς εἰ
καὶ τοῦτο θέμις εἰπεῖν. Ὁμοιότητα γὰρ ἢ
σύγκρισιν ἢ παραβολὴν οὐκ ἐπιδέχεται τὸ
μακάριον ἐκεῖνο, μᾶλλον δὲ μακαριότητος
αὐτῆς ὑπεράνω. Τὸ δὲ ὕστερον τῆς διδασκαλίας καὶ ὑφηγήσεως, τὸ "ὡς ἄνθρωπος,"
ἕνεκα τοῦ παιδεῦσαι τοὺς γηγενεῖς ἡμᾶς ἵνα
μὴ τὰς ὀργὰς καὶ τὰς τιμωρίας μέχρι παντὸς
ἀποτείνωμεν ἀσπόνδως καὶ ἀσυμβάτως ἔ-
χοντες...

Τὸ οὖν "διενοήθη" ἐπὶ θεοῦ οὐ κυριολογεῖται,
τοῦ τὴν γνώμην καὶ τὴν διάνοιαν βεβαιο-
τάτου.

[Ἡ τυχοῦσα τῆς κακίας γένεσις δουλοῖ
τὸν λογισμόν, καὶ ἂν μήπω τέλειον αὐτῆς
ἐκφυτήσῃ τὸ γέννημα.]

Ἴσον γάρ ἐστι τῷ κατὰ τὴν παροιμίαν
λεγομένῳ "πλίνθον πλύνειν ἢ δικτύῳ ὕδωρ
κομίζειν" τὸ κακίαν ἐξελεῖν ἀνθρώπου ψυχῆς.
"Ὅρα γὰρ αἷς ἐγκεχάρακται πάντων ἡ διάνοια", ὥς φησιν, "ἐπιμελῶς" καὶ οὐ παρ-
έργως· τουτέστιν συγκεκόλληται καὶ προσ-
ήρμοσται. Τὸ δὲ σὺν ἐπιμελείᾳ καὶ φρον-
τίδι κατεσκεμμένον ἐστὶ καὶ διηγορευμένον
εἰς ἀκρίβειαν, καὶ τοῦτο οὐκ ὀψὲ καὶ μόλις,

prehenduntur in Lege, ad doctrinam
utilitatemque disciplinae potius quam ad
naturam veritatis. Siquidem quasi duo
sunt capita, quae occurrunt in toto cursu
Legis, primo, ut dicitur : *non sicut homo*,
et altero : *sicut homo*, Ens ipsum in-
struere filium creditur. Primum illud
ad veritatem pertinet ; re enim vera non
sicut homo est deus, neque etiam sicut
sol, neque sicut caelum, neque ut mundus sensibilis, sed sicut deus, si liceat id
quoque proferre ; quoniam similitudinem
aut comparationem aut aenigma non
patitur beatissimus ille ac felicissimus,
imo superat vel ipsam beatitudinem ac
felicitatem [et quidquid his melius poti-
usque cogitari possit.] Alterum vero
pertinet ad doctrinam et directionem,
exposite dictum *sicut homo*, ut notetur
corrigere velle nos terrigenas, ne forte
iram poenamque iugiter luamus impla-
cabili hostilitate sine pace.

Ecce itaque observasse deum in mente
optime dixit : mens enim et ingenium
constantia maiore gaudent.

Sed quasi par est, secundum proverbium
tritum *Laterem lavare*, vel *Rete aquam
haurire*, ac malitiam expellere ab hominis animo [cum suis signis signatis.]
Nam si inest primum, non exsistit obiter,
sed intus insculptum et adhaerens ei.
[Quoniam autem mens potentialis prin-
cipalisque pars est animae, inducit illud
diligenter;] quod autem cum diligentia
et cura perpensum est, cogitatio est
exquisita certo certius. [Diligentia vero
non ad unum tendit malum, sed ut
patet, *ad mala, eaque omnia.*] Neque

ἀλλ' "ἐκ νεότητος"· μονονουχὶ λέγων· "ἐξ αὐτῶν τῶν σπαργάνων," ὥσπερ τι μέρος ἡνωμένον.

The first part from Pitra (*Anal. Sac.* II. 304) e Cod. Coislin. 276 f. 220 b, with the heading φίλωνος ἐκ τοῦ περὶ κοσμοποιΐας γ´ κεφαλαίου, and in Cod. Rup. f. 205 b, φίλωνος, with much variation.

The latter part (Ἡ τυχοῦσα κτέ.) from John Monachus (Mangey II. 663) = Rup. f. 138 a ἐκ τοῦ περὶ μετονομαζομένων. Mangey's conjecture of ἡνωμένον for τεινόμενον in the last line is confirmed by the Latin.

We read οὐ κυριολογεῖται with Rup., although the Armenian attempts to make sense without the negative which was easily lost in the preceding word. The error in the closing words evidently arose from reading μέρος τι ἡνωμένον.

exsistit perfunctorie, sed *a iuventute:* non solummodo, verum etiam ab ipsis cunis; quasi vero aliquatenus unitum.

....

Gen. ix. 4.

Τί ἐστιν "ἐν αἵματι ψυχῆς κρέας οὐ φάγεσθε";

§ 59. Ἔοικεν διὰ τούτου δηλοῦν ὅτι ψυχῆς οὐσία αἷμά ἐστιν· ψυχῆς μέντοι τῆς αἰσθητικῆς οὐχὶ τῆς κατ' ἐξοχὴν γενομένης ἥτις ἐστὶν λογική τε καὶ νοερά. Τρία γὰρ μέρη ψυχῆς· τὸ μὲν θρεπτικόν, τὸ δὲ αἰσθητικόν, τὸ δὲ λογικόν. Τοῦ μὲν οὖν λογικοῦ τὸ θεῖον πνεῦμα οὐσία κατὰ τὸν θεόλογον, φησὶν γὰρ ὅτι ἐνεφύσησεν εἰς τὸ πρόσωπον αὐτοῦ πνοὴν ζωῆς· τοῦ δὲ αἰσθητικοῦ καὶ ζωτικοῦ τὸ αἷμα οὐσία, λέγει γὰρ ἐν ἑτέροις ὅτι ψυχὴ πάσης σαρκὸς τὸ αἷμά ἐστιν· καὶ

Gen. ix. 4.

Quid est "carnem in sanguine animae non comedetis"?

§ 59. Visum est per hoc monere, quod spiritus (s. animae) substantia sanguis est; spiritus tamen sensibilis et vitalis, non eius, qui secundum excellentiam dicitur, is est rationalis et intellectualis. Tres enim partes sunt spiritus (s. animae humanae): una nutritiva, altera sensibilis, tertia rationalis. Rationalis ergo divini spiritus substantia est secundum Theologum (Mosen), nam in ipsa mundi creatione dicit, quod *insufflavit in faciem eius spiraculum vitae,* sicut constitutivum eius. Sensibilis autem et vitalis (spiritus) sanguis est essentia, dicit enim alibi, quod *omni spiritui*

H.

4

κυριώτατα ψυχὴν σαρκὸς αἷμα εἴρηκεν, περὶ
δὲ σάρκα ἡ αἴσθησις καὶ τὸ πάθος οὐχ ὁ
νοῦς καὶ ὁ λογισμός. Οὐ μὴν ἀλλὰ καὶ τὸ
ἐν αἵματι ψυχῆς μηνύει, ὅτι ἕτερόν ἐστιν
ψυχὴ καὶ ἕτερον αἷμα, ὡς εἶναι ψυχῆς μὲν
ἀψευδῶς οὐσίαν πνεῦμα, μὴ καθ᾽ αὑτὸ δὲ
χωρὶς αἵματος τόπον ἐπέχειν, ἀλλ᾽ ἐμφέ-
ρεσθαι καὶ συγκεκρᾶσθαι αἵματι.

From Cod. Reg. 923 fol. 376 b, and
Cod. Rup. f. 279 b.

We may, from the Latin, add καὶ
ζωτικῆς after αἰσθητικῆς.

carnis sanguis est. Proprie profecto carnis
spiritui (s. spiritum) dixit sanguinem, eo
quod in carne sunt sensus et affectiones,
non intellectus, non cogitationes. Verum
et per spiritum sanguinis notificat, quod
aliud est spiritus, et sanguis aliud, ita
ut animae essentia veraciter ac indubie
spiritus sit. Is autem spiritus non per se
seorsum sine sanguine locum tenet (in
corpore), sed contextus est ac commixtus
sanguine.

Gen. ix. 6.

Διατί, ὡς περὶ ἑτέρου θεοῦ, φησι τό, " ἐν
εἰκόνι θεοῦ ἐποίησα τὸν ἄνθρωπον," ἀλλ᾽
οὐχὶ τῇ ἑαυτοῦ;

§ 62. Παγκάλως καὶ σοφῶς τουτὶ κε-
χρησμῴδηται. Θνητὸν γὰρ οὐδὲν ἀπεικο-
νισθῆναι πρὸς τὸν ἀνωτάτω καὶ πατέρα
τῶν ὅλων ἐδύνατο, ἀλλὰ πρὸς τὸν δεύτερον
θεόν, ὅς ἐστιν ἐκείνου λόγος. Ἔδει γὰρ
τὸν λογικὸν ἐν ἀνθρώπου ψυχῇ τύπον ὑπὸ
θείου λόγου χαραχθῆναι, ἐπειδὴ ὁ πρὸ τοῦ
λόγου θεὸς κρείσσων ἐστὶν ἢ πᾶσα λογικὴ
φύσις· τῷ δὲ ὑπὲρ τὸν λόγον ἐν τῇ βελτί-
στῃ καί τινι ἐξαιρέτῳ καθεστῶτι ἰδέᾳ οὐδὲν
θέμις ἦν γεννητὸν ἐξομοιοῦσθαι.

From Euseb. *Praeparatio Evange-
lica*, Lib. VII. c. xiii. ἐκ τοῦ πρώτου μοι
κείσθω τῶν φίλωνος ζητημάτων καὶ λύ-
σεων. (See Mang. II. 625.)

Gen. ix. 6.

Quare tamquam de alio quodam deo
dicit, ad imaginem dei fecisse hominem, non autem ad suam?

§ 62. Optime et sine mendacio hoc
oraculum a deo datum est: mortale enim
nihil formari ad similitudinem supremi
patris universorum poterat, sed ad nor-
mam secundi dei, qui est eiusdem verbum.
Siquidem oportet rationalem hominum
animam typum verbi divini prae se ferre:
quoniam primo verbo deus superior est
rationalissima natura; ille vero qui superior verbo est, in meliori ac singulari
specie locum tenet. Et quomodo poterat
creatura similitudinem eius in se prae-
ferre?

Gen. ix. 13.

§ 64.............................

Ἔστιν οὖν θεοῦ δύναμις ἀόρατος συμβολικῶς τὸ τόξον, ἥτις ἐνυπάρχουσα τῷ ἀέρι
ἀνειμένῳ κατὰ τὰς αἰθρίας καὶ ἐπιτεινομένη
κατὰ τὰς νεφώσεις οὐκ ἐᾷ τὰ νέφη δι᾽ ὅλου εἰς

Gen. ix. 13.

§ 64. ....

Itaque virtus divina invisibilis symbolice
est arcus in nube, solutus sane iuxta
figuram serenitatis et condensatus secundum nubem, ita ut non permittat nubes

ὕδωρ ἀναλύεσθαι τῷ μὴ γενέσθαι καθόλου κατακλυσμόν. κυβερνᾷ γὰρ καὶ ἡνιοχεῖ τὴν πύκνωσιν τοῦ ἀέρος, πεφυκότος μάλιστα τότε ἀπαυχενίζειν καὶ ἐνυβρίζειν διὰ πλησμονῆς κόρου.

From Cat. Lipsiensis i. col. 160 φίλωνος ἐπισκόπου: also in Cod. Burney, fol 37 b, with frequent inaccuracy of transcription.

For the first sentence cf. Procopius (ed. Mai, p. 284).

omnes omnino in aquam resolvi, ne stagnetur terra (ut) sub diluvio, quod diligenter vetat atque disponit, ac quasi fraeno coërcet condensationem aëris, qui tunc magis solitus est rebellem se prodere ob nimiam saturitatem.

The Latin of the passage is also found in Cat. Lippomani f. 153 as follows:

Philo Episcopus. Arcus itaque symbolice invisibilis dei potentia est quae in caelo serenitate laxato et per nebulas extenso existens, non sinit nubes ex toto in aquas resolvi, ita ut in universum diluvium aquarum fiat, gubernat enim et tanquam auriga regit aeris densitatem qui tunc maxime ob satietatem, ut ita dicam, lascivire solet.

Gen. ix. 21.

§ 68. ....

Διττὸν τὸ μεθύειν· ἓν μέν, τὸ ληρεῖν παρ' οἶνον, ὅπερ ἐστὶ φαύλου ἴδιον ἁμάρτημα· ἕτερον δέ, τὸ οἰνοῦσθαι, ὅπερ εἰς σοφὸν πίπτει.

From Mai, *Script. Vet.* vii. 104, e Cod. Vat. 1553 with title ἐκ τοῦ α΄ τῶν ἐν γενέσει ζητημάτων. Quoted also with slight changes in Procopius (Mai, *Auct. Class.* p. 289).

Gen. ix. 21.

§ 68. ....

Duplex enim modus est inebriandi: unum temulentiae abutentis vino, quod delictum est proprium improbo ac pravo: alterum usus vini cadentis in sapientes quoque.

Gen. ix. 22.

§ 71. ....

Οὐ μόνον τοὺς ἀδελφοὺς ἀκηκοέναι, ἀλλὰ καὶ τοὺς περιεστῶτας ἄνδρας ἔξω ὁμοῦ καὶ γυναῖκας. [διὰ τοῦτο Ἰουδαῖοι οὐ συλλούονται τοῖς πατράσι.]

From Cat. Lipsiensis i. col. 163, also in Cat. Burney, fol. 37 b, from φίλωνος

Gen. ix. 22.

§ 71. ....

Non solis fratribus patrem suum tradidisse, verum etiam illis, qui circumstabant eos, viri et mulieres.

4—2

ἐπισκόπου. Cod. Burney adds the following sentence, which is headed ἀδήλου
in the Leipsic Catena, and does not appear to be Philo. Νεώτερον τὸν Χαναὰν
ὁμολογεῖ ὡς προϊδόντα τὴν γύμνωσιν τοῦ
Νῶε καὶ τῷ πατρὶ ἀπαγγείλαντα ἐπείτοιγε
Ἰάφεθ ἔσχατος ἦν τοῦ Χάμ.

Gen. ix. 23.

§ 72. Ὁ εὐχερὴς καὶ ἀπερίσκεπτος τὰ ἐπ'
εὐθείας καὶ πρὸς ὀφθαλμῶν μόνον ὁρᾷ· ὁ
δὲ φρόνιμος καὶ τὰ κατόπιν, τουτέστι τὰ
μέλλοντα· ὥσπερ γὰρ τὰ ὀπίσω τῶν ἔμπροσ-
θεν ὑστερίζει, οὕτω καὶ τὰ μέλλοντα τῶν
ἐνεστώτων. ὧν τὴν θεωρίαν ὁ ἀστεῖος μέτει-
σιν, αὐγαίως πάντοθεν ὀμματωθείς· πᾶς οὖν
σοφὸς οὐκ ἄνθρωπος ἀλλὰ νοῦς καταθεώμε-
νος καὶ περιαθρῶν περιπέφρακται πρὸς τὰ
ἐνεστῶτα καὶ τὰ ἀδοκήτως κατασπιλάζοντα.

From Cod. Rup. fol. 142 φίλωνος· ἐκ
τῶν ἐν γενέσει ζητημάτων.

Is αὐγαίως a corruption of Λυγκέως
[δίκην]?

Gen. ix. 23.

Quid est "Sumentes Sem et Iapheth
vestimentum imposuerunt super duos
humeros suos et perrexerunt retrorsum,
et cooperuerunt nuditatem patris sui,
et non viderunt (eam)"?

§ 72. [Littera evidens est. Ad mentem vero dicendum,] quod levis homo et
nimis festinans tantum id quod coram est
ac in conspectu oculorum videt, sapiens
vero quae a tergo quoque sunt, futura
scilicet. Quoniam sicut posteriora post-
ponuntur anterioribus, sic praesentibus
futura, quorum visio propria est con-
stanti viro sapientique, qui profecto est
alter Lynceus iuxta fabulas undique
oculis praeditus. Omnis ergo sapiens,
qui non ita homo est, quantum intellectus, [retrorsum incedit, id est posteriora
cernit velut in corradiante luce; et] omnia undique certo prospiciens et circa se
conspiciens, armatus comperitur ac con-
clusus munitusque, ne ulla animae pars
nuda aut indecora reperiatur ob eventus
male accidentes.

Quæstiones in Genesim.

Lib. III.

Gen. xv. 9.

§ 3. ....
('Εκ τῶν ἐν γενέσει ζητημάτων.) Ἀτό-
πως δρῶσιν, ὅσοι ἐκ μέρους τινὸς κρίνουσι
τὸ ὅλον, ἀλλὰ τὸ ἐναντίον ἐκ τοῦ ὅλου τὸ μέρος. Οὕτω γὰρ ἄμεινον καὶ σῶμα καὶ πρᾶγμα ·
δογματίζοιτο ἄν. Ἔστιν οὖν ἡ θεία νομο-
θεσία τρόπον τινὰ ζῷον ἡνωμένον, ἣν ὅλην
δι' ὅλου χρὴ μεγάλοις ὄμμασι περισκοπεῖν,
καὶ τὴν βουλὴν τῆς συμπάσης γραφῆς ἀκριβῶς καὶ τηλαυγῶς περιαθρεῖν, μὴ κατακό-
πτοντας τὴν ἁρμονίαν, μηδὲ τὴν ἕνωσιν
διαρτῶντας. Ἑτερόμορφα γὰρ καὶ ἑτερο-
ειδῆ φανεῖται τῆς κοινωνίας στερούμενα.
Dam. Par. 774 from Cod. Rup.

Apparently we should correct σῶμα
into ὄνομα and add οὐ before τὸ ἐναντίον.

Gen. xv. 9.

§ 3. ....
Verum isti, ut mihi videor, ex illis sunt,
qui ex unica parte diiudicant totum, non
vero opposite ex toto partem : quae melior est diiudicatio, qua tam nomen, quam
res omnino probentur.

Est itaque legislatio (h. e. scriptura
sacra), ut ita dixerim, vivens quoddam
unitum : quod totum totis oculis nitide
oportet circumspicere et universum in-
tentionem universae scripturae vere,
certe et manifeste circumcernere, non
dissecando harmoniam neque unionem
disiungendo ; alias aliena omnino et ab-
surda apparerent omnia, communitate
vel aequitate deturbata.......

Gen. xv. 11.

§ 3. ....
Πᾶσα ἡ ὑπὸ τὴν σελήνην φύσις μεστὴ
πολέμων καὶ κακῶν ἐμφυλίων ἐστὶ καὶ
ξένων......

Mai, *Script. Vet.* VII. 98, from Cod.
Vat. 1553, ἐκ τοῦ γ΄ τῶν ἐν γενέσει ζητημάτων.

Gen. xv. 11.

§ 3. ....
Universa enim, quae subter lunam est
natura, plena est praeliis ac malignitati-
bus domesticis et externis......

Gen. xv. 12.

§ 8. ....
Ἕνεκα μὲν τῶν φαύλων οὐδεμία πόλις ἠρέ-
μησεν ἄν. Διαμένουσι δὲ ἀστασίαστοι δι'
ἑνὸς ἢ δευτέρου δικαιοσύνην ἀσκοῦντος
οὗ ἡ ἀρετὴ τὰς πολεμικὰς νόσους ἰᾶται,
γέρας ἀπονέμοντος τοῦ φιλανθρώπου θεοῦ

Gen. xv. 12.

§ 8. ....
Quoniam per malos nec una civitas ac-
quievit in tranquillitate, sed immobiles
factae sunt, quum unus vel alter homo
virtute praeditus exstitit, cuius virtus
civiles morbos sanat, dante deo virtutis

καλοκἀγαθίας, τοῦ μὴ μόνον αὐτόν, ἀλλὰ καὶ τοὺς πλησιάζοντας ὠφελεῖσθαι.

Mangey (II. 661) from John Monachus = Rup. f. 33 b, which reads οἰκοῦντος for ἀσκοῦντος, καλοκαγαθῶν.

Also Anton Melissa, col. 1105, reading συνοικοῦντος, πολιτικὰς νόσους (rightly), φιλαρέτου (which again seems right), ὠφελεῖν.

studiosis ad honorem bonos mores; nec iis solummodo, sed illis quoque, qui (s. quibus) appropinquant ad utilitatem parandam.

Gen. xvi. 6.

§ 26. Οὐ πᾶσα ψυχὴ δέχεται νουθεσίαν, ἀλλ' ἡ μὲν ἵλεως ἀγαπᾷ τοὺς ἐλέγχους καὶ τοῖς παιδεύουσι μᾶλλον οἰκειοῦται· ἡ δὲ ἐχθρὰ μισεῖ καὶ ἀποστρέφεται καὶ ἀποδιδράσκει, τοὺς πρὸς ἡδονὴν λόγους τῶν ὠφελεῖν δυναμένων προκρίνουσα.

Cat. Lips. col. 216 (Προκοπίου).

Gen. xvi. 6.

Quare fugam capessit Agar a facie eius?

§ 26. Non omnis anima admittit observantiam et disciplinam, sed facilis ac suavis proprie mens diligit correptionem et magis familiaris redditur monitoribus suis: infensus autem malevolus odio habet et aversatur effugitque, delectantes sermones potius quam utilitati faventes praeferens ut meliores.

Gen. xvi. 9.

§ 30. ....
Τὸ ὑποτάττεσθαι τοῖς κρείττοσιν ὠφελιμώτατον. Ὁ μαθὼν ἄρχεσθαι καὶ ἄρχειν εὐθὺς μανθάνει. Οὐδὲ γὰρ εἰ πάσης γῆς καὶ θαλάττης τὸ κράτος ἀνάψοιτό τις, ἄρχων ἂν εἴη πρὸς ἀλήθειαν, εἰ μὴ μάθοι καὶ προπαιδευθείη τὸ ἄρχεσθαι.

The first sentence from Mai, *Script. Vet.* VII. 103, e Cod. Vat. 1553, ἐκ τοῦ πρώτου τῶν ἐν τῇ γενέσει ζητημάτων. Also Dam. Par. 359 and Cod. Reg. 923 fol. 74, in each case referred to Greg. Nazianz.

The last part in Dam. Par. 359 as from Philo, and in Cod. Reg. l.c. ἐκ τοῦ α΄ τῶν ἐν γενέσει ζητημάτων.

Gen. xvi. 9.

§ 30. ....
Quoniam obedire et subiici melioribus magis expedit: qui enim didicerit sub potestate esse, cito citius et potestate exercenda imbuitur; nam etsi quis totius terrae marisque vim induatur, vix poterit principatum possidere veritatis, nisi prius discat erudiaturque sub potestate esse.

Gen. xvii. 14.

§ 52. Οὐδὲν τῶν ἀκουσίων ἔνοχον ἀπο-
φαίνει ὁ νόμος, ὁπότε καὶ τῷ φόνον ἀκούσιον
δράσαντι συγγινώσκει...Τὸ δὲ ὀκτὼ ἡμερῶν
μετὰ γέννησιν βρέφος εἰ μὴ περιτέμνηται, τί
ἀδικεῖ, ὡς καὶ θανάτου τιμωρίαν ὑπομένειν;
Ἔνιοι μὲν οὖν φασιν ἀναφορικὸν εἶναι τὸν
τῆς τιμωρίας τρόπον ἐπὶ τοὺς γονεῖς, καὶ
ἐκείνους κολάζεσθαι οἴονται δεινῶς, ὡς ὠλι-
γωρηκότας τῆς τοῦ νόμου διατάξεως. Ἔνιοι
δέ, ὅτι ὑπερβολῇ χρώμενος κατὰ τοῦ βρέφους, ὅσα τῷ δοκεῖν, ἠγανάκτησεν, ἵνα τοῖς
τελείοις καταλύσασι τὸν νόμον ἀπαραίτητος
ἐπάγηται τιμωρία· οὐκ ἐπειδὴ τὸ ἔργον τῆς
περιτομῆς ἀναγκαῖον, ἀλλ' ὅτι ἡ διαθήκη
ἀθετεῖται, τοῦ σημείου, δι' οὗ γνωρίζεται,
μὴ πληρουμένου.

From Catena Inedita Cod. Reg. 1825
(Mangey II. 675) and Cod. Burney fol.
45 as φίλωνος ἑβραίου. Also Cat. Lips.
I. col. 225. The last sentence looks like
an added gloss. Catt. Lips. and Burney
read ἑρμηνείας τρόπον for τιμωρίας τρόπον, apparently correctly. Also Cat.
Lips. reads καταλύουσι in agreement with
the Latin (?). Cod. Burney reads ἀπα-
ραιτήτως ἐπάγηται τιμωρίας. But even
here a short extract is repeated loosely as
follows: φίλων ὁ ἑβραῖός φησιν ὅτι ὑπερβολῇ χρησάμενος κατὰ τοῦ βρέφους φέρει
τὴν ἀγανάκτησιν ἵνα τοῖς τελείοις παραβαί-
νουσιν ἀπαραίτητος ἡ τιμωρία γένηται.

Gen. xvii. 14.

§ 52. De nullo involuntario reum de-
clarat lex, quum et illi, qui involuntariam
perpetraverit occisionem, veniam facit,
[civitatibus distinctis, in quas fugiat ad
inveniendam securitatem; sacratus enim
atque immunis redditur, qui illuc pro-
fugit, unde nemo facultatem habet edu-
cendi citandique in tribunal iudicii.]
Octavo itaque die post nativitatem puer
si non circumcidetur, quid ipse peccabit,
ut poenam mortis quoque luere tene-
atur? Dixerint itaque aliqui, formam
edicti annuere parentes ipsos; illos enim
putant despexisse mandatum legis. Alii
vero: Nimium excessum, aiunt, usurpans super infantes, ut videtur, imposuit,
ut adulti dissolventes legem irrevocabili
modo subiiciantur poenae severissimae.

The Latin of the passage may also be
found in Procopius (ed. Gesner, p. 131),
although there is nothing corresponding
to it in the Greek text as printed by
Mai.

Quæstiones in Genesim.

Lib. IV.

Gen. xix. 1.

§ 30. Τῷ μὲν Ἀβραὰμ φαίνονται τρεῖς, καὶ μεσημβρίας· τῷ δὲ Λὼτ δύο, καὶ ἑσπέρας. Φυσικώτατα διάφορον εἰσηγεῖται ὁ νόμος τελείου καὶ προκόπτοντος· ὁ μὲν οὖν τέλειος τριάδα φαντασιοῦται ἐν ἀσκίῳ φωτὶ καὶ μεσημβρινῷ, μεστὴν διηνεκῆ καὶ πληρεστάτην οὐσίαν· ὁ δὲ δυάδα, διαίρεσιν καὶ τομὴν καὶ κενὸν ἔχουσαν ἐν ἑσπερινῷ σκότει. [Ταῦτα μὲν ὁ ἀκριβέστατος νομομαθὴς καὶ διδάσκαλος.] Pitra, *Anal. Sac.* II. p. xxiii., e Cod. Coislin. (? 276) f. 10, with heading φησὶ γὰρ τοῦτο ὁ ἐν λόγοις ἐξαίρετος Φίλων.

Gen. xix. 2.

§ 33. ....
Στενοχωρεῖται πᾶς ἄφρων, θλιβόμενος ὑπὸ φιλαργυρίας καὶ φιλοδοξίας καὶ φιληδονίας καὶ τῶν ὁμοιοτρόπων ἅπερ οὐκ ἐᾷ τὴν διάνοιαν ἐν εὐρυχωρίᾳ διάγειν.

Dam. Par. 362 ἐκ τοῦ β΄ τῶν ἐν γενέσει, and Cod. Reg. 923 ἐκ τῶν δ΄.

Also Cod. Barocc. 143 reading διαβαίνειν for διάγειν (Mang. II. 674) and in Cod. Rup. f. 73 b without a title.

Gen. xix. 10.

§ 40. ....
Νόμος ἔστω κατὰ τῶν σεμνὰ καὶ θεῖα οὐ σεμνῶς καὶ θεοπρεπῶς ὁρᾶν ἀξιούντων, κόλασιν ἐπιφέρειν ἀορασίας.

Gen. xix. 1.

Quare tribus apparentibus dixerit "venerunt duo angeli in Sodoma vesperi"?

§ 30. Abrahamo apparent tres, et meridie; Lot autem duo, et vespere. Naturalissimam distinctionem enarrat perfecti et proficientis: perfectus enim triade apparitionem sortitur, plena videlicet natura vacuitatis nescia; iste vero dualitatem dissectam ac vacuam.

Gen. xix. 2.

§ 33. ....
Angustus est omnis insipiens, coarctatus ab amore divitiarum, cupiditatis et ambitionis similiumque, quae vix permittunt animae in absoluto statu ambulare.

Gen. xix. 10.

§ 40. ....
Lex enim erit iusta super illos, qui nobilem ac venerabilem vultum divinum dedignantur videre modeste, gloriose et

Dam. Par. 341, where it is ascribed to Clem. Alex.: but in Cod. Reg. 923 f. 62 b, it is ἐκ τοῦ δ' τῶν ἐν γενέσει ζητημάτων.

Cod. Reg. reads μὴ σεμνῶς.

Gen. xix. 14.

§ 43. Οἱ ἐν ταῖς ἀφθόνοις χορηγίαις πλούτου καὶ δόξης καὶ τῶν ὁμοιοτρόπων ὑπάρχοντες, καὶ ἐν ὑγιείᾳ καὶ εὐαισθησίᾳ σώματος καὶ εὐεξίᾳ ζωῆς, καὶ τὰς διὰ πασῶν τῶν αἰσθήσεων ἡδονὰς κρατουμένοι νομίζοντες τῆς ἄκρας εὐδαιμονίας ἀφῖχθαι, μεταβολὴν οὐ προσδοκῶσιν, ἀλλὰ καὶ τοὺς λέγοντας ὅτι πάντα περὶ τὸ σῶμα καὶ ἐκτὸς ἐπικαίρως ἔχει, γέλωτα καὶ χλεύην τίθενται.

Mai, *Script. Vet.* VII. 101, e Cod. Vat. 1553, headed Φίλωνος· ἐκ τῶν δ' τῶν ἐν γενέσει ζητημάτων. We have given ἀφῖχθαι for ἠφίχσθαι of Mai: perhaps the real reading is ἐφικέσθαι.

Gen. xix. 19.

§ 47. ....
Ὁ σοφὸς ἠρεμίαν καὶ ἀπραγμοσύνην καὶ σχολὴν μεταδιώκει, ἵνα τοῖς θείοις θεωρήμασιν ἐν ἡσυχίᾳ ἐντύχῃ. Ὁ φαῦλος πόλιν τε καὶ τὸν κατὰ πόλιν ὄχλον τε καὶ φυρμὸν ἀνθρώπων ὁμοῦ καὶ πραγμάτων μεταδιώκει. Φιλοπραγμοσύναι γὰρ καὶ πλεονεξίαι, δημοκοπίαι τε καὶ δημαρχίαι τῷ τοιούτῳ τιμαί, τὸ δὲ ἡσυχάζειν ἀτιμώτατον.

The first sentence is Dam. Par. 376, also Cod. Reg. 923 f. 85, where it is ἐκ τοῦ α' τῶν ἐν γενέσει, and Maximus II. 599 omitting καὶ σχολὴν μετα. The last part is found in Anton Melissa (Migne, *Patr. Gr.* 136, col. 1193, reading ἀτιμότατον).

H.

---

divino more, ut poenam luant caecitate affligente.

This passage can now be removed from the Clementine fragments: see Zahn, *Supplementum Clementinum*, p. 53.

Gen. xix. 14.

§ 43. Quicumque in abundantia immensarum divitiarum, honorum et consimilium sunt, et in sanitate, robore, et vigore corporis vitam agunt, per omnesque sensus voluptatem coagulant, putantes se propriam felicitatem attigisse, permutationem fore vix exspectant, sed illos, qui dixerint, omnia quae intra et extra corpus sunt, damnosa esse ac brevis temporis, irrident.

Gen. xix. 19.

§ 47. ....
Sapiens enim pacis est amans et nescius dimicationis atque feriatus, ut totus divinis vacet contemplationibus. Improbus autem amat civitatem et civilem turbam ac conturbationem concursumque hominum et rerum; namque amor negotiorum, avaritia, hominibus complacentia atque studium dignitatis possidendae pretiosa illi sunt, et cessare ab iis vile putatum.

5

Gen. xix. 23.

Διὰ τί, "ἐξῆλθεν ὁ ἥλιος ἐπὶ τὴν γῆν, καὶ Λὼτ εἰσῆλθεν εἰς Σηγώρ";

§ 51. Καί φησιν· Ὁ αὐτὸς χρόνος γίνεται καὶ τοῖς προκόπτουσιν εἰς σωτηρίαν, καὶ τοῖς ἀνιάτως ἔχουσι πρὸς κόλασιν. Καὶ ἐν ἀρχῇ δὴ ἡμέρας εὐθὺς ἀνατείλαντος τοῦ ἡλίου τὴν δίκην ἐπάγει, βουλόμενος ἐπιδεῖξαι, ὅτι ἥλιος καὶ ἡμέρα καὶ φῶς καὶ ὅσα ἄλλα ἐν κόσμῳ καλὰ καὶ τίμια μόνοις ἀπονέμεται τοῖς ἀστείοις, φαύλῳ δὲ οὐδενὶ τῶν ἀθεράπευτον κακίαν ἐχόντων.

From Cat. Inedit. Cod. Reg. 1825 (Mang. II. 675), Cat. Burney f. 37 and Cat. Lips. I. col. 251. Cat. Burney reads Διὰ τί δέ—Σέγωρ—ὅσα ἐν κόσμῳ.

....

Φύσει μὲν κοῦφα θεῖον καὶ πῦρ· τὸ δὲ τῆς ἄρας κεκαινουργημένον ἤλλαξε πρὸς τοὐναντίον τὴν κίνησιν.

Cat. Burney f. 46 b as Φίλωνος ἐπισκόπου and omitting καὶ after θεῖον: Cat. Lips. col. 252 as ἀδήλου.

Gen. xix. 26.

§ 52. ....
Χαίρειν ἐπὶ ταῖς τῶν ἐχθρῶν ἀτυχίαις εἰ καὶ δίκαιόν ποτε, ἀλλ' οὐκ ἀνθρώπινον.

....

Dam. Par. 509 ascribed to Nilus, but in Cod. Reg. 923, fol. 154 b, to Philo; and in Mai, *Script. Vet.* VII. 102, from Cod. Vat. 1553 as ἐκ τοῦ γ΄ τῶν ἐν γενέσει ζητημάτων, reading ἑτέρων as in the Armenian. Also given in Tischendorf, *Philonea* p. 154, e Cod. Cahirino, and in Maximus II. 588.

....

Θεοῦ, φησι, κολάζοντος ὡς ἄνθρωποι μὴ

Gen. xix. 23.

Quare dicitur: "Sol egressus est in terram et Lot ingressus est in Zoor (Segor)"?

§ 51. Idem tempus fit tam proficientibus in salutem quam insanabilibus in punitionem, atque in ipso principio diei, oriente sole, iudicium illico inducit —volens indicare, quod sol et dies et lux et quicquid aliud in mundo est pretiosum ac bonum, sapientibus solis distributa sunt, nemini autem illorum, quorum incurabilis est malitia.

(The sentences which follow will be found much abbreviated in Cat. Lips. col. 251 from Procopius.)

....

Siquidem ex natura leve est sulphur, sicut et ignis; verumtamen ob maledictionem nova perpetraturus demutavit in motum contrarium.

Gen. xix. 26.

§ 52. ....
Gaudere autem et pessumdare ob miseriam caeterorum, etsi iure accidat, homini tamen non convenit.

....

Deum, dicit, punientem, o homines, no-

κατανοεῖτε· ὅτι μὲν γὰρ τιμωροῦνται ἐχρῆν γνῶναι· τὸ δὲ περιεργάζεσθαι πῶς, προπετείας καὶ θράσους ἐστίν, οὐκ εὐλαβείας.

From Cat. Lips. col. 248 and Cat. Burney f. 46 b. Φίλωνος ἐπισκόπου.

Gen. xx. 4.

§ 64. ....

Οὐχ ὡς τὸ ἑκουσίως ἁμαρτάνειν ἐστὶν ἄδικον, οὕτω τὸ ἀκουσίως καὶ κατ' ἄγνοιαν εὐθὺς δίκαιον, ἀλλὰ τάχα που μεθόριον ἀμφοῖν, δικαίου καὶ ἀδίκου, τὸ ὑπό τινων καλούμενον ἀδιάφορον. Ἁμάρτημα γὰρ οὐδὲν ἔργον δικαιοσύνης.

Dam. Par. 520. Cod. Reg. 923 with reference to I. Quaest. in Gen. (Δ read as ᴧ). Cod. Vat. removes οὐχ and adds οὐκ before εὐθὺς.

Gen. xx. 10.

§ 67. Οὐ πάντα ἀληθῆ λεκτέον ἅπασιν· ὅθεν καὶ νῦν ὁ ἀστεῖος ὅλον οἰκονομεῖ τὸ πρᾶγμα μεταθέσει καὶ ἀπαλλάγῃ τῶν ὀνομάτων.

From Mai, *Script. Vet.* VII. 106 (Cod. Vat. 1553): ἐκ τῶν ἐν γενέσει ζητημάτων.

Gen. xx. 16.

§ 69. ....

Τὸ δὲ "πάντα ἀλήθευσον" ἀφιλοσόφου καὶ ἰδιώτου παράγγελμα· εἰ μὲν γὰρ ὁ μὲν ἀνθρώπων βίος εὐώδει μηδὲν παραδεχόμενος ψεῦδος, εἰκὸς ἦν ἐπὶ παντὶ πρὸς πάντας ἀληθεύειν· ἐπειδὴ δὲ ὑπόκρισις ὡς ἐν ἑκατέρῳ δυναστεύει καὶ τὸ ψεῦδος παραπέτασμα τῆς ἀληθείας ἐστί, τέχνης δεῖ τῷ σοφῷ πολυτρόπου, καθ' ἣν ὀφελήσει μιμούμενος τοὺς ὑποκριτὰς οἳ ἄλλα λέγοντες ἕτερα δρῶσιν ὅπως διασώσωσιν οὓς δύνανται.

From Mai, *Script. Vet.* VII. 106 (Cod. Vat. 1553). Correct ἑκατέρῳ into θεάτρῳ.

---

lite mirari; satis enim vobis est tantum intelligere quod supplicio mulctati sunt, quod merebantur; at quomodo id passi sint, indagare vel perscrutari, audaciae est et arrogantiae, non vero timoris (dei).

Gen. xx. 4.

§ 64. ....

Non sicut voluntarium peccatum iniquum est, sic involuntarium secundum ignorantiam illico iustum, sed, ut mihi videtur, medium tenet locum inter utrumque, iustum et iniquum, a quibusdam indifferens vocatum; quoniam peccatum nullatenus est opus iustitiae.

Gen. xx. 10.

§ 67. Non omnem veritatem convenit dicere apud omnes. Quamobrem et Sapiens nunc totam rem disponit exponitque alio modo velut nominum mutatione.

....

Gen. xx. 16.

§ 69. ....

Illud tamen *omnia vere loquere* abhorrentis a philosophia et ignorantis mandatum est. Nam si hominum vita optime se haberet nulla accepta falsitate, congruum foret de omnibus apud omnes verum loqui: sed quia fictio malignitatis velut in theatro acquisitam habet et superbiam velatam una cum artificio, artis est opus sapienti multiplicis, ut prosit, similitudinem praeferens ironia utentium, qui aliud dicunt et aliud agunt, ut salvent quos possunt.

Gen. xxiii. 6.

§ 76. ....

Τῶν μὲν ἀφρόνων βασιλεὺς οὐδείς, καὶ ἂν τὸ πάσης γῆς καὶ θαλάσσης ἀνάψηται κράτος· μόνος δὲ ὁ ἀστεῖος καὶ θεοφιλής, καὶ ἂν τῶν παρασκευῶν καὶ τῶν χορηγιῶν ἀμοιρῇ, δι᾽ ὧν πολλοὶ κρατύνονται τὰς δυναστείας. Ὥσπερ γὰρ τῷ κυβερνητικῆς ἢ ἰατρικῆς ἢ μουσικῆς ἀπείρῳ παρέλκον πρᾶγμα οἴακες καὶ φαρμάκων σύνθεσις καὶ αὐλοὶ καὶ κιθάραι, διότι μηδενὶ τούτων δύναται χρῆσθαι πρὸς ὃ πέφυκε, κυβερνήτῃ δὲ καὶ ἰατρῷ καὶ μουσικῷ λέγοιτο ἂν ἐφαρμόζειν δεόντως· οὕτως, ἐπειδὴ τέχνη τίς ἐστι βασιλικὴ καὶ τεχνῶν ἀρίστη, τὸν μὲν ἀνεπιστήμονα χρήσεως ἀνθρώπων ἰδιώτην νομιστέον, βασιλέα δὲ μόνον τὸν ἐπιστήμονα.

As far as θεοφιλής in Dam. Par. 396, and 776 = Cod. Rupef. f. 115 b ἐκ τοῦ α΄ τῶν ἐν γενέσει ζητημάτων and Cod. Reg. 923 fol. 97 ἐκ τοῦ α΄ τῶν ἐν γενέσει (l. ἐκ τοῦ δ΄). The rest of the passage in Dam. Par. 776 (Cod. Rupef.).

Gen. xxiii. 6.

§ 76. ....

Est autem, ut ex insipientibus nullus sit rex, quamvis terrae et maris totam vim subiugarit, sed solus sapiens et dei amans, praeter partes apparatuum armorumque, quibus multi proficiunt per vim violentam. Etenim, sicut nauticae vel medicinae vel musicae si quis imperitus sit, pro argumento sunt ei clavus et medicaminum commixtura et tibia et lyra—nullum enim istorum usurpare potest ad usum destinatum, at navarcho et medico et musico dicitur omnino convenire—: ita profecto, siquidem ars est quaedam regium hoc munus, et artium perfectissima. Nam qui imperitus est et nescius rerum homines iuvantium, rudis atque rusticus est censendus, rex autem dicendus solus peritus gnarusque.

Gen. xxiii. 9.

§ 80. ...... Τὸ σπήλαιον τὸ διπλοῦν δύω εἰσὶν ἀντρώδεις ὑπωρεῖαι· ἡ μὲν ἐκτός, ἡ δὲ εἴσω· ἢ δύω περίβολοι· ὁ μὲν περιέχων, ὁ δὲ περιεχόμενος.

Cat. Lips. col. 288 (Προκοπίου).

Gen xxiii. 9.

Quid est spelunca duplex?

§ 80. ...... Duo sunt sepulcra in illa spelunca sub monte, unum extra, alterum intra; sive duae porticus, una claudens, altera clausa.

Gen. xxiv. 3.

Διατί δὲ μὴ τῷ υἱῷ παραγγέλλει μὴ λαβεῖν Χανανίτιν, ὥσπερ ὕστερον τῷ Ἰακὼβ οἱ γονεῖς, ἀλλὰ τῷ παιδί;

§ 88. ...... Καίτοι τελείου τυγχάνοντος Ἰσαάκ, καὶ ἡλικίαν ἔχοντος γάμου· .... καὶ εἰ

Gen. xxiv. 3.

Quare non ipsi filio praecipit, ne accipiat uxorem Chananeam, sicut postmodum Iacobo parentes eius, sed servo?

§ 88. [Profecto haesitationem dubii atque consilium consideratione dignum

μὲν ἤμελλε πείθεσθαι, εἰκὸς ἦν αὐτῷ μᾶλλον παρεγγυᾶν· εἰ δὲ ἀπειθεῖν, περιττὴ τοῦ παιδὸς ἡ διακονία. τὸ γὰρ εἰπεῖν, ὅτι, χρησμῷ τῆς γῆς ἐξελθών, πέμπειν εἰς αὐτὴν οὐκ ἠξίου τὸν υἱόν, [εἰ καὶ εὔλογον, ὅμως ἀπαρέσκει τισί,] διὰ τὸ μηδ' ἂν τὸν Ἰακώβ, εἰ τοῦτο ἦν ἀληθές, ὑπὸ τῶν γονέων ἐνταῦθα πεμφθῆναι.

Cat. Lips. col. 292 (Προκοπίου).

habet littera;] quoniam perfectus est aetate Isaac, sufficiens ad statum sponsi, [neque erat sub dominio servi. Unum ex duobus aderat: aut consentiebat, aut adversabatur.] Atqui consentienti vadem se praestare conveniens erat patri: quod si non assentiretur, supervacuum esset ministerium servi. Dicere autem, quod quia per iussum divinum ex regione Chaldaeorum migraverat Abraham, quare in eam filium mittere haud aequum censebat, [valde delirum est ac absurdum: primum, quia ob eamdem causam neque rem acceptare sponsoremque esse oportebat plane, sicut etiam ad cognationem, de qua emigrare dictum fuerat;] neque Iacobo licebat adire propter desponsandam uxorem.

Gen. xxiv. 16.

§ 99. ....

Ἀναιδὲς βλέμμα καὶ μετέωρος αὐχὴν καὶ συνεχὴς κίνησις ὀφρύων καὶ βάδισμα σεσοβημένον καὶ τὸ ἐπὶ μηδενὶ τῶν φαύλων ἐρυθριᾶν σημεῖά ἐστι ψυχῆς αἰσχίστης, τοὺς ἀφανεῖς τῶν οἰκείων ὀνειδῶν τύπους ἐγγραφούσης τῷ φανερῷ σώματι.

Dam. Par. 658, and Cod. Reg. 923 f. 292 (ἐκ τοῦ ε´ τῶν ἐν γενέσει).

Cramer, *Anecdota Oxoniensia,* vol. IV. 254 e Cod. Bodl. Clark f. 11 b.

Maximus II. 633.

Anton Melissa(*Patr. Gr.*136,col.1225), referred to Theologi sc. Greg. Nazianz.

Tischendorf, *Philonea* p. 154, e Cod. Cahirino.

We have corrected the text by reading τύπους for τόποις with Cramer, Maximus, and Anton, Tisch., and for ὀφθαλμῶν we read ὀφρύων with the same authorities.

Gen. xxiv. 16.

§ 99. ....

Aspectus vero impudens, et cervix alta, frequensque motus superciliorum, atque gressus lascivus, et nullo modo erubescens de malis ac pudens, indicium est animae turpissimae, quae occultas proprii vituperii figuras pingit describitque evidenter in visibili corpore.

Gen. xxiv. 17.

§ 102. Ἄξιον ἀποδέχεσθαι τὸ μηδενὸς ὀρέγεσθαι τῶν ὑπὲρ δύναμιν· πᾶν γὰρ τὸ συμμετρίαν ἔχον, ἐπαινετόν.........ἀναγκαῖον οὖν τῷ μὲν εὐφυεῖ πλείους εἶναι τὰς διδασκαλίας, ἐλάττους δὲ τῷ ἀφυεῖ, διὰ τὴν ἐν ταῖς ἀνάγκαις ἀρίστην ἰσότητα.........καὶ τοῦτό γέ ἐστι τὸ βιοφελέστατον ἴσον.

Mai, *Script. Vet.* VII. 106, from Cod. Vat. 1553 Φίλωνος· ἐκ τῶν ἐν γενέσει ζητημάτων.

Gen. xxiv. 17.

§ 102. Oportet non desiderare ut recipiantur ampliora suis viribus : omne enim, quod mensuram habet, laudabile est.........quoniam necesse est, ut solertibus amplior sit doctrina, minor autem amentibus, ob aequalitatem exactam, quae consistit in proportione..........et hoc est aequalitas proportionata utilissima vitae.

Gen. xxiv. 18.

§ 104.........Οὐχ ὡς δύναται διδάσκειν ὁ διδάσκαλος, οὕτω καὶ μανθάνειν ὁ γνώριμος. ἐπειδὴ ὁ μὲν τέλειος, ὁ δὲ ἀτελής ἐστιν. ὅθεν προσήκει στοχάζεσθαι τῆς τοῦ παιδευομένου δυνάμεως.

Dam. Par. 435, and Cod. Reg. 923 fol. 116 b referring to Φίλωνος· ἐκ τῆς η΄ τῶν νόμων ἱερῶν ἀλληγορίας. Mai, *Script. Vet.* VII. 99, Φίλωνος· ἐκ τοῦ θ΄ τῶν ἐν γενέσει ζητημάτων.

Gen. xxiv. 18.

§ 104.........Namque non sicut potest docere magister, sic etiam discipulus discere valet, quum ille perfectus sit, iste vero imperfectus. Quare oportet observare et ponderare facultatem eius, qui instruitur.

Gen. xxiv. 22.

§ 110.........Ἀκοῦσαι δεῖ πρῶτον, εἶτα ἐργάσασθαι· μανθάνομεν γὰρ οὐ τοῦ μαθεῖν χάριν, ἀλλὰ τοῦ πρᾶξαι.

Mai, *Script. Vet.* VII. 99.

Gen. xxiv. 22.

§ 110..........Audire primum convenit, deinde operari ; discimus enim, non ut discamus, sed ut operemur.

Gen. xxiv. 52.

§ 130....Δεῖ γὰρ πάσης πράξεως καθαρᾶς ἀρχὴν [εἶναι] τὴν πρὸς θεὸν εὐχαριστίαν καὶ τιμήν· διὰ τοῦτο ὁ παῖς προσκυνεῖ πρότερον, εἶτα χαρίζεται τὰ δῶρα.

Φίλωνος. Ex Cod. Vat. 746 f. 53. Vide Pitra, *Analecta Sacra* II. p. 314.

Gen. xxiv. 52.

§ 130....Oportet omnis operae praeclarae initium facere per gratiarum ad deum actionem laudemque: quamobrem adolescens adorat imprimis dominum, atque deinde offert dona.

Gen. xxiv. 67.

Διατί δὲ οὐκ εἰς τὸν τοῦ πατρὸς οἶκον, ἀλλ᾽ εἰς τὸν τῆς μητρὸς εἰσέρχεσθαι λέγεται Ἰσαὰκ ἐπὶ γάμῳ;

§ 145. ...... Ὅτι ὁ μὲν πατὴρ πλείους ἀγαγόμενος γυναῖκας καὶ πλείους ἔσχεν οἴκους· λέγεται γὰρ οἶκος καὶ τὸ ἐκ γυναικὸς καὶ τέκνων σύστημα.

Cat. Lips. col. 305 (Προκοπίου).

Gen. xxv. 28.

§ 166. Τίς δ᾽ ἂν οὐκ ἀγάσαιτο τὸ "ἠγά-πησε τὸν Ἠσαῦ· ἡ δὲ Ῥεβέκκα ἠγάπα τὸν Ἰακώβ"; Τὸ μὲν γάρ, παρελήλυθε· τὸ δέ, πάρεστιν ἀεί· ἡ μὲν γὰρ ἀποδοχὴ τοῦ φαύλου κἂν συμβῇ ποτε, ὀλιγοχρόνιός ἐστι καὶ ἐφήμερος· ἡ δὲ τοῦ σπουδαίου, ἀθανα-τίζεται· καὶ τὸ μὲν σπουδαῖον, οὐ δι᾽ ἕτερόν τι ἀγαπᾶται· τὸ δὲ μὴ τοιοῦτον, ἐκ τῶν χρειῶν· ἠγάπησε γάρ φησιν ὅτι ἡ θήρα αὐτοῦ βρῶσις αὐτῷ.

From Cat. Lips. col. 315 (Προκοπίου).

Gen. xxv. 29.

§ 168. ....

Καὶ τὸ ῥητὸν τῆς διηγήσεως ἔλεγχον ἔχει ἀκολάστου πρὸς νουθεσίαν τῶν θεραπεύεσ-θαι δυναμένων· ὁ γὰρ τοῦ τυχόντος ἕνεκα προεψήματος ἐκστὰς τῶν πρεσβείων τῷ νεω-

Gen. xxiv. 67.

Quare non in patris sed matris domum intrare dicitur Isaac pro matrimonio?

§ 145. [Qui sane litteram scire ac scrutari volunt, dicent fortassis] quod, quia pater eius multas duxit sibi uxores, virtualiter multas quoque domos haberet. Domus enim [non solum aedificium] di-citur, [sed] ex viro et muliere ac filiis conventus.

Gen. xxv. 28.

Quare dicit, quod "Isaac dilexit Esau, Rebecca autem diligebat Iacob"?

§ 166. Quis non miretur appositionem nominum, quae contra se invicem accu-rate atque apte collocata cernuntur? Illud enim *dilexit* narrandi modo prae-teritum tempus indicat; *diligebat* autem semper adest perseveratque, fine vel con-summatione numquam recepta. Ne forte iure meritoque; quoniam acceptatio mali et turpis etsi occurrat aliquando, exigui temporis est et non diuturna, boni vero quasi immortalis evadit, poenitendi ne-scia.

Cur ob causam aliquam diligit ille? Dixit enim: "quia venatio eius erat cibus ipsi"; at mater sine causa?

§ 167. Sapientissime quidem, quo-niam virtute praeditus non ob aliud quidpiam amatur.......

Gen. xxv. 29.

§ 168. ....

Habet autem littera haud exiguam cor-reptionem hominis avidi prodigi, pro admonitione eorum, qui curari possunt. Non enim ob vile pulmentum coctum

τέρῳ καὶ δοῦλος γαστρὸς ἡδονῆς ἀναγραφεὶς
εἰς ὄνειδος προκείσθω τῶν μήποτε ζῆλον
ἐγκρατείας λαβόντων.

Cat. Lips. I. col. 318 as Φίλωνος but
the editor remarks ἴσως τοῦ ἐπισκόπου.
ἐν γὰρ τοῖς τοῦ Ἑβραίου οὐχ εὑρίσκεται.
Also Cat. Burney f. 55 as Φίλωνος ἐπισκόπου and reading προεψημένων. Pitra,
Anal. Sac. II. 311, gives the same text
from Palat. 203 f. 110 and reads προσ-
λήμματος for προεψήματος.

Gen. xxv. 31.

§ 172. Τὸ μὲν ῥητὸν οἷα τῷ δοκεῖν ἐμφαίνει πλεονεξίαν νεωτέρου σφετερίζεσθαι
ἀδελφοῦ δίκαια ποθοῦντος. Ὁ δὲ σπουδαῖος
οὐ πλεονέκτης ἅτε ὀλιγοδείας καὶ ἐγκρατείας
ἕταιρος. Σαφῶς οὖν ὁ ἐπιστάμενος ὅτι αἱ
ἄφθονοι περιουσίαι τῶν φαύλων χορηγοὶ
τῶν ἁμαρτημάτων καὶ ἀδικημάτων αὐτοῖς
εἰσιν, ἀναγκαιότατον ἡγεῖται τὴν προσανα-
φλέγουσαν ὕλην, ὡς πυρός, τῆς κακίας ἀφαιρεῖν εἰς βελτίωσιν ἠθῶν· ὅπερ οὐ βλάβην
ἀλλὰ μεγίστην ὠφελείαν περιποιεῖ τῷ ζημι-
οῦσθαι δοκοῦντι.

Cat. Lips. I. col. 316 and Cat. Burney
fol. 55 as Φίλωνος ἐπισκόπου. Cod.
Burney reads σφετερίζεσθαι ἀδικῶς—φαυ-
λῶν—πυρρὸς etc.

Gen. xxvi. 3.

§ 180. Ἀδιαφοροῦσιν ὅρκων λόγοι θεοῦ·
καὶ κατὰ τίνος ἂν ὤμοσεν ὁ θεός, ὅτι μὴ
ἑαυτοῦ; λέγεται δὲ ὀμνύναι διὰ τὴν ἡμε-

---

recusavit (Esau) maioritatem, iuniori
eam cedens, sed quia servus deditus erat
voluptati carnis, iure conviciis subiice-
retur, quippe qui numquam aemulator
fuit continentiae.

Gen. xxv. 31.

Quare dicit frater eius: Vende mihi
hodie primogenitium tuum?

§ 172. Littera, quantum suspicari
licet, indicat aviditatem avaritiae iuni-
oris, defraudare nitentis iura fratris
maioris. Verum qui virtutem habet,
non est avarus, quia socius est frugali-
tatis et religiosae abstinentiae atque his
potius proficit. Certus itaque factus,
quod frequens et immensa possessio
superflua improbo occasionem ansam-
que praebent peccati et iustitiae (s. iusto
soli) sunt necessariae, magis expedire
aestimat materiam illam, quae ignis
magis succendendi causa est, auferri ab
improbo velut ab igne pro morum in
melius mutatione; quae non nocet (s.
non est noxa, damnum), sed magnum
emolumentum parat illi, qui putat se
damno affici.

Gen. xxvi. 3.

Quid est "Statuam iuramentum meum,
quod iuravi cum patre tuo"?

§ 180. Primum illud dicendum, quod
dei verba nihil differunt a iuramento.
Et in quem sane iurat deus, nisi in se

τέραν ἀσθένειαν τῶν ὑπολαμβανόντων ὡς ἐπ' ἀνθρώπου διαφέρειν λόγων ὅρκους, οὕτως ἐπὶ θεοῦ....

Cat. Lips. col. 319 (Προκοπίου).

ipsum? Iurare autem dicitur ob nostram imbecillitatem, quippe qui putamus sicut apud homines distingui verbum a iuramento, sic etiam apud deum esse.

Gen. xxvi. 15.

§ 191. ....τοῖς γὰρ ἀβούλοις ἔθος ἐστὶ μήτε στήλας μήτε μνημεῖόν τι ἀπολιπεῖν τῶν καλῶν εἰς εὐδοξίαν συμβαλλόμενον, ἢ ὅτι ῥηγνύμενοι φθόνῳ καὶ βασκανίᾳ τῆς τε περὶ ἐκείνων εὐπραγίας ὀλιγωροῦσι καὶ τῆς αὐτῶν ὠφελείας ἄμεινον ἡγούμενοι βλάπτεσθαι μᾶλλον ἢ ὑφ' ὧν οὐκ εὖ τι θέλουσιν εὐεργετεῖσθαι.

Cat. Burney fol. 55 b, also Cat. Lips. I. col. 323 (reading ἔτι θέλουσιν). Described as Φίλωνος ἐπισκόπου. The translator read συμβαλλομένων.

Gen. xxvi. 15.

Cur puteos quos foderant servi patris eius, obstruunt eos Philistaei et implent?

§ 191. [Littera proponit duplicem causam: unam et primam, quia] inconsultorum mos est, nec columnas neque monumentum, qualecumque sit, sinere manere bonis ad felicem gloriam contendentibus; alteram vero eam, quia instigati livore invidiae ob eorum nimiam prosperitatem pessumdant et suum emolumentum, melius aestimantes damnum potius sustinere, quam a caeteris, quos nolunt, aliquid boni invenire.

Gen. xxvi. 18.

Ἐμφραγέντα φρέατα πάλιν ὀρύσσει ὁ Ἰσαάκ.

§ 193. Ὅτι φύσει φιλάνθρωπος ὁ ἀστεῖος καὶ εὐμενὴς καὶ συγγνώμων, οὐδενὶ μνησικακῶν τὸ παράπαν, ἀλλὰ νικᾶν τοὺς ἐχθροὺς ἀξιῶν ἐν τῷ ποιεῖν εὖ μᾶλλον ἢ βλάπτειν.

Cat. Lips. I. col. 323. Cat. Burney fol. 55 b. Anton Melissa (*Patr. Gr.* 136 col. 1077).

Gen. xxvi. 18.

Cur obstructos puteos rursum fodit?

§ 193. Ad litteram quia natura humanus, benevolus et indulgens est sapiens, nullius omnino memor malitiae, sed devictis hostibus aequum ducit bonum facere potius, quam damnum.

Note that between § 195 and § 196 eleven sections are missing in the Armenian of Aucher and are supplied by him in Latin from the Basle (1538) edition of the Quaestiones. Observe also that in the neighbourhood of the passage quoted above there should apparently be one which has served as a basis for the following in the (Latin) Catena of Zephyrus.

Philo Episcopus. Discat quicumque cupit inter Abrahae filios annumerari, ingenii esse humani, discat adversarium suum non contentione rixarum superare sed benignitate. Ex hoc potissimum loco Isaac natura deprehenditur simplex et libera qua maxime Deum delectari: monemur ex eo quod illi e vestigio occurrens promissa stabilivit.

Gen. xxvi. 26.

Κατάσκοποι μᾶλλον ἢ ἔνσπονδοι γενησό-μενοι, καὶ πρὸς ἑκάτερον παρεσκευασμένοι· πόλεμον μὲν, εἰ ἀσθενοῦντα κατίδοιεν, εἰρή-νην δέ, εἰ δυνατώτερον ἑαυτῶν.

From Cat. Ined. cod. Reg. 1825 (Mang. II. 675).

Cat. Lips. I. col. 325 with the remark that this and three following passages are not among the edita of Philo and do not seem to belong to him. Cod. Burney f. 56 (φίλωνος ἑβραίου).

Cf. Procopius (ed. Gesner, p. 158).

Gen. xxvi. 26.

Videntur mihi exploratores potius, quam pro foedere amicitiarum advenisse, in utroque parati ad praelium, si infir-mum viderint: ad pacem, si potentiorem.

The Latin is printed from Aucher p. 397.

Also Latinè in Cat. Franc. Zephyri p. 82 as follows: non tam ut societatem inirent quam ut specularentur hominis opes, parati quidem ad bellum si tenuem invenissent, ad foedus, si potentem. Qui nunc dicuntur Philistaei, sacra scrip-tura modo Chananaeos modo Cappado-ces vocat.

Cf. Gen. xxvi. 29.

Οὐ διὰ τὸν ἔπαινον· οὐ γὰρ κολακείαν ἤ τινα ἄλλην θεραπείαν ὁ σοφὸς ἀσπάζεται, ἀλλὰ ἀποδεξάμενος αὐτῶν τὴν μετάνοιαν.

Cat. Reg. 1825 (Mang. II. 675).

Cat. Lips. coll. 326, 327, and Cat. Burney, f. 56, adding σωτηρίαν τὴν ἀπὸ τῶν ὅρκων (cod. Burn. ἀνθρώπων) ἔχοντες.

Gen. xxvi. 29.

Non pro laude sua hospitio rogat, nec novit blandire strenuus, aut procacem medelam sapiens affectatur, [sed pro-positis iracundiis quibus exagitati prae-sidere terrena sortiti sunt, nunc confite-tur unum universitatis deum, benedic-tum eum confitentur, sed continuatione sermonis etiam praeteritum aevum de-clarant, quoniam et nunc et a principio ipse est sine immutatione, vel diminu-tione benedictionis, quem nosipsi suspec-tum habuimus, nunc vero absit omnis invidia.] Suscepta igitur eorum poeni-tentia.

Aucher II. 397.

Catena of Zephyrus, p. 82, non quod laudaretur ab illis; nullo enim obsequio vel adulatione sapiens commovetur, sed illorum poenitentiam amplexatus.

Gen. xxvi. 32.

'Αμήχανον ὑπὸ φύσεως ἀνθρωπίνης εὑρεθῆναι τῆς οἰασοῦν ἐπιστήμης τὸ τέλος·
οὐδὲν γὰρ ἄνθρωπος ἄκρως οἶδεν ἀλλ' οἴεται
μόνον εἰδέναι· τὸ δὲ τέλος τῆς γνώσεως
ἀνάκειται μόνῳ θεῷ.

Mai, *Script. Vet.* VII. 107 from Cod.
Vat. 1553. Φίλωνος· ἐκ τῶν ἐν γενέσει
ζητημάτων.

Gen. xxvii. 3.

§ 198. ....

Δυοῖν ὄντων υἱῶν, τοῦ μὲν ἀγαθοῦ, τοῦ
δὲ ὑπαιτίου, τὸν μὲν ὑπαίτιον εὐλογήσειν
φησίν· οὐκ ἐπειδὴ τοῦ σπουδαίου προκρίνει
τοῦτον, ἀλλ' ὅτι ἐκεῖνον οἶδε δι' αὑτοῦ
κατορθοῦν δυνάμενον, τοῦτον δὲ τοῖς ἰδίοις
τρόποις ἁλισκόμενον, μηδεμίαν δὲ ἔχοντα
σωτηρίας ἐλπίδα, εἰ μὴ τὰς εὐχὰς τοῦ πα-
τρός· ὧν εἰ μὴ τύχοι, πάντων ἂν εἴη κακο-
δαιμονέστατος.

Cat. Inedit. Reg. 1825 (Mang. II. 676)
adding τῶν before υἱῶν.

Cat. Lips. I. col. 330 φίλωνος (ἴσως
ἐπισκόπου) and Cat. Burn. f. 56 b (φίλωνος ἑβραίου).

Gen. xxvi. 32.

Ita etiam disciplinam sectantes finem
explorant, quod est impossibile hominibus revelari......quod nihil perfecte homo
nosse potest.........se existimat tantum
scire, finis enim scientiae deo tantum
recondita est.

Gen. xxvii. 3.

§ 198. ....

Quippe quod duo sunt filii: unus
bonus, alter sub causa (s. crimine, culpa).
Istum itaque, qui sub causa est, benedicere ait, non quod plus quam bonum
praeferat hunc, sed quia scit illum per
se solum posse recte rem perficere; istum
vero ut a suis moribus detentum im-
peditumque, spem salutis habere in sola
patris oratione: quam si non assequatur,
prae omnibus miser erit.

In Catena Zephyri, p. 83, as follows:

In deteriorem filium deflectit pater
benedictionem non quia meliori praeferret
sed providens alterum sua virtute semper
felicem fore, alterum suis moribus pro-
labentem in peius, benedictionis peda-
mento indigere. Sara (? Rebecca) igitur
filium quibus dignus erat noluit frau-
dari. Isaac alterius defectum emendare
cupiebat.

In Catena Lippomani f. 288 b as follows:

Philo Hebraeus. Isaac cum duos filios
haberet unum bonum alterum peccatorem, peccatorem tamen benedicere voluit, non quia illum bono praeferret, sed
quia noverat bonum bonitate propria sibi
ipsi satis auxilio fore, malum filium
benedictione adiuvare volebat, sine qua
non nisi infelicissimus esse poterat.

Gen. xxvii. 8—10.

Gen. xxvii. 8—10.

Quid est "Nunc igitur, fili mi, audi me, et vadens ad gregem sume inde mihi duos haedos caprarum teneros et bonos, et faciam eos escas patri tuo, sicut amavit: atque comedens benedicat te, antequam moriatur"?

§ 200. Ἐντεῦθέν ἐστι μαθεῖν τὸ τοῦ σώματος μέγεθος, καὶ τὴν ἐκ κατασκευῆς φυσικὴν εὐεξίαν· ὁ γὰρ ἐν γήρᾳ δύο πίοσιν ἐρίφοις κεχρημένος προεψήμασι, τίς ἂν ὑπῆρχεν ἐν τῇ νεότητι; καὶ ταῦτα ὢν ἐγκρατὴς καὶ οὐκ ἄπληστος.

Cat. Lips. col. 331 (Προκοπίου) and cf. Procopius (ed. Gesner, p. 159).

§ 200. Corporis magnitudo una cum sanitate viscerum patet etiam ex cibi confectione; duos enim haedos pingues exhibere ingens ac procerum corpus indicat una cum fortissima vi, quae omnem medicam virtutem superabat. Nam si senescens duorum haedorum superabat escas, quanto magis quum iuvenis esset: non ob aviditatem edacitatis.

Gen. xxvii. 12.

Gen. xxvii. 12.

§ 202. Ἄξιον καὶ τὴν μητέρα τῆς εὐνοίας θαυμάσαι, τὰς κατάρας ὁμολογοῦσαν εἰσδέξασθαι τὰς ὑπὲρ ἐκείνου, καὶ τὸν υἱὸν τῆς εἰς ἀμφοτέρους τοὺς γονεῖς τιμῆς. Ἀνθέλκεται γὰρ ὑπὸ τῆς πρὸς ἑκάτερον εὐσεβείας· τὸν μὲν γὰρ πατέρα ἐδεδίει, μὴ δόξῃ φενακίζειν καὶ ὑφαρπάζειν ἑτέρου γέρας, τὴν δὲ μητέρα, μὴ καὶ ταύτης νομισθῇ παρακούειν λιπαρῶς ἐγκειμένης· ὅθεν ἄγαν εὐλαβῶς καὶ ὁσίως φησίν· οὐχ "ὁ πατήρ με καταράσεται" ἀλλ' "ἐγὼ τὰς κατάρας ἐπ' ἐμαυτὸν ἄξω."

Cat. Inedit. Reg. 1825 (omitting τοὺς γονεῖς and reading ἐκδέξασθαι). At the end is added a sentence which is ascribed to Procopius in Cat. Lips., ἐθάρρει μὲν τῇ ἐπαγγελίᾳ τοῦ θεοῦ τῇ λεγούσῃ· Ὁ μείζων δουλεύσει τῷ ἐλάσσονι. Πάλιν δὲ ἐφοβεῖτο ὡς ἄνθρωπος, μήπως ἡ εὐλογία τοῦ πατρὸς ὡς δικαίου μεταθήσῃ τὴν ἀπόφασιν τοῦ θεοῦ.

§ 202. Aequum est et matrem mirari propter benevolentiae curam, quum promiserit in se acceptare maledictionem ei pertinentem; et filium propter utriusque genitoris reverentiam, quoniam huc illuc trahebatur, ne putaretur tamquam illudere patri et aliena desiderare, neque matrem negligere ac verba eius nihili facere videretur, cui (s. quae) supplex sese commendabat. Quare dicit nimis timide et condigne: non *pater me conviciabitur*, sed *ego maledictionem super me inducam*.

Cat. Lips. I. col. 331, reading φαινακί-
ζειν, ἐπ᾽ ἐμ. ἔξω. Cat. Burn. fol. 56 b.
Procopius (ed. Gesner, p. 159).

Gen. xxvii. 16.

§ 204. Ὥσπερ τὰς ἄλλας ἀρετὰς ὁ ἀστεῖος, οὕτως καὶ τὴν ἀνδρείαν καθαρῶς ἐπι-
τετηδευκώς, ἐάν που ταύτην ἐπισκιάζῃ χάριν,
καιρῶν οἰκονομίᾳ χρῆται, μένων μὲν ἐν ὁμοίῳ
καὶ τῆς ἐξ ἀρχῆς προθέσεως οὐκ ἀναχωρῶν,
διὰ δὲ τῶν ἀβουλήτων συντυχίας ἐναλλάτ-
των ὥσπερ ἐν θεάτρῳ μορφὴν ἑτέραν ὑπὲρ
ὠφελείας τῶν ὁρώντων· ἰατρὸς γὰρ τῶν
κατὰ τὸν βίον πραγμάτων ὁ ἀστεῖος, ὃς
ἕνεκα τῶν καιρῶν φρονίμως ἐνεργεῖ τὰ
ἀφροσύνης, καὶ σωφρόνως τὰς ἀκολασίας
καὶ τὰς δειλίας ἀνδρείως καὶ δικαίως τὰς
ἀδικίας· καὶ γὰρ ἐρεῖ ποτε τὰ ψευδῆ οὐ
ψευδόμενος καὶ ὑβρίσει μὴ ὢν ὑβριστής.

Mai, *Script. Vet.* VII. 106 e Cod. Vat.
1553 : Φίλωνος· ἐκ τοῦ ς΄ τῶν ἐν γενέσει
ζητημάτων.

Gen. xxvii. 16.

§ 204. ...ut caeteras virtutes, sic etiam
fortitudinem sancte usurpans exercens-
que. Quod si contingat, ut istam quoque
occultet et pilosam reddat, ob necessi-
tatem temporis dispensationem usurpans,
perstat in sua similitudine, vix cedens
primitivae suae propositioni, sed tantum
ob involuntaria accidentia transmutabit
tamquam in spectaculo formam alio
modo propter utilitatem spectatorum.
[Id enim et medicorum mos est facere,
quippe qui infirmorum demutant cibos,
loca et rationem vivendi, quam habebant
ante morbum.] Medicus autem est circa
res mundi sapiens, pro tempore agens
res, quae in sapientia insipientes videntur, et castitate venereae, fortitudine
formidabiles, et iustitia iniustae putan-
tur : ita ut aliquando mentiens non men-
tiatur, decipiat non fallens, et convi-
cietur sine convicio.

Gen. xxvii. 18.

§ 206. ....
Λεγέτω καὶ ὁ στρατηγὸς ἢ τὰ πολεμο-
ποιοῦντα εἰρήνην πραγματευόμενος, ἢ τὰ
εἰρήνης πολεμεῖν διανοούμενος· ὑποδυέσθω
καὶ βασιλεὺς ἰδιώτου σχῆμα, εἰ μὴ δύναιτο
ἑτέρως τὸ συμφέρον τῇ τε ἀρχῇ καὶ τοῖς
ὑπηκόοις λαβεῖν· καὶ ὁ δεσπότης δούλου,
εἵνεκα τοῦ μηδὲν ἀγνοῆσαι τῶν κατὰ τὴν
οἰκίαν δρωμένων.

Mai, *Script. Vet.* VII. 106, ut supra.

Gen. xxvii. 18.

§ 206. ....
Dicat et dux militiae, qui bellum facit,
velle pacis negotium operari vel in tempore pacis aciem parare cogitans. In-
duat et rex habitum privati, si nequit
alio modo utilitatem imperii subditorum-
que auspicari; et dominus (formam)
servi, ne ignoret omnino res domi actas.

Gen. xxvii. 34.

§ 227. Οὐκ ἐπὶ τῷ μὴ τυχεῖν τῶν εὐλο-
γιῶν οὕτω δυσχεραίνει, ὡς ἐπὶ τῷ τὸν ἀδελφὸν αὐτοῦ ἀξιωθῆναι. Βάσκανος γὰρ ὢν
ἐπιμελέστερον προκρίνει τῆς ἰδίας ὠφελείας
τὴν ἐκείνου ζημίαν. Ταῦτα γὰρ ἐμφαίνεται
διὰ τοῦ μέγα καὶ πικρὸν ἀνοιμῶξαι καὶ
ἐπιλέγειν· Εὐλόγησον δὴ καὶ ἐμέ, πάτερ.

Catena Inedita Reg. 1825 (Mang. II.
676).

Cat. Lips. I. col. 339 referred to Procopius, reading ἐκβοῆσαι for ἀνοιμῶξαι.

Cat. Burney fol. 57 b, φίλωνος ἑβραίου,
reading βοῆσαι for ἀνοιμῶξαι and κἀμοὶ
for καὶ ἐμέ.

Gen. xxvii. 35.

§ 228. Ἀλλ᾿ εἴ γε μετὰ δόλου ἔλαβεν,
εἴποι τις ἄν, οὐκ ἐπαινετός. Τί οὖν φησί·
Καὶ εὐλογημένος ἔσται; Ἀλλ᾿ ἔοικεν αἰνίτ-
τεσθαι διὰ τοῦ λεχθέντος ὅτι οὐ πᾶς δόλος
ὑπαίτιός ἐστιν, ἐπεὶ καὶ λῃστὰς νυκτοφύ-
λακες, καὶ πολεμίους στρατηγοί, οὓς ἀδόλως
συλλαβεῖν οὐκ ἔστιν, ἐνεδρεύοντες κατορθοῦν
δοκοῦσι. Καὶ τὰ λεγόμενα στρατηγήματα
τοιοῦτον λόγον ἔχει καὶ τὰ τῶν ἀθλητῶν ἀγω-
νίσματα· καὶ γὰρ ἐπὶ τούτων ἡ ἀπάτη νενόμισ-
ται τίμιον, καὶ οἱ δι᾿ ἀπάτης περιγενόμενοι
τῶν ἀντιπάλων βραβείων ἀξιοῦνται καὶ στε-
φάνων. Ὥστε οὐ διαβολὴ τὸ "μετὰ δόλου,"
ἀλλ᾿ ἐγκώμιον ἰσοδυναμοῦν τῷ "μετὰ τέχνης"· οὐδὲν γὰρ ἀτέχνως πράττει ὁ σπουδαῖος.

Cat. Reg. Inedit. 1825 (Mang. II. 676).

Cat. Lips. I. col. 340 as ἀδήλου, Cat.
Burney, f. 57 b, not headed as Philo,
both reading ἴσως εἴποι τις, οὐκ· ἔστω for
ἔσται· περιγινόμενοι.

Gen. xxvii. 34.

Quare, quando audivit Esau, exclama-
vit voce magna et amara valde, et dixit,
"Benedic et me, pater"?

§ 227. Littera id praefert: Non
tantum quod consecutus non sit benedictionem, aegre fert conturbaturque,
quantum quod frater eius dignus est effectus. Quandoquidem invidiosus erat,
maiori curae esse sibi putat damnum
eius, quam utilitatem propriam : id enim
indicat, quum alta voce acerbeque ex-
clamat et dicit rursum : *Benedic etiam me.*

Cf. Cat. Lippomani f. 294. Philo
Hebraeus. Esau non tam cordi erat
paterna benedictio, quam ne frater Iacob
sibi praeferretur atque in potioribus bonis
esset, invidus enim cum esset, exclama-
vit, Benedic etiam mihi pater.

Gen. xxvii. 35.

§ 228. Atqui si *fraudulenter* accepit,
dixerit forte quisquam, non laudabilis
erat. Quomodo ergo asserit, dicens :
Erit benedictus? Caeterum videtur de-
signare per dictum, quod non omnis
fraudulentus (visus) reus est. Quod
autem ita se res habeat, ecce cum la-
trones excubitor et inimicos pugnantes
duces militiae sine fraude nequeant pre-
hendere et vincere, insidias parantes rem
perficiunt oppido magnam, eam inquam,
quae insidiosa actio appellatur. Similem
habet rationem et luctatorum congressus,
siquidem et istis illusio vel fraus putatur
honorifica, et qui per dolum vincunt ad-
versarios praemium coronamque merentur. Non ergo sicut fallacia vituperio
digna est habenda talis fraus, sed pro
laude aequaliter valet et ratio sapientis,
qui arte, non autem sicut iners operatur.

Quæstiones in Exodum.

Lib. I.

Exod. xii. 2.

§ 1. ....

Ὅταν οἱ τῶν σπαρτῶν καρποὶ τελειωθῶσιν, οἱ τῶν δένδρων γενέσεως ἀρχὴν λαμβάνουσιν, ἵνα δολιχεύωσιν αἱ τοῦ θεοῦ χάριτες τὸν αἰῶνα, παρ' ἄλλων ἄλλαι διαδεχόμεναι καὶ συνάπτουσαι τέλη μὲν ἀρχαῖς, ἀρχὰς δὲ τέλεσιν, ἀτελεύτητοι ὦσιν.

Dam. Par. 789 (Cod. Rupef. f. 142 b) ἐκ τοῦ α΄ τῶν ἐν ἐξόδῳ.

Exod. xii. 2.

§ 1. ......Quando ergo satorum fructus perficiantur ab arboribus, tunc principium generationis accipiunt, ut prolongentur dei gratiae perpetuo aliis post alia se invicem excipientibus et adhaerente fine initiis initioque finibus.

Exod. xii. 4.

§ 6. Ὑπερβολαὶ καὶ ἐλλείψεις ἀνισότητα ἐγέννησαν. ἀνισότης δέ, ἵνα αὐτὸς μυθικώτερον χρήσωμαι τοῖς ὀνόμασιν, μητὴρ ἀδικίας ἐστίν, ὡς ἔμπαλιν ἰσότης δικαιοσύνης· ὑπερβολῆς δὲ καὶ ἐλλείψεως μέσον τὸ αὐταρκές· ἐν ᾧ τὸ ἱερὸν γράμμα περιέχεται τὸ Μηδὲν ἄγαν.

Mai, *Script. Vet.* VII. 106, from Cod. Vat. 1553. Φίλωνος· ἐκ τοῦ α΄ τῶν ἐν ἐξόδῳ ζητημάτων, reading χρήσομαι.

Exod. xii. 4.

§ 6. Primum quidem excessus defectusque aequitatis sive paritatis generavit inaequitatem atque imparitatem. Ut autem et ego fabulosum quicquam usurpem de his nominibus, mater istius iniustitia est, sicut itidem paritas sive aequalitas iustitia est. Inter autem excessum et defectum medium tenet *sufficiens*, in quo divinus liber hoc constituit, ut *Nihil sit nimis.*

Exod. xii. 5.

§ 7. ....

Λέγεται ὑπὸ φυσικῶν ἀνδρῶν, οὐδὲν ἕτερον εἶναι θῆλυ ἢ ἀτελὲς ἄρσεν.

Dam. Par. 777 (Cod. Rupef. f. 134) ἐκ τῶν ἐν ἐξόδῳ ζητημάτων. Anton Melissa (*Patr. Gr.* col. 1088), reading ἄῤῥεν.

Exod. xii. 5.

§ 7. ......quapropter etiam a physicis dicitur non aliud esse femina, nisi masculum imperfectum.

....

Ἔνιοι προκόψαντες ἐπ' ἀρετὴν ὑπενόστησαν πρὶν ἐφικέσθαι τοῦ τέλους, τὴν ἄρτι φυο-

.... Quidam progredientes in virtute, antequam finem consequantur, retrogressi sunt fugitivi; quoniam ani-

μένην ἀριστοκράτειαν ἐν ψυχῇ καθελούσης τῆς παλαιᾶς ὀλιγοκρατείας, ἢ πρὸς ὀλίγον ἠρεμήσασα πάλιν ἐξ ὑπαρχῆς μετὰ πλείονος δυνάμεως ἀντεπέθετο.

Dam. Par. 343, reading ἐναπέθετο. In Cod. Reg. 923, f. 84, this is given as ἐκ τοῦ αʹ τῶν ἐν ἐξαγω (sc. ἐξαγωγῇ) ζητημάτων. Philo frequently uses the term ἐξαγωγή as a synonym for ἔξοδος.

Anton Melissa (*Patr. Gr.* col. 1117), reading ὀχλοκρατίας for παλαιᾶς ὀλιγοκρατείας.

Exod. xii. 11.

§ 19. ....

Αἱ μὲν γὰρ ζῶναι στάσιν ἐμφαίνουσι καὶ συναγωγὴν ἡδονῶν καὶ τῶν ἄλλων παθῶν ἃ τέως ἀνεῖτο καὶ κεχάλαστο· οὐκ ἀπὸ δὲ σκοποῦ προσέθηκε τὸ δεῖν ζώννυσθαι κατὰ τὴν ὀσφύν· ὁ γὰρ τόπος ἐκεῖνος εἰς φάτνην ἀποκέκριται πολυκεφάλῳ θρέμματι τῶν ἐν ἡμῖν ἐπιθυμιῶν...

From Pitra, *Anal. Sac.* II. 313, e Cod. Vat. 1611, f. 181.

Exod. xii. 17.

§ 21. ....

Ἄνδρες ἀγαθοί, τροπικώτερον εἰπεῖν, κίονές εἰσι δήμων ὅλων, ὑπερείδοντες, καθάπερ οἰκίας μεγάλας, τὰς πόλεις καὶ τὰς πολιτείας.

From Joh. Monachus (Mang. II. 661) as ἐκ τοῦ περὶ μέθης,=Rup. f. 33 b, reading κρείττονες for κίονες which was emended by Mangey. The passage will be found again with the same heading in Rup. f. 200 b.

Anton Melissa (*Patr. Gr.* 136, col. 1105).

mae supernatam virtutis vim destruxit antiquus error, qui ad tempus cessans iterum magna vi molitus est.

Exod. xii. 11.

§ 19. ....

Quia *zona* constrictionem indicat collectionemque cupiditatum et caeterarum affectionum, quae quasi solutae occupant totam animam; unde non frustra adiecit zona accingi debere lumbum, quia is locus ut praesepium habetur bestiae multicapitis in nobis cupiditatis.

Exod. xii. 17.

§ 21. ....

Quoniam viri boni columnae sunt populorum, cunctis pro fulcro exsistentes, tamquam domus magnarum urbium et urbanitatis.

Quæstiones in Exodum.

Lib. II.

<table>
<tr><td>

Exod. xx. 25.

Τί ἐστι, "τὸ γὰρ ἐγχειρίδιόν σου" καὶ τὰ ἑξῆς;

§ 1. Οἱ τὴν φύσιν παρεγχειρεῖν τολμῶντες καὶ τὰ ἔργα τῆς φύσεως ἐγχειρήμασιν ἰδίοις μεταμορφοῦντες τὰ ἀμίαντα μιαίνουσι. Τέλεια γὰρ καὶ πλήρη τὰ τῆς φύσεως, προσθήκης οὐδεμιᾶς δεόμενα.

Catena Inedita, Reg. 1825 (Mang. II. 677), reading τὸ ἐγχ.

Cat. Lips. I. col. 785 (φίλωνος ἑβραίου).

</td><td>

Exod. xx. 25.

Quid est "Quia manus instrumentum iniecisti super illud, et inquinatum est"?

§ 1. Qui in naturam manum mittere praesumunt operaque naturae manumissione sua mutantes efformant, impollutum polluunt : perfecta enim plenaque sunt naturae propria, nec decisione, nec additione, neque quoquam egentes.

Also in part in Cat. Lippomani in Genesim, f. 197.

Philo Hebraeus. Hi qui naturam transmutari audacter aggrediuntur, hi mihi impolluta polluere videntur. Naturae namque opera perfecta absolutaque sunt, quaeque nulla additione indigeant.

</td></tr>
<tr><td>

Exod. xxii. 20.

§ 2. Ἐμφανέστατα παρίστησιν, ὅτι προσήλυτός ἐστιν, οὐχ ὁ περιτμηθεὶς τὴν ἀκροβυστίαν, ἀλλ᾽ ὁ τὰς ἡδονὰς καὶ τὰς ἐπιθυμίας καὶ τὰ ἄλλα πάθη τῆς ψυχῆς. Ἐν Αἰγύπτῳ γὰρ τὸ Ἑβραῖον γένος οὐ περιτέτμητο, κακωθὲν δὲ πάσαις κακώσεσι τῆς παρὰ τῶν ἐγχωρίων περὶ τοὺς ξένους ὠμότητος, ἐγκρατείᾳ καὶ καρτερίᾳ συνεβίου· οὐκ ἀνάγκῃ μᾶλλον ἢ ἐθελουσίῳ γνώμῃ, διὰ τὴν ἐπὶ τὸν σωτῆρα θεὸν καταφυγήν, ὃς ἐξ ἀπόρων καὶ ἀμηχάνων ἐπιπέμψας τὴν εὐεργέτιν δύναμιν ἐρρύσατο τοὺς ἱκέτας. Διὰ τοῦτο προστίθησιν· "Ὑμεῖς γὰρ οἴδατε τὴν

</td><td>

Exod. xxii. 20.

Quare admonens "Advenam non vexabis" inducit dicens "Advenae enim fuistis in terra Aegyptiorum"?

§ 2. Manifeste declarat, advenam utique esse non qui circumciderit praeputium, sed cupiditates et voluptates caeterasque affectiones animi. Quoniam in Aegypto Hebraeorum gens non erat circumcisa, sed afflicta omni afflictione ab incolis regionis, in peregrina vagatione patienti animo cum iis degens, non ex necessitate, sed ultro. Quia salvator deus, confugientibus illis ad se, ex inopinata ac inexplebili spe misit beneficam virtutem et salvavit suppliciter rogantes. Quare adiicit, quod *vos conscii estis*

</td></tr>
</table>

Rom. ii. 28

H.

7

ψυχὴν τοῦ προσηλύτου." Τίς δὲ προσηλύτου διάνοιά ἐστιν; Ἀλλοτρίωσις τῆς
πολυθέου δόξης, οἰκείωσις δὲ τῆς πρὸς τὸν
ἕνα καὶ πατέρα τῶν ὅλων τιμῆς. Δεύτερον
ἐπήλυδας ἔνιοι καλοῦσι τοὺς ξένους. Ξένοι
δὲ καὶ οἱ πρὸς τὴν ἀλήθειαν αὐτομοληκότες,
τὸν αὐτὸν τρόπον τοῖς ἐν Αἰγύπτῳ ξενιτεύ-
σασιν. οὗτοι μὲν γὰρ ἐπήλυδες χώρας,
ἐκεῖνοι δὲ νομίμων καὶ ἐθῶν εἰσί, τὸ δὲ
ὄνομα κοινὸν ἑκατέρων "ἐπηλύδων" ὑπο-
γράφεται.

Cat. Reg. 1825 (Mang. II. 677).

Cat. Lips. I. col. 810, φίλωνος ἑβραίου,
reading οἰκέτας for ἱκέτας, ηὐτομοληκότες,
and in the last line ἐπηλύδες.

Cat. Burn. f. 136.

Exod. xxii. 21.

Χήραν καὶ ὀρφανὸν ἀπείρηται κακοῦν.

§ 3. Οὐδένα μέν, οὐδὲ τῶν ἄλλων, οὔτε
ἄρρενα οὔτε θήλειαν, ἀφίησιν ἀδικεῖν ὁ
νόμος· ἐξαιρέτου δὲ προνοίας μεταδίδωσιν
χήραις καὶ ὀρφανοῖς, ἐπειδὴ τοὺς ἀναγκαίους
βοηθοὺς καὶ κηδεμόνας ἀφήρηνται, χῆραι
μὲν ἄνδρας, ὀρφανοὶ δὲ γονεῖς. Βούλεται
γὰρ τῇ φυσικῇ κοινωνίᾳ χρωμένους, τὰς
ἐνδείας ὑπὸ τῶν ἐν περιουσίᾳ ἀναπληροῦσθαι.

Mai, *Script. Vet.* VII. 104, from Cod.
Vat. 1553, Φίλωνος· ἐκ τοῦ τελευταίου τῶν
ἐν ἐξόδῳ ζητημάτων, and omitting the last
sentence. Mai gives Οὐ δυναμένου δὲ for
the opening words. Cod. Reg. 923, f.
32 b, gives the part from ἐξαιρέτου...
γονεῖς, reading however ἀνδρός, γονέων,
and Rup. f. 220 b, Cat. Inedit. Reg.
1825 (Mang. II. 678), omit as far as
νόμος, and so Cat. Lips. I. col. 805, and
Cat. Burney fol. 136, which also leave
out from χῆραι...γονεῖς.

animi advenae (Exod. xxiii. 9). Caeterum
quae advenae mens, nisi abalienatio a
voluntate serviendi multis diis, familia-
ritasque ad unum deum atque in honorem patris universorum ? Secundo ad-
venas aliqui nuncupant *alienos:* alieni
vero et qui ad veritatem per se concur-
rerunt, non eodem modo, qui in Aegypto
peregrinatione degerunt: nam isti pere-
grini mundo sunt, illi vero legi et con-
suetudini ; nomen tamen commune utro-
rumque *advenarum* adscribitur.

Exod. xxii. 21.

Quare omnem viduam et pupillum in-
hibet vexare ?

§ 3. Neminem ne ex alienis quidem,
nec masculum neque feminam, sinit
iniuria afficere. Meliorem tamen pecu-
liaremque curam praestat *viduis* et *pu-
pillis :* quoniam necessariis adiutoribus
curatoribusque destituti sunt, viduae
viris, et pupilli parentibus. Vult ergo,
ut naturali aequitate usurpata, egestati
ab. iis qui in abundantia sunt, satisfieri.

....
....

Ψυχαὶ δέ, ὅταν προσκολληθῶσι θεῷ, ἐκ γυναικῶν γίνονται παρθένοι, τὰς μὲν γυναικώδεις ἀποβάλλουσαι φθορὰς τῶν ἐν αἰσθήσει καὶ πάθει· τὴν δὲ ἄψευστον καὶ ἀμιγῆ παρθένον, ἀρέσκειαν θεοῦ, μεταδιώκουσι· κατὰ λόγον οὖν αἱ τοιαῦται ψυχαὶ χηρεύουσιν, ἄνδρα τὸν τῆς φύσεως ὀρθὸν νόμον προσσυμβιοῦσιν καὶ πατέρα τὸν αὐτόν, ἃ χρὴ πράττειν παραγγέλλοντα καθάπερ ἐγγόνοις μετὰ τῆς ἀνωτάτω κηδεμονίας.

Pitra, *Anal. Sac.* II. 308, from Coislin. 276, f. 183. The MS. has ἄψαυστον, which Pitra corrects by means of the Armenian.

Exod. xxii. 27.

§ 6. ....
Προνοεῖται τῶν ἰδιωτῶν ὡς μὴ περιπίπτοιεν ἀνηκέστοις τιμωρίαις· οἱ γὰρ κακῶς ἀκούσαντες ἄρχοντες τοὺς εἰπόντας οὐ μετὰ δίκης ἀμυνοῦνται· καταχρήσονται δυναστείαις εἰς πανωλεθρίαν. Ἐπεί, φησίν, οὐ περὶ παντὸς ἄρχοντος ἔοικε νομοθετεῖν ἀλλ᾽ ὡσανεὶ τοῦ λαοῦ τοῦδε ἢ ἔθνους ἡγεμόνα σπουδαῖον ὑποτίθεται, διὰ πλειόνων, καταχρηστικῶς δὲ δυνατοὺς ἢ ἱερεῖς ἢ προφήτας ἢ ἁγίους ἄνδρας ὡς Μωϋσέα· Ἰδοὺ γάρ, ἔθηκά σε θεὸν Φαραώ, ἐλέχθη πρὸς Μωϋσῆν.

Cat. Burney f. 136, reading ἀπόντας for εἰπόντας, πανολεθρίαν, ἐπειδὴ, ὑπερτίθεται.
Cat. Lips. I. col. 805 (φίλωνος ἑβραίου).
Οὐδὲν οὕτως εὐάγωγον εἰς εὔνοιαν ὡς ἡ τῶν εὐεργετημάτων εὐφημία.

From Anton Melissa (*Patr. Gr.* 136, col. 1149).

Exod. xxiii. 1.

§ 9. Μάταιόν φησιν οὔτε ἀκοαῖς οὔτε ἄλλῃ τινὶ τῶν αἰσθήσεων προσιτέον· ἐπακο-

Animae vero quum deo induuntur (vel initiantur) ex mulieribus virgines existunt, muliebribus sepositis corruptoribus, quae in sensibus et cupiditatibus sunt. Qui vero infallibilem inviolabilemque virginem, veracem scilicet Sapientiam dei, sequuntur, contraria eiiciunt (vitia). Iure itaque huiusmodi mentes viduae fiunt et orbantur ex mortalibus, habentque acquisitum sibi tam virum, naturae rectam legem, quocum vivunt, tam (l. quam) patrem eundem, qui, quae oportet facere, praecipit tamquam filiis una cum superna providentia.

Exod. xxii. 27.

§ 6. ....
Secundo cura gerenda omnium aliorum hominum, ne subeant inexorabilem poenam; quoniam maledictionem audientes principes a dicentibus, non per iudicium vindictam capiunt, sed absolutam usurpant vim ad damnificandum omnino. Non pro omni principe videtur legem ferre, sed de eo qui praeest universo populo, atque ducem gentis secundum Iudaeos, virtute praeditum hominem praepositum, innuit multis rebus.........

Nihil enim est adeo inducens ad curam habendam, sicut bonae famae laus.

Exod. xxiii. 1.

Quid est "non suscipies auditionem mendacem"?
§ 9. Inaniter nihil, nec auribus neque aliis sensibus, suscipiendum est:

λουθοῦσι γὰρ ταῖς ἀπάταις αἱ μέγισται ζημίαι. Διὸ καὶ παρ' ἐνίοις νομοθέταις ἀπείρηται μαρτυρεῖν ἀκοῇ, ὡς τὸ μὲν ἀληθὲς
ὄψει πιστευόμενον, τὸ δὲ ψεῦδος ἀκοῇ.

  Cat. Reg. Inedit. 1825.   Mangey sug-
gests προσετέον, πιστούμενον.

  Cat. Lips. ι. col. 807.

  Cat. Burney fol. 136 b.

  Cf. Procopius (ed. Gesner, p. 284).

quoniam errorem illusionis permagna
sequuntur detrimenta. Quamobrem
etiam nonnulli legislatorum statuere,
non testari per auditum (s. ex fama),
quasi vero verum per oculos fidele comperitur, mendacium autem per auditus.

Exod. xxiii. 3.

§ 10.   Πενία καθ' ἑαυτὴν μὲν ἐλέου
χρῄζει εἰς ἐπανόρθωσιν ἐνδείας, εἰς δὲ κρίσιν
ἰοῦσα βραβευτῇ χρῆται τῷ τῆς ἰσότητος
νόμῳ· θεῖον γὰρ ἡ δικαιοσύνη καὶ ἀδέκαστον.
Ὅθεν καὶ ἐν ἑτέροις εὖ εἴρηται, ὅτι ἡ κρίσις
τοῦ θεοῦ δικαία ἐστίν.

  Cat. Reg. Inedit. 1825.   Cat. Lips. ι.
col. 807.   Cat. Burney f. 136 b.

  Cf. Procopius (ed. Gesner, p. 284).

Exod. xxiii. 3.

§ 10.   Paupertas per se misericordiam
desiderat ad erectionem egestatis: in
iudicium vero veniens iudice utitur paritatis lege; quoniam divina quaedam est
iustitia, dona minime accipiens.   Unde
quibusdam optime dictum est: *Iudicia
dei sunt.*

Exod. xxiii. 20.

§ 13. ....
Οἱ ἀφυλάκτως ὁδοιποροῦντες διαμαρτάνουσιν
τῆς ὀρθῆς καὶ λεωφόρου ὡς πολλάκις εἰς ἀνο-
δίας καὶ δυσβάτους καὶ τραχείας ἀτραποὺς
ἐκτρέπεσθαι. Τὸ παραπλήσιόν ἐστιν ὅτε καὶ
αἱ ψυχαὶ τῶν νέων παιδείας ἀμοιροῦσιν,
καθάπερ ῥεῦμα ἀνεπίσχετον ὅπη μὴ λυσι-
τελὲς ῥεμβεύονται.

  Cod. Reg. 923, fol. 302 b, from the
Quaest. in Exod., reading ἀμοιρῶσιν,
ἀνέπισχετο (sic).

....

  Ὁ πεινῶν καὶ διψῶν ἐπιστήμης καὶ τοῦ
μαθεῖν ἃ μὴ οἶδεν, τὰς ἄλλας μεθιέμενος
φροντίδας, ἐπείγεται πρὸς ἀκρόασιν, καὶ
νύκτωρ καὶ μεθ' ἡμέραν θυρωρεῖ τὰς τῶν
σοφῶν οἰκίας.

  Dam. Par. 613, Cod. Reg. f. 230.

Exod. xxiii. 20.

§ 13. ....
Quicumque sine cautela viam faciunt,
aberrant ab ipsa recta propriaque semita,
saepe per impervia, dura et anfracta
deviantes.   Huic aequale est pariter,
quando et anima patiatur aliquid iuve-
nile, etsi pium: quum enim expers sit
disciplinae, fertur torrentis instar sine
impedimento, eo quo vix expedit.

  (Aucher prints saepe saepius.)

....

  Esuriens sitiensque ad intelligentiam
disciplinae atque ad discendum quae
nescit, caeteris omissis curis, properat
ad auscultationem, et nocte ac die ostia
custodit domuum sapientum.

....

Exod. xxiii. 18.

§ 14. Ἀντὶ τοῦ οὐ δεῖ ζυμωτὸν παρεῖναι ἐπὶ τῶν θυσιαζομένων, ἀλλὰ πάντα τὰ προσαγόμενα εἰς θυσίαν ἤτοι προσφορὰν ἄζυμα δεῖ εἶναι, αἰνίττεται διὰ συμβόλου δύο τὰ ἀναγκαιότατα· ἐν μὲν τὸ καταφρονεῖν ἡδονῆς, ζύμη γὰρ ἥδυσμα τροφῆς, οὐ τροφή· ἕτερον δὲ τὸ μὴ δεῖν ἐπαίρεσθαι φυσωμένους διὰ κενῆς οἰήσεως. Ἀνίερον γὰρ ἑκάτερον, ἡδονή τε καὶ οἴησις, μητρὸς μιᾶς ἀπάτης ἔγγονα.

Τὸ αἷμα τῶν θυσιῶν δεῖγμα ψυχῆς ἐστι σπενδομένης θεῷ, μιγνύναι δὲ τὰ ἄμικτα οὐχ ὅσιον.

Cat. Reg. Inedit. 1825 (= Mang. II. 678).

Cat. Lips. I. col. 816, reading καίνης for κενῆς.

Cat. Burney f. 138.

Cf. Procopius (ed. Gesner, p. 287).

Exod. xxiii. 18.

§ 15. Κελεύει τὰ στέατα αὐθήμερον ἀναλίσκεσθαι γινόμενα ὕλην ἱερᾶς φλογός.

Cat. Burney f. 138.

Cat. Lips. I. col. 816 as ἀδήλου.

A sentence is added by Cat. Burney which is given to Cyril by Cat. Lips., and belongs to the next verse of the chapter.

Διὰ τὸ συγγνωμόνας αὐτοῖς φαίνεσθαι τῷ θεῷ εὐχαριστοῦντας ἢ καὶ εἰς ἀποτροφὴν ἱερέως καὶ λευϊτῶν.

Exod. xxiii. 18.

Quid est "Non immolabis in fermento sanguinem victimae"?

§ 14. [Alias quoque similiter huic statuit, jubens,] in aram, super quam sacrificia offeruntur, fermentum non adhiberi, subindicans per utrumque symbolum necessarium: contemnere voluptates, quoniam fermentum dulcificum cibi est, non cibus; alterum etiam, quod non oportet fastu efferri praeter (s. propter) communem opinionem. Siquidem foeda et odiosa est utraque, voluptas cupiditatis et superbia (velut) opinio stultitiae, unius eiusdemque matris, illusionis, partus. Sanguis autem victimae oblatae indicium est animae deo consecratae: at miscere immixta nefas.

In Catena Zephyri (p. 141) as follows:

Phil. Id est nihil fermentati super hostiam adhibebis. Quaecumque offeruntur azyma esse oportet. Et sanguis sacrorum cum animae sit indicium illius quae deo mactatur cum re profana commisceri non debet.

Exod. xxiii. 18.

Quid est "Non dormiet adeps solemnitatis meae usque ad mane"?

§ 15. Littera iussum dat adipem eo die consumi, materia facta divino igni.

Catena Zephyri: adipes autem eodem die iubet absumi, ne desit sacra materia flammae.

Exod. xxiii. 22.

§ 16. ....

Φωνὴν θεοῦ τὸν πρὸ μικροῦ λεχθέντα ἄγγε-
λον ὑπονοητέον μηνύεσθαι. Τοῦ γὰρ λέ-
γοντος ὁ προφήτης ἄγγελος κυρίου ἐστίν.
Ἀνάγκη γὰρ τὸν ἀκοῇ ἀκούοντα, τουτέστι
τὸν τὰ λεγόμενα βεβαίως παραδεχόμενον,
ἔργοις ἐπιτελεῖν τὰ λεχθέντα. Λόγου γὰρ
πίστις ἔργον· ὁ δὲ καὶ τοῖς εἰρημένοις κατα-
πειθὴς καὶ ἐνεργῶν τὰ ἀκόλουθα, σύμμαχον
καὶ ὑπερασπιστὴν ἐξ ἀνάγκης ἔχει τὸν δι-
δάσκαλον, ὅσα μὲν τῷ δοκεῖν, βοηθοῦντα τῷ
γνωρίμῳ, τὸ δὲ ἀληθὲς τοῖς αὐτοῦ δόγμασι
καὶ παραγγέλμασιν, ἅπερ οἱ ἐναντίοι καὶ
ἐχθροὶ βούλονται καθαιρεῖν.

Cat. Reg. Inedit. 1825 (=Mang. II. 678).
Cat. Lips. I. col. 818.
Cat. Burney f. 139, where the passage
has been glossed by a Christian com-
mentator.
Cf. Procopius (ed. Gesner, p. 288).

Exod. xxiii. 24.

§ 17. Στῆλαί εἰσι τὰ δόγματα συμβολικῶς, ἅπερ ἑστάναι καὶ ἐρηρεῖσθαι δοκεῖ.
Τῶν δὲ κατεστηλιτευμένων δογμάτων τὰ μὲν
ἀστεῖά ἐστιν, ἃ καὶ θέμις ἀνακεῖσθαι καὶ
βεβαίαν ἔχειν τὴν ἵδρυσιν· τὰ δὲ ἐπίληπτα,
ὧν τὴν καθαίρεσιν ποιεῖσθαι λυσιτελές.
Τὸ δὲ "καθαιρῶν καθελεῖς" καὶ "συντρίβων
συντρίψεις" τοιοῦτον ὑποβάλλει νοῦν. Ἔνιά
τινες καθαιροῦσιν ὡς ἀναστήσοντες, καὶ
συντρίβουσιν ὡς αὖθις ἁρμοσόμενοι· βούλεται δὲ τὰ καθαιρεθέντα ἅπαξ καὶ συντρι-
βέντα μηκέτι τυχεῖν ἀνορθώσεως, ἀλλ' εἰς
ἅπαν ἠφανίσθαι τὰ ἐναντία τοῖς ἀγαθοῖς καὶ
καλοῖς.

Cat. Reg. Inedit. 1825 (Mang. II. 678).

Exod. xxiii. 22.

§ 16. ....

Vocem dei quo paulo ante dictum an-
gelum existimandum est denotare; qui
enim ab isto dicitur propheta, angelus est
veraciter. Necesse est ergo ei qui *au-
diendo audit*, id est constanter recipit
dicta, opera quoque ea perficere; nam
sermonis fides opera est. Qui vero dictis
consentiens in operam ducit ordinatum
per enunciationem, protectorem neces-
sario sibi acquirit magistrum, ut putatur, adiuvante amico (vel adiuvantem
alumno), re tamen vera propria voluntate legis, quam adversarii et inimici op-
tarunt destruere.

Exod. xxiii. 24.

Quid est, quod "Destruendo destrues
et conterendo conteres statuas eorum"?

§ 17. *Statuae* sunt symbolice gratae
leges, quae statutae fulcitaeque constanter videntur. Acceptarum autem legum,
statuae instar erectarum, sunt quaedam,
quae probandae sunt quasque aequum
est stare et firmum habere situm sta-
tionis; sunt item, quae improbandae
sunt, quas sane destrui expedit. [Huius-
modi sunt, quaecumque insipientia contra prudentiam statuit, et quaecumque
incontinentia adversus sobrietatem, et
quaecumque iniustitia pro iustitia, et
simul quicquid malitiae contra virtutem
est.] Verum illud "*Destruendo destrues
et conterendo conteres*" huiusmodi inducit

Cat. Lips. ı. col. 820.
Cat. Burney fol. 139.
Cf. Procopius (ed. Gesner, p. 288).

sententiam: Quoniam est aliquid, quod destruunt ad rursum erigendum, confringuntque ut iterum coaptent, is tamen vult semel destructum confractumque non amplius reparationem consequi, sed semper in corruptione iacere, quicquid contrarium est bono optimoque.

Exod. xxiii. 25.

Exod. xxiii. 25.

Cur dicet "Benedicam panem tuum et aquam, et avertam infirmitates a te"?

§ 18. Τροφὴν καὶ ὑγιείαν αἰνίττεται·
τροφὴν μὲν δι᾽ ἄρτου καὶ ὕδατος· ὑγιείαν
διὰ τοῦ μαλακίαν ἀποστρέφειν. δεύτερον,
ἐγκράτειαν εἰσηγεῖται, τὴν τῶν ἀναγκαίων
μετουσίαν, μόνον ἐπειπών·...πρὸς δὲ τούτοις,
μάθημα ἡμᾶς αἰσιώτατον ἀναδιδάσκει· δη-
λῶν ὅτι οὔτε ἄρτος οὔτε ὕδωρ καθ᾽ ἑαυτὰ
τρέφουσιν· ἀλλ᾽ ἔστιν ὅτε καὶ βλάπτουσι
μᾶλλον ἢ ὠφελοῦσιν, ἐὰν μὴ θεῖος λόγος
καὶ τούτοις χαρίσηται τὰς ἀφελητικὰς δυνά-
μεις· ἧς χάριν αἰτίας φησὶν "εὐλογήσω τὸν
ἄρτον σου καὶ τὸ ὕδωρ"· ὡς οὐχ ἱκανὰ καθ᾽
ἑαυτὰ τρέφειν ἄνευ θείας [deest?] καὶ ἐπι-
φροσύνης.

Cat. Lips. ı. col. 820, inscribed ἀδήλου.
Cf. Procopius, p. 289.

§ 18. Cibum et sanitatem subsignat: cibum per *panem et aquam*, sanitatem vere per *aversionem infirmitatum*. Secundo religiosam abstinentiam enunciat perceptione necessariorum ciborum, haec tantum dicens,.......................doctrinam nobis dignissimam rite docet, admonens, quod nec panis nec aqua per se nutriunt, sed aliquando etiam damnum ferunt magis quam utilitatem, nisi divinum verbum istis quoque concedat perutilem virtutem. Quamobrem et dixit: Benedicam pani tuo et aquae tuae: eo quod non sunt sufficientes per se solum nutrire sine divina conciliatione cum anima.

Exod. xxiii. 26.

Exod. xxiii. 26.

Quare dicet "non erit in te semine carens et sterilis"?

§ 19. Ἀγονίαν καὶ στείρωσιν ἐν κατά-
ραις τάττων Μωϋσῆς οὐ φησιν ἔσεσθαι
παρὰ τοῖς τὰ δίκαια καὶ νόμιμα δρῶσιν·
ἆθλον γὰρ τοῖς τὸ ἱερὸν γράμμα τοῦ νόμου
φυλάττουσι παρέχει τὸν ἀρχαιότερον νόμον
τῆς ἀθανάτου φύσεως, ὃς ἐπὶ σπορᾷ καὶ
γενέσει τέκνων ἐτέθη πρὸς τὴν τοῦ γένους
διαμονήν.

Mai, *Script. Vet.* vıı. p. 105, from

§ 19. Infoecunditate ac sterilitate in maledictionis ordine positis non erit, inquit, apud eos, qui iusta legitimaque operantur: quoniam in praemium conservantibus divinam scripturam legis praestat principalem legem immortalis Naturae, quae in semine et generatione filiorum posita fuit ad generis perpetuitatem.

Cod. Vat. 1553, Φίλωνος, ἐκ τοῦ β' τῶν ἐν γενέσει ζητημάτων (cod. reads ἀγωνίαν).

Exod. xxiii. 27.

Καὶ τὸν φόβον ἀποστελῶ ἡγούμενόν σου.

§ 21. Τὸ μὲν ῥητὸν ἐμφανές· εἰς κατάπληξιν ἐχθρῶν ἰσχυρὰ δύναμις ὁ φόβος, ὑφ' οὗ μᾶλλον ἡ τῆς τῶν ἀντιπάλων ἐφόδου ῥώμη ἁλίσκεται. Τὸ δὲ πρὸς διάνοιαν οὕτως· δυοῖν οὐσῶν αἰτιῶν, ὧν ἕνεκα τὸ θεῖον ἄνθρωποι τιμῶσιν, ἀγάπης καὶ φόβου, τὸ μὲν ἀγαπᾶν ἐστιν ὀψίγονον· τὸ δὲ φοβεῖσθαι συνίσταται πρότερον, ὥστε οὐκ ἀπὸ σκοποῦ λέλεχθαι τὸ ἡγεῖσθαι τὸν φόβον, τῆς ἀγάπης ὕστερον καὶ ὀψὲ προσγενομένης.

Pitra, *Anal. Sac.* II. 313, e Cod. Palat. Vat. 203 f. 261, reading ὀψέως. Also Cat. Lips. I. col. 822 and Cat. Burney fol. 139 b.

Exod. xxiii. 27.

Quare dicit: "Timorem mittam, qui te antecedet"?

§ 21. Littera manifesta est, quia horror inimicorum valida est vis ac terror, quo maxime adversariorum vis apprehensa convincitur. Ad mentem vero duae sunt rationes, quibus divinitatem homines honorant: amore et timore. Amare autem est tardius, in senioribus locum habens; timere vero fit prius. Non ergo inaniter dictum est *praecurrere timorem*, quum amor posterior sit et sero acquiratur.

Exod. xxiii. 28.

§ 24. ....
Σύμβολον δὲ ὑποληπτέον εἶναι τοὺς σφῆκας ἀνελπίστου δυνάμεως θείᾳ πομπῇ σταλησομένης, ἥτις, ἀφ' ὑψηλοτέρων κατ' ἄκρον τὸ οὖς ὑποφέρουσα τὰς πληγάς, εὐστοχήσει πᾶσι τοῖς βλήμασι, καὶ διαθεῖσα οὐδὲν ἀντιπείσεται τὸ παράπαν.

Cat. Reg. Inedit. 1825 (Mang. II. 679). Cat. Lips. I. col. 823.
Cat. Burney fol. 139 b, all reading ἀντιπεσεῖται for which Mangey conjectures rightly ἀντιπείσεται.

Exod. xxiii. 28.

§ 24. ....
Et allegorice notum est, quod crabronem oportet indicium existimare inexspectatae subitaneaeque virtutis divinitus missae, quae de excelsis magna vi inducens caedem, furit in percutiendo, atque hoc facto nihil contrarium patiantur ullo modo.

Exod. xxiii. 29.

§ 25. ....
Ἐὰν τοῦ ἄρτι πρῶτον εἰσαγομένου καὶ μανθάνοντος σπουδάσῃς, πᾶσαν τὴν ἁμά-

Exod. xxiii. 29.

§ 25. ....
Si nondum progressum habens in doctrina operam naves, ut cunctis peccatis

θειαν ἐκτεμών, ἀθρόαν ἐπιστήμην εἰσοικίσαι, τοὐναντίον οὗ διανοῇ πράξεις· οὔτε γὰρ
τὴν ἀφαίρεσιν ἑνὶ καιρῷ γινομένην ὑπομενεῖ,
οὔτε τὴν ἄφθονον ῥύμην καὶ φορὰν τῆς
διδασκαλίας χωρήσει, ἀλλὰ καθ' ἑκάτερον
τό τε ἐκτεμνόμενον καὶ προστιθέμενον ὀδυνη-
θεὶς καὶ περιαλγήσας ἀφηνιάσει. Τὸ δὲ
ἡσυχῇ καὶ μετρίως ἀφαιρεῖν μέν τι τῆς
ἀπαιδευσίας, προστιθέναι δὲ τῆς παιδείας τὸ
ἀνάλογον, ὠφελείας γένοιτ' ἂν ὁμολογουμέ-
νης αἴτιον.

The passage thus far is found in John
Monachus (Mangey II. 663) = Cod. Rup.
f. 137, reading σαυτοῦ for ἐὰν τοῦ, σπου-
δάσεις, ἀμαθείαν, ἀφαίρησιν, ὑπομεῖναι, χω-
ρῆσαι and omitting τι before ἀπαιδευσίας, etc. Also in Pitra *Anal. Sac.* II.
312 from Cod. Palat. 203 f. 261 and
Cod. Vat. 1553 f. 129. The latter MS.
seems to be the one used by Mai *Script.
Vet.* VII. 100, but it should be observed
that Mai, as well as Cod. Rup., adds a
passage (given below) which Pitra omits,
and which certainly corresponds to the
Latin, while Pitra adds a long extract
which seems to be Philo but remains for
the present unidentified. Observe that
Mai reads τοῦ ἄρτι, σπουδάσῃ, ἢ διανοῇς,
νέαν for ἐνί, γενομένην, omits ὑπομενεῖ,
χωρήσει, reads τότε for τό τε, ἀπεράσει
for ἀφηνιάσει, ἡσυχῶς for ἡσυχῇ, after
ἀφαιρεῖν μὲν adds κατ' ὀλίγον and omits
τι (correctly ?), reads προστιθήναι and
ὡμολογουμένης. The passage as far as
διδασκαλίας is also found in Cat. Lips. I.
col. 823 and Cat. Burney fol. 140 with
some variations.

Ὁ δὲ ἀγαθὸς ἰατρὸς οὐ μιᾷ ἡμέρᾳ τῷ νοσ-
οῦντι πάντα ἀθρόα τὰ ὑγιεινὰ προσφέρειν ἂν
ἐθελήσειεν, εἰδὼς βλάβην ἐργαζόμενος μᾶλ-

abscissis simul in anima intellectionem
disciplinae ex adverso habitare facias,
haud prudenter egeris; non enim susti-
nebit ablationem uno momento factam,
neque immensam influxionem doctrinae
portabit, sed secundum utramque, tum
abscissionem, tum additionem, afflic-
tus doloreque affectus animus resiliet.
Qui vero tranquille ac moderate eiicit
paulatim ineruditionem, addita disci-
plina honestae utilitatis ex confesso
causa exsistet.

Procopius (ed. Gesner, p. 290) has
abbreviated the above into the sentence
"nec tolerare possunt doctrinam nimiam."
That he is working upon this passage of
Philo will be evident on comparing the
opening sentences of the section, e.g.,
Philo…"quandoquidem fugiunt bestiae
tanquam proprium dominum hominem:
quare quum populo repletae sint civitates,
minime adveniunt, &c."

Procopius, "nam ferae fugitant domi-
cilia multorum hominum ut qui natura
illis imperitent. Caeterum solitudines et
solitaria loca frequentare consueverunt."

Quoniam nec medicus peritissimus
aegroto una die omnem simul sanitatem
tribuere studet, satis conscius, quod

H.

8

λον ἥπερ ὠφέλειαν, ἀλλὰ διαμετρησάμενος τοὺς καιροὺς ἐπιδιανέμει τὰ σωτήρια καὶ ἄλλοτε ἄλλα προστιθεὶς πράως ὑγιείαν ἐμποιεῖ.

From Mai and Cod. Rup., ut supra: also Dam. Par. 567 and Cod. Reg. f. 210 b. Mai omits ἀθρόα, and reads ὑγίειαν for ὠφέλειαν. The rest give ἐπιφέρειν for προσφέρειν and some minor changes.

detrimentum potius facit quam utilitatem; sed mensuratis temporibus distribuit salutem, atque alia in hora aliam inferens medicinam mite sanitatem operatur.

Exod. xxiii. 33.

§ 26. Ὥσπερ οἱ προσπταίσαντες, ἀρτίοις βαίνειν ποσὶν ἀδυνατοῦντες, μακρὰν τοῦ κατὰ τὴν ὁδὸν τέλους ὑστερίζουσι προσκάμνοντες· οὕτω καὶ ἡ ψυχὴ τὴν πρὸς εὐσέβειαν ἄγουσαν ὁδὸν ἀνύειν κωλύεται, προεντυγχάνουσα ταῖς ἀσεβέσιν ἀνοδίαις. Αὗται γάρ εἰσιν ἐμπόδιοι καὶ προσπταισμάτων αἰτίαι, δι᾽ ὧν κυλλαίνων ὁ νοῦς ὑστερίζει τῆς κατὰ φύσιν ὁδοῦ. Ἡ δὲ ὁδός ἐστιν ἡ ἐπὶ τὸν πατέρα τῶν ὅλων τελευτῶσα.

Dam. Par. 774 (Cod. Rupef.) ἐκ τοῦ α΄ τῶν ἐν ἐξόδῳ ζητημάτων.

Exod. xxiii. 33.

Cur offendiculum appellat alienorum deorum servitutem?

§ 26. Sicut qui scandalizantur sanis pedibus, eo ipso quod non possunt longius procedere, fine itineris destituuntur, iam prius desistentes: sic et animus ad pietatem conductus facere eam viam impedietur, prius impingens invia impietatis, quoniam haec sunt obstacula et scandali causae. Quare claudicans mens desistit ex naturae via. Via autem illa est, quae ad patrem fertur sicut ad finem.

Exod. xxiv. 1.

§ 28. Οὐχ ὁρᾷς, ὅτι τοῦ πυρὸς ἡ δύναμις τοῖς μὲν ἀφεστηκόσι μεμετρημένον διάστημα παρέχει φῶς, κατακαίει δὲ τοὺς ἐγγίζοντας; Ὅρα, μὴ τοιοῦτόν τι πάθῃς τῇ διανοίᾳ, μή σε ὁ πολὺς πόθος ἀδυνάτου πράγματος ἀναλώσῃ.

From Dam. Par. 748 (Cod. Rup. f. 22 b).

Exod. xxiv. 1.

Quare dicit "adorabunt a longe dominum"?

§ 28. Quemadmodum qui prope ignem sunt, comburuntur, qui vero procul stant a longe mensurato intervallo, securitatem habent; *sic res habetur in animis.*

Exod. xxiv. 10.

§ 37. ....

Οὐδεὶς αὐχήσει τὸν ἀόρατον θεὸν ἰδεῖν, εἴξας ἀλαζονείᾳ.

From John Monachus (Mang. ii. 662) = Cod. Rup. f. 55. Mangey reads ἀλογιστίᾳ but the MS. has ἀλαζονείᾳ.

Exod. xxiv. 11.

§ 38. Τὸ μὲν ῥητὸν διήγημα φανερὰν ἔχει τὴν ἀπόδοσιν ὡς ἁπάντων σώων διατηρηθέντων, τὸ δὲ πρὸς διάνοιαν τὸ πάντας περὶ τὴν εὐσέβειαν συμφώνους εἶναι καὶ ἐν μηδενὶ τῶν ἀγαθῶν διαφωνεῖν.

Cat. Reg. Inedit. 1825 (Mang. ii. 679), reading σύμφρονας, Cat. Lips. i. col. 829, Cat. Burney fol. 141.

All the Catenae add somewhat to the above.

Exod. xxiv. 12.

§ 40. ....

Ἐνίοις ἀψίκορος ἐγγίνεται λογισμός, οἳ πρὸς ὀλίγον ἀναπτεροφορηθέντες αὐτίκα ὑπενόστησαν, οὐκ ἀναπτάντες μᾶλλον ἢ ὑποσυρέντες εἰς ταρτάρου, φησίν, ἐσχατιάς. Εὐδαίμονες δὲ οἱ μὴ παλινδρομοῦντες.

Dam. Par. 784 (= Rup.) Φίλωνος· ἐκ τῶν ἐν ἐξόδῳ ζητημάτων.

Exod. xxiv. 10.

Quid est "Viderunt locum, ubi stabat deus Israel, et sub pedibus eius sicut opus lateris sapphiri et sicut visio firmamenti caeli puritate"?

§ 37. Haec omnia Theologo decentia ac condigna (sunt) in primis; quia nemo glorietur invisibilem videre deum, indulgens superbiae.

Exod. xxiv. 11.

Quare dicit "De electis videntibus nemo recessit (s. discrepavit)"?

§ 38. Littera expositionem habet manifestam quod omnes integri servati fuerint. Ad mentem autem [electa gens secundum animam immortalis est, quo (in quam) pervenit sapientia et omnis virtus, et prae omnibus regina virtutum, pietas. Mors vero animae est dissonantia ad probitatem et defectus harmoniae].

Cf. Procopius (ed. Gesner, p. 291). Omnes incolumes conservati sunt: si vero spiritualem sensum huic elicere voles, indicat omnes in religionis negotio consensisse uno animo.

Exod. xxiv. 12.

§ 40. ....

Quoniam in quibus fuit vitium cito sese satiandi contemplatione, modicum sursum volantes dei initiatione, statim retrocesserunt, non tantum volantes, quantum deorsum tracti, nempe in Tartari profunditatem. [Qui vero non redeunt a sancta divinaque civitate, in quam transmigrarunt, principali duce usi sunt deo in habitationem constantem.]

8—2

Exod. xxiv. 16.

§ 45. Ἐναργέστατα δυσωπεῖ τοὺς ἐγγὺς ὑπὸ ἀσεβείας εἴτε ἠλιθιότητος οἰομένους τοπικὰς καὶ μεταβατικὰς κινήσεις εἶναι περὶ τὸ θεῖον. Ἰδοὺ γὰρ ἐμφανῶς οὐ τὸν οὐσιώδη θεόν, τὸν κατὰ τὸ εἶναι μόνον ἐπινοούμενον, κατεληλυθέναι φησίν, ἀλλὰ τὴν δόξαν αὐτοῦ. Διττὴ δὲ ἡ περὶ τὴν δόξαν ἐκδοχή· ἡ μὲν παρουσίαν ἐμφαίνουσα τῶν δυνάμεων, ἐπεὶ καὶ βασιλέως λέγεται δόξα ἡ στρατιωτικὴ δύναμις· ἡ δὲ τῇ δοκήσει αὐτοῦ μόνον καὶ ὑπολήψει δόξης θείας, ὡς ἐνειργάσθαι ταῖς τῶν παρόντων διανοίαις φαντασίαν ἀφίξεως θεοῦ, ὡς ἥκοντος εἰς βεβαιοτάτην πίστιν τῶν μελλόντων νομοθετεῖσθαι.

From Cat. Reg. Inedit. 1825 (Mang. II. 679), Cat. Lips. I. col. 832.

. . . .

Ἄβατος καὶ ἀπροσπέλαστος ὄντως ἐστὶν ὁ θεῖος χῶρος, οὐδὲ τῆς καθαρωτάτης διανοίας τοσοῦτον ὕψος προσαναβῆναι δυναμένης ὡς θίξει μόνον ἐπιψαῦσαι.

From Dam. Par. 748 = Cod. Rup. 22 b ἐκ τοῦ αὐτοῦ, ἤτοι τοῦ τελευταίου τῶν ἐν ἐξόδῳ ζητουμένων.

Exod. xxiv. 16.

§ 46. Τὸν ἴσον ἀριθμὸν ἀπένειμε καὶ τῇ τοῦ κόσμου γενέσει καὶ τῇ τοῦ ὁρατικοῦ[1] γένους ἐκλογῇ, τὴν ἑξάδα· βουλόμενος ἐπιδεῖξαι, ὅτι αὐτὸς καὶ τὸν κόσμον ἐδημιούργησε καὶ τὸ γένος εἵλετο.

. . . .

[1] This interpretation is found in Philo, *passim*: viz. Israel=homo videns Deum= (איש ראה אל).

Exod. xxiv. 16.

Quid est "Et descendit gloria dei super montem Sina"?

§ 45. Evidenter pudore afficit eos, qui sive impie sive stulte existimant localem ac mutabilem motum inesse divinitati. Ecce enim manifeste non substantiam dei, quae secundum essentiam solam intelligitur, descendentem ait, sed gloriam suam. Duplex autem est gloriae notitia: una, quatenus essentiam ostendit virtutum, nam et regis dicitur gloria virtus exercitus; altera, quatenus opinionem causat solam putandi videre gloriam divinam, faciens in occurrentium mente apparitionem adventus dei, quasi vero, qui non ibi fuerit, ecce iam venerit ad firmam fidem legis tradendae.

. . . .

Itaque inascensibilis atque inaccessibilis utique est divinus locus, ita ut neque purissimi intellectus tanta celsitudo ad eum ascendere queat, sed solummodo appropinquare satagere.

Exod. xxiv. 16.

Cur operitur mons nube sex dies, septimo autem Moses sursum vocatur?

§ 46. Parem numerum, sex videlicet, impertiit tam mundi creationi, quam theoricae gentis electioni, volens ostendere imprimis, quod ipse et mundum fecit et gentem virtute electam.

. . . .

Ἡ δὲ ἀνάκλησις τοῦ προφήτου δεύτερα γένεσίς ἐστι τῆς προτέρας ἀμείνων.

....

Ἑβδόμῃ δὲ ἀνακαλεῖται ἡμέρᾳ, ταύτῃ διαφέρων τοῦ πρωτοπλάστου· ὅτι ἐκεῖνος μέν, ἐκ γῆς καὶ μετὰ σώματος συνίστατο· οὗτος δέ, ἄνευ σώματος· διὸ τῷ μὲν γηγενεῖ, ἀριθμὸς οἰκεῖος ἀπενεμήθη ἑξάς· τούτῳ δέ, ἡ ἱερωτάτη φύσις τῆς ἑβδομάδος.

From Cat. Lips. I. col. 832 (Προκοπίου). Again a passage of Philo transferred by Procopius to his Commentary. Cf. Procop. (ed. Gesn. p. 292).

Exod. xxiv. 17.

§ 47. ....

Τὸ δὲ εἶδος τῆς δόξης Κυρίου φησὶν ἐμφερέστατον εἶναι φλογί, μᾶλλον δὲ οὐκ εἶναι, ἀλλὰ φαίνεσθαι τοῖς ὁρῶσι· τοῦ θεοῦ δεικνύντος ὅπερ ἐβούλετο δοκεῖν εἶναι πρὸς τὴν τῶν θεωμένων κατάπληξιν, μὴ ὢν τοῦτο ὅπερ ἐφαίνετο. Ἐπιφέρει γοῦν "τὸ ἐνώπιον τῶν υἱῶν Ἰσραήλ," ἐναργέστατα μηνύων, ὅτι φαντασία φλογὸς ἦν, ἀλλ᾽ οὐ φλὸξ ἀληθής. Ὥσπερ δὲ ἡ φλὸξ πᾶσαν τὴν παραβληθεῖσαν ὕλην ἀναλίσκει, οὕτως, ὅταν ἐπιφοιτήσῃ εἰλικρινὴς τοῦ θεοῦ ἔννοια τῇ ψυχῇ, πάντας τοὺς ἑτεροδόξους ἀσεβείας λογισμοὺς διαφθείρει, καθοσιοῦσα τὴν ὅλην διάνοιαν.

Catena Inedita Reg. 1825 ; and Cat. Lips. I. col. 832 (Mang. II. 679).

Exod. xxiv. 18.

§ 49. ....

Ὅτι ἔμελλε κατάκριτος ἔσεσθαι ἡ ἀποικισθεῖσα γενεά, καὶ ἐπὶ τεσσαράκοντα ἔτεα φθείρεσθαι· μυρία μὲν εὐεργετηθεῖσα, διὰ μυρίων δὲ ἐπιδειξαμένη τὸ ἀχάριστον.

Catena Inedita Reg. 1825 (Mang. II.

Sursum autem vocatio prophetae secunda est nativitas (sive regeneratio) priore melior.

....

Septimus enim vocatur dies, hoc differens a protoplasta terrigena, quia ille de terra, et una cum corpore in existentiam veniebat, is autem ex aethere et sine corpore. Quare terrigenae numerus familiaris distributus fiat sexenarius, heterogenae vero superior natura septenarii.

Exod. xxiv. 17.

§ 47. ....

Huius virtutis species similis est flammae : imo non est, sed apparet videntibus, monstrante deo, non quod est secundum essentiam, sed sicut volebat putari esse ad videntium stuporem. Adiicit ergo illud *in conspectu filiorum Videntis*[1], manifestius declarans, quod apparentia flammae erat, non flamma vera......ad mentem vero, sicut flamma omnem materiam immissam consumit, sic quando manifeste adveniat dei meditatio in animas, omnem cogitationem a pietate alienam devastat, in decentiam reducens totam mentem.

[1] Here the Armenian text must be the right one : cf. previous note.

Exod. xxiv. 18.

§ 49. ....

Damnanda erat gens transmigrans et per annos quadraginta corruptionem subitura, multiplici invento beneficio et multipliciter ingratitudine demonstrata.

680), and Cat. Lips. I. col. 833, reading
τεσσαρακονταετίαν.

Cf. Procopius *in loc.*

Exod. xxiv. 18.

§ 49. ....
Ὑπὲρ ὧν ἐν ἰσαρίθμοις ἡμέραις ἱκέτευε τὸν
πατέρα, καὶ μάλιστα παρὰ τοιοῦτον καιρόν,
ἐν ᾧ δίδονται νόμοι, καὶ φορητὸν ἱερόν, ἡ
σκηνή. Τίσι γὰρ οἱ νόμοι; ἆρά γε τοῖς
ἀπολλυμένοις; Ὑπὲρ τίνων δὲ αἱ θυσίαι;
[ἆρα] τῶν μικρὸν ὕστερον φθαρησομένων;
προῄδει γὰρ ὡς προφήτης τὰ ἐσόμενα.

From Cat. Lips. I. col. 834 (Προκοπίου).

Cf. Procopius (ed. Gesner, p. 292).

Exod. xxiv. 18.

§ 49. ....
Aequali itaque tempore dierum pro annis
sursum perstat, precibus ac intercessione
reconcilians patrem: maxime in tali
tempore, in quo et lex divina datur et
portatile templum verbis erigitur, Testi-
monii Tabernaculum dictum. Cui enim
erat lex? num eis, qui perituri erant?
Aut cuius gratia erant oracula? an
eorum, qui paulo post deperdendi erant?
Caeterum mihi videtur, quod dicat ali-
quis: Praesciebatne illud quod futurum
postmodum erat ei iudicium?

Exod. xxv. 2.

§ 50. Τὴν καρδίαν ἀντὶ τοῦ ἡγεμονικοῦ
παρείληφεν ἡ γραφή. ....
Mai, *Script. Vet.* VII. 103, from Cod.
Vat. 1553 as Φίλωνος. ἐκ τοῦ τελευταίου
τῶν ἐν ἐξόδῳ ζητημάτων.

....
Ὁ μὴ ἐκ προαιρέσεως ἀπάρχων θεῷ, καὶ ἂν
τὰ μεγάλα πάντα κομίζῃ μετὰ τῶν βασιλι-
κῶν θησαυρῶν, ἀπαρχὰς οὐ φέρει. Οὐ γὰρ
ἐν ὕλαις, ἀλλ' ἐν εὐσεβεῖ διαθέσει τοῦ κομί-
ζοντος ἡ ἀληθὴς ἀπαρχή.

John Monachus (Mangey II. 670) ἐκ
τοῦ τελευταίου τῶν ἐν ἐξόδῳ ζητημάτων.

εὐσεβεῖ is an emendation of Mangey
for εὐσεβείᾳ. Should we not also read
μέταλλα for μεγάλα?

Exod. xxv. 2.

§ 50. *Cor* nunc pro principali (in homine) in medium sumit.

....
Qui vero invitus obtulerit, [oblivioni tra-
ditur, se ipsum fallens]: quum argentum
quidem aut aliud quicquam introduxerit,
primitias tamen minime adduxerit.

From the Latin there is some ground
for supposing the last sentence in the
Greek to be a gloss.

Exod. xxv. 11.

§ 55. ....

Οἱ ἀστέρες στρέφονται καὶ εἱλοῦνται κύκλον· οἱ μὲν κατὰ τὰ αὐτὰ τῷ σύμπαντι οὐρανῷ, οἱ δὲ καὶ κινήσεσιν ἰδίαις (add ἃς) ἔλαχον ἐξαιρέτοις.

John Monachus (Mang. II. 670) ἐκ τοῦ β′ τῶν ἐν ἐξόδῳ ζητημάτων.

Exod. xxv. 11.
§ 55. ....

Ὁ τῶν ἀνθρώπων βίος, ὁμοιούμενος πελάγει, κυματώσεις καὶ στροφὰς παντοίας προσεπιδέχεται, κατά τε εὐπραγίας, καὶ κακοπραγίας. Ἵδρυται γὰρ οὐδὲν τῶν γηγενῶν, ἀλλ' ὧδε καὶ ἐκεῖσε διαφέρεται, οἷα σκάφος θαλαττεῦον ὑπ' ἐναντίων πνευμάτων.

Ex Anonymi Collectione Florilega MS. Barocc. 143 (Mang. II. 674), (om. καὶ κακ.). Ascribed to Nilus in Dam. Par. 506 but in Reg. 923 f. 156 b. to the ii. Quaest. in *Genesim.* Dam. Par. reads προσδέχεται, Cod. Reg. προσενδέχεται: and Dam. Par. reads πραγμάτων for πνευμάτων. The last is probably a mistake of Lequien, as the Latin gives *ventis.*

Exod. xxv. 18.

Τίνα τὰ χερουβίμ;

§ 62. Τὰ χερουβὶμ ἑρμηνεύεται μὲν ἐπί-
cod. om. ῇ γνῶσις πολλή, ῇ ἐν ἑτέροις ὄνομα ἐπιστήμη πλουσία καὶ κεχυμένη. Σύμβολα δέ ἐστι δυεῖν τοῦ ὄντος δυνάμεων ποιητικῆς τε καὶ βασιλικῆς. Πρεσβυτέρα δὲ ἡ ποιητικὴ τῆς
cod. αἴτε βασιλικῆς κατ' ἐπίνοιαν. Ἰσήλικες γὰρ αἴγε περὶ τὸν θεὸν ἅπασαι δυνάμεις, ἀλλὰ προεπινοεῖται πῶς ἡ ποιητικὴ τῆς βασιλικῆς· βασιλεὺς γάρ τις οὐχὶ τοῦ μὴ ὄντος, ἀλλὰ τοῦ γεγονότος· ὄνομα δὲ ἔλαχεν ἐν τοῖς

Exod. xxv. 11.
Quid est "cymacia tortilia" quae iubet circa arcam construere?

§ 55. Obumbrat per illius modi coronam stellas, quippe quae circumferuntur, quaedam per se una cum caelo universo, quaedam vero peculiari etiam motu, quem sortitae sunt seorsum.

Exod. xxv. 11.
§ 55. ....

Tertio humana vita, similis reperta vastissimo mari, fluctuationes aestusque circulorum omnigenos suscipit secundum fortunas. Siquidem nihil terrenum constans est, sed huc et illuc vacillans titubat ad modum navis mare lustrantis contra ventos contrarios.

Exod. xxv. 18.
Quid sit "Cherubim"?

§ 62. Interpretatur *scientia multa,* in caetera nomina intelligentiam ac copiam suam refundens. Symbolum autem est duplicis virtutis, creativae et regiae; maior tamen est creativa secundum cogitationem. Quamvis enim coaetaneae sint quae circa deum sunt virtutes, verum prius intelligitur creativa quam regia. Rex enim est quisquam non eius, qui non est, sed eius, qui factus est. Titu-

ἱεροῖς γράμμασιν ἡ μὲν ποιητικὴ θεός, τὸ γὰρ ποιῆσαι θεῖναι ἔλεγον οἱ παλαιοί· ἡ δὲ βασιλικὴ κύριος, ἐπειδὴ τὸ κῦρος ἁπάντων ἀνακεῖται τῷ βασιλεῖ.

Tischendorf, *Philonea*, 144: from Cod. Vat. 379, f. 385. This and the following passages were first edited by Grossmann in an inaugural dissertation (Leipsic 1856).

lum autem sortita est in sacris scripturis creativa (virtus), ut *deus* appellaretur; quoniam apud maiores (Graecorum) loco verbi *facere* (ut creare) dicebatur *ponere* (Graece *thyne*, Arm. *tnel:* hinc *theos, deus*). Regia vero (virtus) *dominus* vocatur, quoniam titulus domini ab omnibus consecratum est regi.

Exod. xxv. 18.

Διατί χρυσοῦ τορευτά;

§ 63. Ὁ μὲν χρυσὸς σύμβολον τῆς τιμιωτάτης οὐσίας, ἡ δὲ τορεία τῆς ἐντέχνου καὶ ἐπιστημονικῆς φύσεως· ἔδει γὰρ τὰς πρώτας τοῦ ὄντος δυνάμεις ἰδέας ἰδεῶν ὑπαρχούσας καὶ τῆς καθαρωτάτης καὶ ἀμιγοῦς καὶ τιμαλφεστάτης καὶ προσέτι τῆς ἐπιστημονικωτάτης φύσεως μεταλαχεῖν.

Tischendorf, *ut supra*.

Exod. xxv. 18.

Quare "aurei tornatiles"?

§ 63. *Aurum* symbolum est pretiosae substantiae, *tornatile* vero artificiosae ac intelligentia praeditae naturae. Oportet enim primas entis virtutes, species specierum[1] esse, et puriores, simplices ac pretiosissimas, insuper etiam intelligentiorem essentiam sortiri.

[1] S. ideas idearum. Aucher.

Exod. xxv. 18.

Διατί ἐπ' ἀμφοτέρων τῶν κλιτῶν τοῦ ἱλαστηρίου τὰ χερουβὶμ ἥρμοττε;

§ 64. Τοὺς ὅρους τοῦ παντὸς οὐρανοῦ καὶ κόσμου δυσὶ ταῖς ἀνωτάτω φρουραῖς ὠχυρῶσθαι, τῇ τε καθ' ἣν ἐποίει τὰ ὅλα θεός, καὶ τῇ καθ' ἣν ἄρχει τῶν γεγονότων. Ἔμελλε γὰρ ὡς οἰκειοτάτου καὶ συγγενεστάτου κτήματος προκήδεσθαι ἡ μὲν ποιητική, ἵνα μὴ λυθείη τὰ πρὸς αὐτῆς γενόμενα, ἡ δὲ βασιλική, ὅπως μηδὲν μήτε πλεονεκτῇ μήτε πλεονεκτῆται, νόμῳ βραβευόμενα τῷ τῆς ἰσότητος, ὑφ' ἧς τὰ πράγματα διαιωνίζεται· πλεονεξία μὲν γὰρ καὶ ἀνισότης ὁρμητήρια πολέμου, λυτικὰ τῶν ὄντων· τὸ δὲ εὔνομον καὶ τὸ ἴσον εἰρήνης σπέρματα, σωτηρίας αἴτια καὶ τῆς εἰσάπαν διαμονῆς.

Tischendorf, *ut supra*.

Grossmann gives διαμονίζεται, τέρματα.

Exod. xxv. 18.

Cur in ambobus lateribus altaris Cherubim collocabat?

§ 64. Terminos totius caeli mundique duabus ac superioribus custodiis muniri (designat): una secundum illud, quo omnia faciebat deus; et altera, secundum quod princeps est creaturarum. Quoniam velut familiari ac cognatae possessioni prius curam habitura erat creativa (virtus), ne dissolverentur per eam creata; regia vero ne quidpiam redundasset, symbolice concilians victoriam indicio paritatis, qua res perseverant. Siquidem excessu imparitateque incursiones bellorum dissolutiones sunt entium, bene vero ordinatae atque aequae, pacis semina, salutis causae atque perpetuo perseverandi.

Exod. xxv. 20.

Διατί φησιν· ἐκτείνει τὰς πτέρυγας τὰ
χερουβὶμ ἵνα συσκιάζῃ;

§ 65. Αἱ μὲν τοῦ θεοῦ πᾶσαι δυνάμεις
πτεροφυοῦσι, τῆς ἄνω πρὸς τὸν πατέρα ὁδοῦ
γλιχόμεναί τε καὶ ἐφιέμεναι· συσκιάζουσι
δὲ οἷα πτέρυξι τὰ τοῦ παντὸς μέρη· αἰνίττεται δὲ ὡς ὁ κόσμος σκέπαις καὶ φυλακτη-
ρίοις φρουρεῖται, δυσὶ ταῖς εἰρημέναις δυνά-
μεσι τῇ τε ποιητικῇ καὶ βασιλικῇ.

Tischendorf, *ut supra,* p. 146.

John Monach. (Mang. ii. 656) referring to ii. Quaest. in *Gen.* gives the first
sentence as also Pitra, *Anal. Sac.* ii.
p. xxiii. e Cod. Coislin. (?) f. 60, with
the same reference.

Exod. xxv. 20.

Διατί τὰ πρόσωπα τῶν χερουβὶμ εἰς ἄλ-
ληλα ἐκνεύει καὶ ἄμφω πρὸς τὸ ἱλαστήριον;

§ 66. Παγκάλη τίς ἐστι καὶ θεοπρεπὴς
ἡ τῶν λεχθέντων εἰκών· ἔδει γὰρ τὰς δυνάμεις τήν τε ποιητικὴν καὶ βασιλικὴν εἰς
ἀλλήλας ἀφορᾶν, τὰ σφῶν κάλλη κατανο-
ούσας καὶ ἅμα πρὸς τὴν ὠφελείαν τῶν γεγονότων συμπνεούσας· δεύτερον ἐπειδὴ ὁ θεὸς
εἷς ὢν καὶ ποιητής ἐστι καὶ βασιλεύς, εἰκότως αἱ διαστᾶσαι δυνάμεις πάλιν ἕνωσιν
ἔλαβον· καὶ γὰρ διέστησαν ὠφελίμως, ἵνα
ἡ μὲν ποιῇ, ἡ δὲ ἄρχῃ· διαφέρει γὰρ ἑκάτε-
ρον· καὶ ἡρμόσθησαν ἑτέρῳ τρόπῳ κατὰ
τὴν τῶν ὀνομάτων ἀΐδιον προσβολὴν ὅπως
καὶ ἡ ποιητικὴ τῆς βασιλικῆς καὶ ἡ βασιλικὴ τῆς ποιητικῆς ἔχηται· ἀμφότεραι γὰρ
συννεύουσιν εἰς τὸ ἱλαστήριον εἰκότως· εἰ
μὴ γὰρ ἦν τοῖς νῦν οὖσιν ἵλεως ὁ θεός, οὔτ'
ἂν εἰργάσθη τι διὰ τῆς ποιητικῆς οὔτ' ἂν
εὐνομήθη διὰ τῆς βασιλικῆς.

Tischendorf, *ut supra,* p. 147.

For εἰς ἀλλήλας the MS. has εἰς ἀλλη-
γορίαν.

H.

Exod. xxv. 20.

Quare dicit, "Extendat alas Cherubim
ut obumbret"?

§ 65. Dei virtutes omnes alatae com-
periuntur, supernam ad patrem viam
desiderantes. Obumbrare vero alarum
instar universi partes subsignat, quippe
quod mundus tegatur per custodiam
ambarum virtutum quae sunt, ut dictum
est, creativa et regia.

Exod. xxv. 20.

Cur facies Cherubim ad se invicem
respiciunt, et ambo (vultus) in propitiatorium?

§ 66. Optime atque decentissima est
dictorum forma: nam conveniens fuit,
ut virtutes creativa et regia se mutuo
respicerent, propriam pulchritudinem cer-
nentes, et simul in utilitatem factorum
ambo conspirarent. Secundo quia deus
unus est tum creator tum rex, iure
distinctam virtutem sumpsere; dis-
tinctae autem fuere utiliter ut una
faceret altera imperaret. Quia vero
separatae sunt, concinnatae quoque fue-
runt alio modo cum nominibus, perpe-
tuam inter se habentes connexionem, ita
ut tam creativa spectatrix sit principa-
tivae, tam creativae regia. Sicut autem
se mutuo respiciunt, ita etiam iure propitiatorium; quoniam si non erat simul
convenientium propitius deus, nec fecisset
quicquam per creativam neque disposuis-
set per regiam.

9

Exod. xxv. 22.

Τί ἐστι· γνωσθήσομαί σοι ἐκεῖθεν ;

§ 67. Γνῶσιν καὶ ἐπιστήμην ὁ εἰλικρι-
νέστατος καὶ προφητικώτατος νοῦς λαμβάνει
τοῦ ὄντος οὐκ ἀπ' αὐτοῦ τοῦ ὄντος, οὐ γὰρ
χωρήσει τὸ μέγεθος, ἀλλ' ἀπὸ τῶν πρώτων
αὐτοῦ καὶ δορυφόρων δυνάμεων· καὶ ἀγα-
πητὸν ἐκεῖθεν εἰς τὴν ψυχὴν φέρεσθαι τὰς αὐ-
γάς, ἵνα δύνηται διὰ τοῦ δευτέρου φέγγους τὸ
πρεσβύτερον καὶ αὐγοειδέστερον θεάσασθαι.
Tischendorf, *ut supra*, p. 148.

Exod. xxv. 22.

Τί ἐστι· λαλήσω ἄνωθεν τοῦ ἱλαστηρίου
ἀνὰ μέσον τῶν Χερουβίμ;

§ 68. Ἐμφαίνει διὰ τοῦτο πρῶτον μὲν
ὅτι καὶ τῆς ἵλεω καὶ τῆς ποιητικῆς καὶ
πάσης δυνάμεως ὑπεράνω τὸ θεῖόν ἐστιν·
ἔπειτα δὲ ὅτι λαλεῖ κατὰ τὸ μεσαίτατον τῆς
τε ποιητικῆς καὶ βασιλικῆς· τοῦτο δὲ
τοιοῦτον ὑπολαμβάνει νοῦς[1]· ὁ τοῦ θεοῦ
λόγος μέσος ὢν οὐδὲν ἐν τῇ φύσει καταλεί-
πει κενόν, τὰ ὅλα πληρῶν καὶ μεσιτεύει καὶ
διαιτᾷ τοῖς παρ' ἑκατέρα διεστάναι δοκοῦσι,
φιλίαν καὶ ὁμόνοιαν ἐργαζόμενος· ἀεὶ γὰρ
κοινωνίας αἴτιος καὶ δημιουργός[2]. Τὰ μὲν
Cf. Heb. οὖν περὶ τὴν κιβωτὸν κατὰ μέρος εἴρηται·
ix. 5 δεῖ δὲ συλλήβδην ἄνωθεν ἀναλαβόντα τοῦ
γνωρίσαι χάριν τίνων ταῦτά ἐστι σύμβολα
διεξελθεῖν· ἦν δὲ ταῦτα συμβολικά. Κιβωτὸς καὶ τὰ ἐν αὐτῇ θησαυριζόμενα νόμιμα
καὶ ἐπὶ ταύτης τὸ ἱλαστήριον καὶ τὰ ἐπὶ
τοῦ ἱλαστηρίου Χαλδαίων γλώττῃ λεγόμενα
Χερουβίμ, ὑπὲρ δὲ τούτων κατὰ τὸ μέσον
φωνὴ καὶ λόγος καὶ ὑπεράνω ὁ λέγων. Εἰ
δέ τις ἀκριβῶς δυνηθείη κατανοῆσαι τὰς

Exod. xxv. 22.

Quid est, "Innotescam vobis inde"?

§ 67. Scientiam et intelligentiam
magis lucida ac prophetica mens recipit
entis, non ab ipso (immediate) ente,—
vix enim portabit maiestatem—sed ex
primis eius ministralibus virtutibus.
Placet autem inde ad animas pervenire
splendores, ut possit per secundos splendores maiorem atque splendidissimum
cernere.

Exod. xxv. 22.

Quid est "Loquar tibi desursum ex
propitiatorio, e medio duorum Cherubim"?

§ 68. Ostendit hoc imprimis, quod
propitiam, creativam omnemque virtutem superat divinitas; deinde vero, quod
loquitur quasi de medio creativae (*add* et
regiae). Hoc autem huiusmodi quidpiam
arbitratur mens. Dei verbum, eo quod
in medio est conveniente, nihil omnino in
natura relinquit vacuum, omnia implens,
atque fit mediator arbiterque utriusque
partis a se invicem, ut putatur, disiunc-
tae, amore et concordia facta; semper
enim communionis est causa et pacificum.
Porro de arca secundum partes eius dis-
seruimus; oportet tamen cuncta simul
resumere propter notificationem, quorum
haec symbola fuerint, obiter significando.
Symbolica namque haec erant: arca et
lex in ea recondita, supraque istam propitiatorium; deinde super propitiatorium
Cherubim Chaldaica lingua dicti; superius autem e regione medii Vox et
Verbum, et supra illud Dicens. Quod
si itaque accurate haec perspicere atque

---

[1] Grossmann νοῦν.

[2] Gr. add εἰρήνης (rightly).

τούτων φύσεις, δοκεῖ μοι πᾶσι τοῖς ἄλλοις
ἀποτάξασθαι ὅσα ζηλωτά, κάλλεσι θεοειδεσ-
τάτοις περιληφθείς. Σκοπῶμεν δὲ ἕκαστον
οἷόν ἐστι. Τὸ πρῶτον ὁ καὶ ἑνὸς καὶ μονά-
δος καὶ ἀρχῆς πρεσβύτερος. Ἔπειτα ὁ τοῦ
ὄντος λόγος[1], ἡ σπερματικὴ τῶν ὄντων οὐσία·
ἀπὸ δὲ τοῦ θείου λόγου, καθάπερ ἀπὸ
πηγῆς, σχίζονται αἱ[2] δύο δυνάμεις. Ἡ
μὲν ποιητική, καθ᾽ ἣν ἔθηκε τὰ πάντα καὶ
διεκόσμησεν ὁ τεχνίτης, αὕτη θεὸς ὀνομάζε-
ται· ἡ δὲ βασιλική, καθ᾽ ἣν ἄρχει[3] τῶν
γεγονότων ὁ δημιουργός, αὕτη καλεῖται
κύριος· ἀπὸ δὲ τούτων τῶν δυεῖν δυνάμεων
ἐκπεφύκασιν ἕτεραι· παραβλαστάνει γὰρ
τῇ μὲν ποιητικῇ ἡ ἵλεως, ἧς ὄνομα εὐεργέτις, τῇ δὲ βασιλικῇ ἡ νομοθετική, ὄνομα δὲ
εὐθυβόλον ἡ κολαστήριος· ὑπὸ δὲ ταύτας
καὶ περὶ ταύτας ἡ κιβωτός· ἔστι δὲ κιβωτὸς
κόσμου νοητοῦ σύμβολον. Ἔχει δὲ τὰ
πάντα ἰδρυμένα ἐν τοῖς ἐσωτάτοις ἁγίοις
συμβολικῶς ἡ κιβωτός, τὸν ἀσώματον κόσμον, τὰ νόμιμα ἃ κέκληκε μαρτύρια, τὴν
νομοθετικὴν καὶ κολαστήριον δύναμιν, τὸ
ἱλαστήριον, τὴν ἵλεω καὶ εὐεργέτιν, τὰς
ὑπεράνω τήν τε ποιητικὴν ἥτις ἐστὶ πίστις
τῆς ἵλεω καὶ εὐεργέτιδος, καὶ τὴν βασι-
λικήν, ἥτις ἐστὶ ῥίζα τῆς κολαστηρίου καὶ
νομοθετικῆς· ὑπεμφαίνεται δὲ μέσος ὢν
ὁ θεῖος λόγος, ἀνωτέρω δὲ τοῦ λόγου ὁ
λέγων· ἔστι δὲ καὶ ὁ τῶν κατειλεγμένων
ἀριθμὸς ἑβδομάδι συμπληρούμενος νοητὸς
κόσμος, καὶ δυνάμεις δύο συγγενεῖς ἥ τε
κολαστήριος καὶ εὐεργέτις, καὶ ἕτεραι πρὸ
τούτων δύο ἥ τε ποιητικὴ καὶ ἡ βασιλική,
συγγένειαν ἔχουσαι μᾶλλον πρὸς τὸν δημι-

intelligere quis poterit horum naturas,
ultro ego renunciabo caetera omnia, quaecumque aemulationem merentur deiformi
pulchritudine circumdata. Verumtamen
consideremus singula, utcumque se ha-
beant. Primus est (Ens) ille, qui maior
(natu) est etiam uno vel unico et principio. Deinde Entis Verbum, seminativa
entium vere essentia. Ex Ente vero
Verbo tamquam ex fonte disruptae sca-
turiunt ambae virtutes. Una est creativa, secundum quod posuit (creavit
scilicet) omnia et ornavit artifex; is
deus appellatur. Altera regia, secundum quod princeps est factorum a crea-
tore; is vocatur *dominus.* Ex his ergo
duabus virtutibus germinant aliae. Quoniam germinat apud creativam propi-
tia cuius nomen est proprium benefica;
apud vero regiam legislativa, cui nomen
datur conveniens percussiva: sub his
autem et iuxta haec arca. Arca autem
est intelligibilis mundi symbolum et
habet omnia collocata sede in adyto
sanctorum: symbolice inquam arca in-
corporeum mundum: et legem, quam
nuncupavit testimonium, legislativam et
percussivam virtutem, propitiam ac bene-
ficam superioremque creativam, quae est
fons propitiae et beneficae: atque regiam, quae est radix percussivae et legis-
lativae. Excellit tamen, eo quod in medio
est, divinum verbum, verbum autem superat qui dicit. Quibus dinumeratis sep-
tenarius completur numerus : mundus
videlicet intellectualis et virtutes, quatenus cognatae sunt, percussiva et benefica, atque duae aliae his anteriores, creativa ac regia, cognationem habente ma-

---

[1] τοῦ ὄν. λόγου Gross.   [2] αἱ added by Tisch.   [3] αἱ ἀρχαὶ sic Gross.

ουργὸν ἢ τὸ γεγονός· καὶ ἕκτος ὁ λόγος καὶ
ἕβδομος ὁ λέγων· ἐὰν δὲ ἄνωθεν τὴν κατα-
ρίθμησιν ποιῇ, εὑρήσεις τὸν μὲν λέγοντα
πρῶτον, τὸν δὲ λόγον δεύτερον, τρίτον δὲ
τὴν ποιητικὴν δύναμιν, τετάρτην δὲ τὴν
ἀρχήν, εἶτα δὲ ὑπὸ μὲν τῇ ποιητικῇ πέμπτην
τὴν εὐεργέτιν, ὑπὸ δὲ τῇ βασιλικῇ ἕκτην
τὴν κολαστήριον, ἕβδομον δὲ τὸν ἐκ τῶν
ἰδεῶν κόσμον.

Tischendorf, *ut supra*, p. 148—152.

Exod. xxvii. 1.
§ 99. ....
Οὔτε πλοῦτον ἀσπάζεται τὸ θεῖον, οὔτε
πενίαν ἀποστρέφεται......

Pitra, *Anal. Sac.* II. 308, from Cod.
Coislin. 276, f. 208.

Exod. xxvii. 21.
§ 105. ....
Οὐδὲν οὔτε ἥδιον οὔτε σεμνότερον ἢ θεῷ
δουλεύειν, ὃ καὶ τὴν μεγίστην βασιλείαν
ὑπερβάλλει· καί μοι δοκοῦσιν οἱ πρῶτοι
βασιλεῖς ἅμα καὶ ἀρχιερεῖς γενέσθαι, δη-
λοῦντες ἔργοις, ὅτι χρὴ τοὺς τῶν ἄλλων
δεσπόζοντας δουλεύειν τοῖς λατρεύουσι θεῷ.

From Dam. Par. 775 (Cod. Rupef.,
f. 113), ἐκ τοῦ β' τῶν ἐν ἐξόδῳ ζητημάτων.

Exod. xxviii. 2.
§ 107. ....
Δόξα, ὡς ὁ παλαιὸς λόγος, ψευδής ἐστι
ὑπόληψις καὶ δόκησις ἀβέβαιος.

Mai, *Script. Vet.* VII. 102 (Cod. Vat.
1553), ἐκ τῶν ἐν ἐξόδῳ ζητημάτων.

Exod. xxviii. 32.
§ 118. ....
Οἱ λάλοι, τὰ ὀφείλοντα ἡσυχάζεσθαι ῥηγ-
νύντες, τρόπον τινὰ ὑπὸ γλωσσαλγίας προ-
χέουσιν εἰς ὦτα ἀκοῆς οὐκ ἄξια...

Dam. Par. 576 and Cod. Reg. 923,
f. 231; in each case headed Φίλωνος.

---

iorem creativa, [et gente singulisque;]
atque verbum; septimus autem qui dicit.
Quod si de superiore inchoabis, primo
Dicens, et secundo Verbum, tertio virtus
creativa, quarto principativa, deinde sub
creativa quinto benefica, et sub regia
sexto percussiva, septimus autem est
mundus ex speciebus constans.

Exod. xxvii. 1.
§ 99. ....
Non enim opulentiam amat divinitas,
nec paupertatem taedet.......

Exod. xxvii. 21.
§ 105. ....
Quum nihil sit iucundum ac suave neque
gloriosum magis, quam deo servire, quod
excellit magnum etiam regnum. Mihi
autem videtur priscos reges simul et
pontifices fuisse, palam per suum ministerium facientes, quod oportet eos, qui
aliorum dominantur, per se colere deum
officiose.

Exod. xxviii. 2.
§ 107. ....
Gloria autem, ut antiquus sermo vult,
falsa est opinio; opinio vero inconstans
per se imperfecta (est).

Exod. xxviii. 32.
§ 118. ....
Servanda sunt, *ne laceretur*. Quod evenit
gulosis et loquacibus, qui ubi oportebat
continere, lacerant: ut ex garrulitate
quidam frustra effundunt intima, quae
non erant auditu digna.

We come now to the passages which are for one reason or another to be ascribed to the books of Questions and Solutions but which have not yet been identified.

Quæstiones in Genesim.

Τῶν φαύλων πλούσιος οὐδεὶς καὶ ἂν τὰ πανταχοῦ μέταλλα κέκτηται· ἀλλ᾽ εἰσὶ πάντες οἱ ἄφρονες πένητες.

Dam. Par. 362 and Cod. Reg. 923, fol. 76, in each case with reference to II. Quaest. in Gen.

Μεῖζον ἀνθρώπῳ κακὸν ἀφροσύνης οὐδέν ἐστι, τὸ ἴδιον τοῦ λογιστικοῦ γένους, τὸν νοῦν, ζημιωθέντι.

Dam. Par. 363 and Cod. Reg. 923, fol. 76, in both cases as from the *sixth* book of the Questions on Genesis.

Also Tischendorf, *Philonea*, p. 152, e cod. Cahirino, and Maximus (II. 670).

Dam. Par. reads τοῦ ἰδίου τοῦ λογισμοῦ, Maximus, τῷ ἴδιον.

Μελέτη τροφὸς ἐπιστήμης.

Dam. Par. 405.

Cod. Reg. 923, fol. 105, and Mai, *Script. Vet.* VII. 99 (Cod. Vat. 1553) read τροφός ἐστιν in both cases. Mai's codex says expressly ἐκ τῶν ἐν γενέσει ζητημάτων.

Οὐ θέμις τὰ ἱερὰ μυστήρια ἐκλαλεῖν ἀμυήτοις (thus far Dam. Par. 533), ἄχρις ἂν καθαρθῶσιν τελείᾳ καθάρσει (thus far Cod. Reg. 923), ὁ γὰρ ἀνοργίαστος καὶ εὐχερής, ἀσώματον καὶ νοητὴν φύσιν ἀκούειν ἢ βλέπειν ἀδυνατῶν, ὑπὸ τῆς φανερᾶς ὄψεως ἀπατηθεὶς μωμήσεται τὰ ἀμώμητα. Τοῖς ἀμυήτοις ἐκλαλεῖν μυστήρια καταλύοντός ἐστι τοὺς θεσμοὺς τῆς ἱερατικῆς τελετῆς.

Dam. Par. 533.

Cod. Reg. 923, f. 25 b, reading ἄχρι καθαρσῶσι (C for Θ).

Dam. Par. 782 (Cod. Rupef. f. 189): by the last two expressly referred to II. Quaest. in Gen.

Ὥσπερ κίονες οἰκίας ὅλας ὑπερείδουσιν, οὕτω καὶ αἱ θεῖαι δυνάμεις τὸν σύμπαντα κόσμον καὶ τοῦ ἀνθρωπείου τὸ ἄριστον καὶ θεοφιλέστατον γένος.

Dam. Par. 749 (Cod. Rupef. f. 29), ἐκ τοῦ α΄ τῶν ἐν γενέσει ζητημάτων.

Ἐάν τις κατ᾽ οἰκίαν ἢ κώμην ἢ πόλιν ἢ ἔθνος γένηται φρονήσεως ἐραστής, ἀνάγκη τὴν οἰκίαν καὶ τὴν πόλιν ἐκείνην ἀμείνονι βίῳ χρήσασθαι· ὁ γὰρ ἀστεῖος κοινὸν ἀγαθόν ἐστιν ἅπασιν, ἐξ ἑτοίμου τὴν ἀφ᾽ ἑαυτοῦ προτείνων ὠφελείαν.

Dam. Par. 750 (Cod. Rupef. f. 33 b) from I. Quaest. in Gen.

Οὕτως γὰρ ὁ σοφίας ἐραστὴς οὐδενὶ τῶν εἰκαιοτέρων, καὶ ἂν συμπεφυκὼς τυγχάνῃ, σύνεστιν ἢ συνδιατρίβει πονηροτάτῳ, διεζεύγμενος τῶν πολλῶν διὰ λογισμῶν, δι᾽ οὓς οὔτε συμπλεῖν, οὔτε συμπολιτεύεσθαι οὔτε συζῆν λέγεται.

Dam. Par. 754 (Cod. Rupef.), ἐκ τοῦ ε΄ τῶν αὐτῶν.

Ἀνθρώποις τὸ εὐμετάβλητον διὰ τὴν ἐν τοῖς ἐκτὸς ἀβεβαιότητα συμβαίνειν ἀνάγκη. Οὕτω γοῦν φίλους ἑλόμενοι πολλάκις καὶ βραχύν τινα αὐτοῖς διατρίψαντες χρόνον, οὐδὲν ἐγκαλεῖν ἔχοντες ἀπεστράφημεν ὡσεὶ ἐχθρῶν.

Dam. Par. 776 (Cod. Rupef.) ἐκ τῶν ἐν
γενέσει ζητουμένων.

Τὸ ἐπαισθάνεσθαι τῶν ἐσφαλμένων καὶ
ἑαυτοῦ καταμέμφεσθαι πρὸς δικαίου ἀνδρός·
τὸ δὲ ἀνεπαισθήτως διακεῖσθαι—ἀργαλεώ-
τερα ποιεῖ τῇ ψυχῇ τὰ δεινά—πρὸς κακοῦ
ἀνδρός.

Dam. Par. 777 (Cod. Rupef.) ἐκ τῶν
αὐτῶν, the preceding passage being from
the Questions on Genesis.

Ἐκ τῶν ἐν γενέσει ζητημάτων.

Ἐπειδὴ πρὸς πολλὰ τῶν κατὰ τὸν βίον
τυφλὸς ὁ τῶν μὴ πεφιλοσοφηκότων νοῦς,
χρηστέον τοῖς βλέπουσι τὰς τῶν πραγμάτων
ἰδέας πρὸς ὁδηγίαν.

Dam. Par. (Cod. Reg. 923, fol. 315 b)
referred to Philo on Genesis and reading
χρητέον: and John Monach. (Mang. II.
667) = Rup. f. 256 b, ἐκ τῶν ἐν γεν. ζητ.

Ἐν θεῷ μόνον τὸ τέλειον καὶ ἀνενδεές,
ἐν δὲ ἀνθρώπῳ τὸ ἐπιδεὲς καὶ ἀτελές. Δι-
δακτὸς γὰρ ὁ ἄνθρωπος, καὶ ἂν γὰρ σοφώ-
τατος ἄλλος ἀπ᾿ ἄλλου, ἀλλ᾿ οὐκ ἀδιδάκτως,
οὐδὲ αὐτοφυῶς· καὶ εἰ ἐπιστημονικώτερος
ἕτερος ἑτέρου, οὐκ ἐμφύτως, ἀλλὰ μεμαθη-
μένως.

Dam. Par. (Cod. Reg. 923, fol. 335)
from Quaest. in Gen. reading ἀνθρώποις,
σοφώτερος ἄλλος ἀλλήλου.

Joh. Monach. (Mang. II. 667) = Rup.
f. 262 b.

Ἀμήχανον ἁρμονίαν καὶ τάξιν καὶ λόγον
καὶ ἀναλογίαν καὶ τοσαύτην συμφωνίαν καὶ
τῷ ὄντι εὐδαιμονίαν ἀπαυτοματισθεῖσαν γενέσθαι. Ἀνάγκη γὰρ εἶναι ποιητὴν καὶ
πατέρα, κυβερνήτην τε καὶ ἡνίοχον, ὃς γε-
γέννηκεν καὶ γεννηθέντα σώζει.

Joh. Monach. (Mang. II. 669) ἐκ τοῦ α´
τῶν ἐν γεν. ζητημ.

Τὰ αὐτὰ καθήκοντα πολλάκις ἐνεργοῦσιν
ὅ τε ἀστεῖος καὶ ὁ φαῦλος, ἀλλ᾿ οὐκ ἀπὸ τῆς
αὐτῆς διανοίας ἀμφότεροι· ὁ μὲν γὰρ κρίνων
ὅτι καλόν, ὁ δὲ μοχθηρὸς μνώμενός τι τῶν
εἰς πλεονεξίαν.

Mai, *Script. Vet.* VII. 100 (Cod. Vat.
1553). Φίλωνος· ἐκ τῶν ς´ ἐν γεν. ζητημ.
Also in Rup. f. 337 b, reading καθηκόντως,
μοχθηρῶς and omitting ἀμφότεροι.

Εἰώθασιν οἱ ἄνθρωποι ἐκ πλουσίων γενό-
μενοι πένητες ἐξαίφνης ἢ ἐξ ἐνδόξων καὶ
μεγάλων ἄδοξοι καὶ ταπεινοὶ ἢ ἐξ ἀρχόντων ἰδιῶται ἢ ἐξ ἐλευθέρων δοῦλοι, ταῖς
τύχαις συμμεταβάλλειν τὰ φρονήματα, φά-
σκοντες οὐ προνοεῖσθαι τῶν ἀνθρωπίνων
πραγμάτων τὸ θεῖον, οὐ γὰρ ἂν χρήσασθαι
μεγάλαις καὶ ἀπροσδοκήτοις μεταβολαῖς
καὶ κακοπραγίαις· ἀγνοοῦντες πρῶτον μὲν
ὅτι τούτων οὐδέν ἐστι κακὸν οὐδὲ γὰρ τά-
ναντία ἀγαθά, ὅτι μὴν τὸ δοκεῖν οὐκ ἀλή-
θεια· δεύτερον δὲ ὅτι πολλάκις ταῦτα συμ-
βαίνει διὰ νουθεσίαν, ἕνεκα τῶν ἀδιαφόρων
ἐξυβρίζοντων· οὐ γὰρ πάντες φέρειν τὰ
ἀγαθὰ δύνανται· τρίτον δέ, ὡς ἔφην, πρὸς
ἀπόπειραν ἠθῶν· ἀκριβεστάτη γὰρ βάσανος,
οἱ πρὸς ἑκάτερα καιροί.

Mai, *Script. Vet.* VII. 101 (Cod. Vat.
1553). Φίλωνος· ἐκ τοῦ α´ τῶν ἐν γεν.
ζητημ.

Τὸ ἐπιορκεῖν ἀνόσιον καὶ ἀλυσιτελέστα-
τον.

Dam. Par. 784 (Cod. Rupef.) ἐκ τῶν ἐν
γενέσει ζητημάτων, also Dam. Par. 751
(Cod. Rupef.), apparently referred to
the Questions on Exodus.

Οὐδὲν ἐναντίον καὶ μαχόμενον ταῖς ὁσιω-
τάταις τοῦ θεοῦ δυνάμεσίν ἐστιν οὕτως, ὡς
ἀδικία.

Dam. Par. 787 (Cod. Rupef. f. 238) ἐκ
τοῦ β´ τῶν ἐν γενέσει ζητημάτων.

Οἱ ἑαυτῶν μόνον ἕνεκα πάντα πράττοντες φιλαυτίαν, μέγιστον κακόν, ἐπιτηδεύουσιν, ὃ ποιεῖ τὸ ἄμικτον, τὸ ἀκοινώνητον, τὸ ἄφιλον, τὸ ἄδικον, τὸ ἀσεβές. τὸν γὰρ ἄνθρωπον ἡ φύσις κατεσκεύασεν, οὐχ ὡς τὰ μονωτικὰ θηρία, ἀλλ' ὡς ἀγελαῖα καὶ σύννομα, κοινωνικώτατον, ἵνα μὴ μόνῳ ἑαυτῷ ζῇ, ἀλλὰ καὶ πατρὶ καὶ μητρὶ καὶ ἀδελφοῖς καὶ γυναικὶ καὶ τέκνοις καὶ τοῖς ἄλλοις συγγενέσι καὶ φίλοις, καὶ δημόταις καὶ φυλέταις καὶ πατρίδι καὶ ὁμοφύλοις καὶ πᾶσιν ἀνθρώποις, ἔτι μέντοι καὶ τοῖς μέρεσι τοῦ παντός, καὶ τῷ ὅλῳ κόσμῳ καὶ πολὺ πρότερον τῷ πατρὶ καὶ ποιητῇ· δεῖ γὰρ εἶναι, εἴγε ὄντως ἐστὶ λογικός, κοινωνικόν, φιλόκοσμον, φιλόθεον, ἵνα γένηται καὶ θεοφιλής.

Joh. Monach. (Mangey II. 662).

Mai, *Script. Vet.* VII. 108 (Cod. Vat. 1553), gives this passage as ἐκ τοῦ β' τῶν ἐν γεν. ζητημάτων, and reads φιλαυτίᾳ τὸ, om. τὸ ἄφιλον, reads τὰ ἀγελαῖα, ἑαυτῷ μόνῳ, om. καὶ μητρὶ, om. καὶ φίλοις...φυλέταις, om. ἔτι...κόσμῳ and last sentence. Cod. Reg. 923 fol. 20 b: as Φίλωνος; with some slight errors of transcription.

Maximus (II. 686) gives the first sentence, reading φιλαυτίας so as to connect it with the following words.

Further in Dam. Par. 721 the whole passage is ascribed to the Abbot Isaiah, and there are a few variations in the reading.

τρεπτοὶ πολύτρεπτον διαπερῶντες βίον, καὶ συμφορὰς καθημέραν ἐνειλούμενοι, ἥκιστα τῆς εὐδαιμονίας ἠφῖχθαί (l. ἀφῖχθαί) τινα πρὸ τέλους ὑπολαμβάνομεν.

Mai, *Script. Vet.* VII. 102 (Cod. Vat. 1553). Φίλωνος· ἐκ τῶν ἐν γεν. ζητημ.

Συγκρύπτεται διὰ φιλίαν νόθου πράγματος καὶ ἀδόκιμον τὸ γνήσιον καὶ δοκιμώτατον.

Mai, *Script. Vet.* VII. 103. Φίλωνος· ἐκ τοῦ δ' τῶν ἐν γεν. ζητημ.

Τοὺς ἄρξαντας εἴτε τῶν ἀγαθῶν εἴτε καὶ πονηρῶν βουλευμάτων, καὶ μάλιστα ὅταν ἐφαρμόσῃ τοῖς βουλεύμασι τὰ ἔργα, ἴσους ἡγητέον τοῖς καὶ τελειώσασιν αὐτά· τὸ μὲν γὰρ μὴ φθάσαι πρὸς τὸ πέρας ἐλθεῖν, ἕτερα καὶ πολλὰ αἴτια· ἡ δὲ γνώμη καὶ σπουδὴ τῶν προελομένων ἔφθακεν δυνάμει καὶ πρὸς τὸ πέρας.

Mai, *Script. Vet.* VII. 105 (Cod. Vat. 1553). Φίλωνος· ἐκ τοῦ β' τῶν ἐν γεν. ζητημ.

Φίλων καὶ συγγενῶν ἔργον ἐπελαφρίζειν τὰ πταίσματα.

Mai, *Script. Vet.* VII. 107. Φίλωνος· ἐκ τῶν ἐν γεν. ζητημ.[1]

Ὁ εὐλαβέστερος τρόπος οὐχ οὕτως ἐπὶ τοῖς ἰδίοις ἀγαθοῖς γέγηθεν ὡς ἐπὶ τοῖς τοῦ πέλας κακοῖς ἀνιᾶται ἢ φοβεῖται· ἀνιᾶται μὲν ὅτ' ἀνάξιος ὢν ἀτυχῇ, φοβεῖται δὲ ὅτ' ἂν ἐπιτηδέως κακοπαθῇ.

Mai, *Script. Vet.* VII. 107. Φίλωνος· ἐκ τοῦ δ' τῶν ἐν γεν. ζητημ.

Τί οὖν ἐνεθυμήθη; ὅτι διὰ τὸ εὐαρεστεῖν πεποίηται ὁ ἄνθρωπος, οὐ κατ' ἀντιστροφήν, διότι ἐποίησεν, ἀλλ' ὡς μὴ ἐμμεῖναν τὸ ποίημα τῇ εἰς εὐαρέστησιν ποιήσει. Πρὸς οὖν τὸ ποίημα ὁ λόγος, ὥσπερ σοφιστὴς διαλογεῖται, οὐ διότι πεφύτευκεν ὁ θεὸς ἀλλ' ὅτι προελθὸν διὰ ῥᾳθυμίαν διαμαρτάνει τῆς ἐγχειρίσεως.

Pitra, *Anal. Sac.* II. 307 (Cod. Coislin. 276, f. 221). Ἐκ τῶν εἰς γεν. ζητημ.

The following passage seems to belong to the Questions on Genesis XIV. 18, being found in a codex which quotes the

---

[1] I see now that this is *De Providentia* II. 15.

Questions on Gen. IV. 4 and seems to have no other Philonea. This part of the Questions is lost in the Armenian.

Τὰ γὰρ τοῦ πολέμου ἀριστεῖα δίδωσι τῷ ἱερεῖ καὶ τὰς τῆς νίκης ἀπαρχάς. ἱεροπρεπεστάτη δὲ καὶ ἁγιωτάτη πασῶν ἀπαρχῶν ἡ δεκάτη διὰ τὸ παντέλειον εἶναι τὸν ἀριθμόν, ἀφ' οὗ καὶ τοῖς ἱερεῦσι καὶ νεωκόροις αἱ δεκάται προστάξει νόμου καρπῶν καὶ θρεμμάτων ἀποδίδονται, ἄρξαντος τῆς ἀπαρχῆς Ἀβραάμ, ὃς καὶ τοῦ γένους ἀρχηγέτης ἐστίν.

Cramer, *Catena in Heb.* p. 580, e Cod. Paris. 238.

The following passage is ascribed to the Questions on Genesis but incorrectly: it is *De Posteritate Caini* § 8.

Πέφυκεν ὁ ἄφρων ἐπὶ μηδενὸς ἑστάναι παγίως καὶ ἐρηρεῖσθαι δόγματος. Ἄλλοτε γοῦν ἀλλοῖα δοξάζει, καὶ περὶ τῶν αὐτῶν ἐστὶν ὅτε μηδενὸς συμβεβηκότος καινοτέρου, τἀναντία. καί ἐστιν ἡ ζωὴ αὐτοῦ πᾶσα κρεμαμένη, βάσιν ἀκράδαντον οὐκ ἔχουσα ἀλλὰ πρὸς τῶν ἀντισπώντων καὶ ἀντιμεθελκόντων ἀεὶ φορουμένη πραγμάτων.

Dam. Par. 448 with large omissions.

Dam. Par. 750 (Cod. Rupef. f. 35) refers to Quaest. in Gen., omits παγίως, reads κοινοτέρου, om. φορουμένη.

Mai, *Script. Vet.* VII. 100 (Cod. Vat. 1553), refers ἐκ τοῦ η' καὶ θ' τῆς νόμων ἀλληγορίας and reads ἐνερίσθαι δόγματος.

Maxim. II. 670 reads the passage abbreviated as in Dam. Par. 448: ἐπὶ μηδενὸς αἰσθάνεσθαι πράγματος ἢ ἑστάναι, and αὐτῶν ζωὴ πᾶσα.

Also Cat. Lips. col. 1601.

Unidentified passages from the Questions on Exodus.

Ἀμήχανον ἀνθρωπίνῃ φύσει τὸ τοῦ Ὄντος πρόσωπον θεάσασθαι. Τὸ δὲ πρόσωπον οὐ κυριολογεῖται, παραβολὴ δέ ἐστιν εἰς δήλωσιν τῆς καθαρωτάτης καὶ εἰλικρινεστάτης τοῦ Ὄντος ἰδέας, ἐπειδὴ καὶ ἄνθρωπος οὐδενὶ γνωρίζεται μᾶλλον ἢ προσώπῳ κατὰ τὴν ἰδίαν ποιότητα καὶ μορφήν. Οὐ γάρ φησιν ὁ θεός, ὅτι "οὐκ εἰμὶ ὁρατὸς τὴν φύσιν"— τίς δὲ μᾶλλον ὁρατὸς ἢ ὁ τὰ ἄλλα πάντα γεννήσας ὁρατά;—"πεφυκὼς δὲ τοιοῦτος εἰς τὸ ὁρᾶσθαι ὑπ' οὐδενὸς ἀνθρώπων ὁρῶμαι" φησι. Τὸ δὲ αἴτιον ἡ ἀδυναμία τοῦ γενητοῦ. Καὶ ἵνα μὴ περιπλέκων μηκύνω· Θεὸν γενέσθαι δεῖ πρότερον—ὅπερ οὐδὲ οἷόν τε—, ἵνα θεὸν ἰσχύσῃ τις καταλαβεῖν. Ἐὰν δὲ ἀποθάνῃ μέν τις τὸν θνητὸν βίον, ζήσῃ δὲ ἀντιλαβὼν τὸν ἀθάνατον, ἴσως ὃ μηδέποτε εἶδεν ὄψεται. Αἱ φιλοσοφίαι

πᾶσαι κατά τε τὴν Ἑλλάδα καὶ βάρβαρον ἀκμάσασαι, ζητοῦσαι τὰ φύσεως, οὐδὲ τὸ βραχύτατον ἠδυνήθησαν τηλαυγῶς ἰδεῖν. Σαφὴς δὲ πίστις αἱ διαφωνίαι, αἱ διαμάχαι καὶ ἑτεροδοξίαι τῶν ἑκάστης αἱρέσεως ἀνασκευαζόντων καὶ ἀνασκευαζομένων μέρη· καὶ πᾶσιν ὁρμητήρια πολέμων γεγόνασιν αἱ τῶν αἱρεσιομάχων οἰκίαι[1], τυφλοῦσαι τὸν δυνάμενον βλέπειν ἀνθρώπινον νοῦν ταῖς ἀντιλογικαῖς ἔρισιν, ἀμηχανοῦντα τίνα δεῖ προσέσθαι καὶ τίνα διώσασθαι. Δεῖ τὸν βουλόμενον φαντασιωθῆναι τὸν τῶν ὅλων ἄριστον, στῆναι τὸ πρῶτον κατὰ ψυχήν, ἱδρυνθέντα παγίως γνώμῃ μιᾷ, καὶ μηκέτι πρὸς πολλὰ πλάζεσθαι, ἔπειτα δὲ στῆναι ἐπὶ φύσεως καὶ γνώμης ξηρᾶς καὶ ἀγόνου παντός[2], ὅσα φθαρτά· ἐὰν γὰρ προσήσεταί τι τῶν μαλακωτέρων, σφαλήσεται τῆς προθέσεως. Ἀ-

---

[1] l. σκιαί.

[2] l. πάντων.

δυνατήσει καὶ τὸ ὀξυωπέστατον βλέπον
ἰδεῖν τὸ ἀγένητον, ὡς τυφλωθῆναι πρότερον
ἢ θεάσασθαι, διὰ τὴν ὀξυαύγειαν καὶ
τὸν ἐπεισρέοντα χείμαρρον τῶν μαρμαρυ-
γῶν.

Dam. Par. 748 (Cod. Rupef. f. 22 b),
ἐκ τοῦ τελευταίου τῶν ἐν ἐξόδῳ ζητουμένων.
προσέσθαι, ἐπεισρέοντα are corrections by
Mangey for προέσθαι, ἀπεισρέοντα.

Ἡ φορὰ τῶν κακιῶν ἀνακυκᾷ καὶ στροβεῖ
τὴν ψυχήν, ἴλιγγον αὐτῇ περιτιθεῖσα τὸν
καλύπτοντα καὶ καμμύειν ἐκβιαζόμενον τὴν
φύσει μὲν πρέπουσαν ὄψιν, ἐπιτηδεύσει δὲ
τυφλουμένην.

Dam. Par. 751 (Cod. Rupef.) ἐκ τῶν
ἐν ἐξόδῳ ζητημάτων.

Αἱ περὶ τῶν τοῦ θεοῦ ἀρετῶν ἐναγώνιοι
ζητήσεις βελτιοῦσι τὴν διάνοιαν καὶ ἀθλοῦ-
σιν ἄθλους ἡδίστους ἅμα καὶ ὠφελιμωτάτους,
καὶ μάλιστα ὅταν μή, ὡς οἱ νῦν, τὴν ψευδώ-
νυμον κλῆσιν ὑποδυόμενοι μέχρι τοῦ δοκεῖν
ὑπερμαχοῦσι τῶν δογμάτων, ἀλλὰ πάθει
γνησίῳ μετ' ἐπιστήμης ἰχνηλατοῦσιν ἀλήθειαν.

Τὸ ἐμμελὲς καὶ εὔρυθμον οὐκ ἐν φωνῇ
μᾶλλον ἢ διανοίᾳ ἐπιδείκνυσθαι πειρωμένους.
Ὁ τοῦ σοφοῦ λόγος οὐκ ἐν ῥήμασι ἀλλ' ἐν
τοῖς δηλουμένοις πράγμασιν ἐπιδείκνυσιν τὸ
κάλλος.

Τοὺς ἐντυγχάνοντας τοῖς ἱεροῖς γράμμασιν
οὐ δεῖ συλλαβομαχεῖν, ἀλλὰ πρὸ τῶν ὀνομάτων καὶ ῥημάτων τὴν διάνοιαν σκοπεῖν,
καὶ τοὺς καιροὺς καὶ τρόπους, καθ' οὓς
ἕκαστα λέγεται. Πολλάκις γὰρ αἱ αὐταὶ
λέξεις ἑτέροις καὶ ἑτέροις πράγμασιν ἐφαρ-
μόζουσιν, καὶ κατὰ τὸ ἐναντίον διαφέρουσαι
λέξεις ἐπὶ τοῦ αὐτοῦ τιθέμεναι πράγματος
συνᾴδουσιν.

All from Dam. Par. 774 (Cod. Rupef.)
referred respectively to the first, second

and last books of the Questions on
Exodus.

Περιέχει τὰ πάντα, ὑπ' οὐδενὸς περιεχόμενος. Ὡς γὰρ ὁ τόπος περιεκτικὸς σωμάτων ἐστὶ καὶ καταφυγή, οὕτω καὶ ὁ θεῖος
λόγος περιέχει τὰ ὅλα καὶ πεπλήρωκεν.

Dam. Par. 752 (Cod. Rupef.), ἐκ τοῦ
τελευταίου τῶν ἐν ἐξόδῳ ζητημάτων.

Ἐντὸς φέρει τὸν ὄλεθρον ὁ τῇ κακίᾳ
συζῶν ἐπεὶ σύνοικον ἔχει τὴν ἐπίβουλον καὶ
πολέμιον. Ἱκανὸς γὰρ πρὸς τιμωρίαν ἡ τοῦ
φαύλου συνείδησις, οἴκοθεν ὡς ἐκ πληγῆς
δειλίαν προτείνουσα τῇ ψυχῇ.

Dam. Par. 782 (Cod. Rupef.), ἐκ τῶν
ἐν ἐξόδῳ ζητουμένων.

Τοῦ φαύλου ὁ βίος ἐπίλυπος καὶ περιδεής,
καὶ ὅσα κατὰ τὰς αἰσθήσεις ἐνεργεῖ, φόβοις
καὶ ὀδύναις ἀνακέκραται.

Dam. Par. 782 (Cod. Rupef.), referred
to Quaest. in Exod.

Lequien (p. 784) gives a long passage
as ἐκ τῶν ἐν ἐξόδῳ ζητημάτων, but a reference to Rup. f. 222 b will, I think, shew
the heading to be an editorial addition.

Αἱ τοῦ θεοῦ χάριτες οὐ μόνον ἀναγκαῖα
παρέχονται, ἀλλὰ καὶ πρὸς περιττὴν καὶ
δαψιλεστέραν ἀπόλαυσιν.

Dam. Par. 789 (Cod. Rupef. f. 277),
from II. Quaest. in Exod.

Μυρία γε, οὐ λέγω τῶν ἀναγκαίων ἀλλὰ
καὶ τῶν βραχυτάτων εἶναι δοκούντων, ἐκ-
φεύγει τὸν ἀνθρώπινον νοῦν.

Joh. Monach. (Mang. II. 662), ἐκ τοῦ
α΄ τῶν ἐν ἐξόδῳ ζητ.

The reference is to Cod. Rup. f. 55,
where there is however no other heading
than τοῦ αὐτοῦ.

Μία ἀνάπαυσις ψυχῆς ἐστιν ἡ κρατίστη
εἰς τὸν ἱερὸν τοῦ ὄντος πόθον, ἡγεμόνι χρῆ-

H.

10

σθαι θεῷ καὶ βουλευμάτων καὶ λόγων καὶ πράξεων.

Πέρας εὐδαιμονίας τὸ ἀκλινῶς καὶ ἀρρεπῶς ἐν μόνῳ θεῷ στῆναι.

Joh. Monach. (Mang. II. 669) = Rup. f. 178 b, ἐκ τοῦ τελευταίου τῶν ἐν ἐξόδῳ ζητημ.

Πολλὰ ἀσωμένοις καὶ ἀδημονοῦσιν ἔθος ἐστὶ ψεύδεσθαι τῶν παθῶν οὐκ ἐπιτροπευόντων ἀληθεύειν εἰ τὸ ψεῦδος οἰκεῖόν ἐστιν.

Mai, *Script. Vet.* VII. 96 (Cod. Vat. 1553), ἐκ τοῦ αʹ τῶν ἐν ἐξόδῳ ζητημάτων.

Τὸ τῶν φαύλων ἄκριτον καὶ ἀνίδρυτον ἐν γνώμαις διασυνίστησιν μαχομένους μὲν λόγους ἀλλήλοις μαχομένας δὲ πράξεις καὶ μηδέποτε συμφωνούσας ἑαυταῖς·

Mai, *Script. Vet.* VII. 100 (Cod. Vat. 1553), ἐκ τοῦ αʹ τῶν ἐν ἐξόδῳ ζητημ.

Τὰ βουλήματα τῶν ἀγαθῶν δεῖ βεβαιοῦσθαι τελευτησάντων οὐδὲν ἧττον ἢ ζώντων.

Mai, *Script. Vet.* VII. 101 (Cod. Vat. 1553), ἐκ τοῦ αʹ τῶν ἐν ἐξόδῳ ζητημ.

Τὸ μὲν "πρωτότοκον" πρὸς τὸ μητρῷον γένος, τίκτει γὰρ γυνή· τό τε "πρωτογενὲς" πρὸς τὸ πατρῷον, γεννᾷ γὰρ ἄρρεν· τὸ δὲ "διανοῖγον πᾶσαν μήτραν" ἵνα μὴ γενομένης πρωτοτόκου θυγατρός, εἶθ᾿ ὕστερον ἐπιγενομένου υἱοῦ, τὸν υἱὸν ἐν πρωτοτόκοις καταριθμήσει τίς, ὡς τῆς ἄρρενος ἄρχοντα γενεᾶς· ὁ γὰρ νόμος φησίν, οὐ διοίγνυσι τὴν μήτραν ὁ τοιοῦτος τὴν εὐθὺς ἐκ παρθενίας.

Mai, *Script. Vet.* VII. 105 (Cod. Vat. 1553), ἐκ τοῦ δʹ τῶν ἐν ἐξόδῳ ζητημ. The passage evidently belongs to Exod. xiii. 2.

Τὰ μέτρα πλεονάζοντα τὸν ὅρον ὑπερβαίνει ὡς γίνεσθαι τὴν μὲν ἄμετρον φρόνησιν, πανουργίαν· τὴν δὲ σωφροσύνην, φειδωλίαν· τὴν δὲ ἀνδρίαν, θρασύτητα.

Mai, *Script. Vet.* VII. 106 (Cod. Vat. 1553), ἐκ τῶν ἐν ἐξόδῳ ζητημ.

Ἡ εὐφυΐα πλεονάζουσα τῇ ῥύμῃ τῆς φορᾶς πρὸς πολλὰ δὴ τῶν ἀλυσιτελῶν εἴωθε χωρεῖν· ἐν δὲ ταῖς διδασκαλίαις οὐκ ἐλάττω τὰ οὐκ ἀναγκαῖα τῶν ἀναγκαίων ἐστί· διὸ προσήκει τὸν ἔφορον καὶ ψυχῆς ὑφηγητήν, ὥσπερ γεωργὸν ἀγαθόν, τὰ ὑπερβάλλοντα περικόπτειν.

Mai, *Script. Vet.* VII. 108 (Cod. Vat. 1553), ἐκ τοῦ αʹ τῶν ἐν ἐξόδῳ ζητημάτων.

Ὁ σοφιστικός, γνώμης ὢν ἑτέρας, λόγοις οὐ συνᾴδουσι χρῆται· διέξεισι μὲν γὰρ ἀπνευστὶ τοὺς ἀρετῆς ἑκάστης ἐπαίνους, οἷα λόγῳ πολὺς ἐπὶ θήρᾳ τῶν ἀκουόντων· ὁ δὲ βίος ἐστὶν αὐτῶν πάντων ἀνάπλεος ἁμαρτημάτων· καί μοι δοκεῖ τῶν ἐπὶ σκηναῖς ὑποκριτῶν διαφέρειν οὐδέν, οἳ πολλάκις ἠμελημένοι καὶ ἄφρονες, ἄνθρωποι διεφθαρμένοι τινὲς δὲ καὶ θεραπεύοντες, εἰς ἥρωας ἀσκοῦνται· μικρὸν δὲ ὕστερον ἀποθέμενοι τὴν σκευήν, τὰ τῆς ἰδίας ἀδοξίας ἀναφαίνουσι σημεῖα.

Mai, *Script. Vet.* VII. 106 (Cod. Vat. 1553), ἐκ τοῦ αʹ τῶν ἐν ἐξόδῳ ζητημάτων.

Ὅρασις παρὰ τὰς ἄλλας αἰσθήσεις καὶ ταύτῃ διαφέρει, ὅτι αἱ μὲν ἄλλαι τοῖς αἰσθητοῖς ἐγκαταμίγνυνται, οἷον ἡ γεῦσις ἀνακιρνᾶται τοῖς χυμοῖς καὶ ἡ ὄσφρησις τοῖς ἐπαναδιδομένοις ἀτμοῖς καὶ αἱ ἀκοαὶ ταῖς φωναῖς ἐκδυομέναις εἰς τὰ ὦτα· οὔτε γὰρ αὐτὴ διὰ τοῦ βάθους τῶν σωμάτων χωρεῖ, ψαύει δὲ τῶν ἐπιφανειῶν μόνον κατὰ τὴν προσβολήν, οὔτε τὰ σώματα εἰς τὴν ὄψιν εἰσδύεται.

Mai, *Script. Vet.* VII. 109 (Cod. Vat. 1553), ἐκ τοῦ αʹ τῶν ἐν ἐξόδῳ ζητημάτων.

Οὐ πάντων κοινωνητέον πᾶσιν οὔτε λόγων
οὔτε πραγμάτων καὶ μάλιστα ἱερῶν· πολλὰ
γὰρ προϋπάρξαι δεῖ τοῖς ἐφιεμένοις τῆς
μετουσίας τούτων· πρῶτον μέν, τὸ μέγιστον
καὶ ἀναγκαιότατον, πρὸς τὸν ἕνα καὶ ὄντως
ὄντα θεὸν εὐσέβειαν καὶ ὁσιότητα, τὴν ἐπὶ
τοῖς ἀγάλμασι καὶ ξοάνοις καὶ συνόλως
ἀφιδρύμασι, τελεταῖς τε ἀτελέστοις καὶ
μυστηρίοις ἀνοργιάστοις, ἀνήνυτον πλάνην
ἀπωσαμένοις· δεύτερον δέ, καθαρθῆναι τὰς
ἁγνευτικὰς καθάρσεις κατά τε σῶμα καὶ
ψυχὴν διὰ νόμων πατρίων καὶ ἠθῶν· τρίτον,
ἀξιόπιστον τοῦ συνασμενισμοῦ παρασχεῖν
ἐνέχυρον, ἵνα μὴ τραπέζης μεταλαβόντες
ἱερᾶς, ἀσώτων μειρακίων τρόπον, ὑπὸ κόρου
καὶ πλησμονῆς ἐναλλοιώθωσιν ἐμπαροινοῦν-
τες, οἷς οὐ θέμις.

Pitra, *Anal. Sac.* II. 308 (Cod. Coislin.
276, f. 205), ἐκ τοῦ πρώτου τῶν ἐν ἐξόδῳ
ζητημάτων.

Also in Dam. Par. 782 (Cod. Rupef.),
reading καὶ μέγιστον, om. ὄντως, r. ἀγνευ-
ούσας, and by an eye-error to τρόπον,
reading τροφῆς for τραπέζης.

Φθαρτὸν καλῶ τὸν μὴ ἐφιέμενον ἀφθαρ-
σίας, ἀλλ' ὀστρέου τρόπον ἐνειλούμενον
ὀστρακοδέρμῳ, ὅπερ ἐστὶν ὁ σωματικὸς ὄγκος
καὶ ὁ τῶν θνητῶν βίος.

Ἐκ τοῦ τελευταίου τῶν ἐν ἐξόδῳ ζητημάτων.

Pitra, *Anal. Sac.* II. 308 (Cod. Coislin.
276, f. 245), and Cod. Rup. f. 240,
Μάταιον οὐδὲν οὔτε ἀκοαῖς οὔτε ἄλλῃ τινί
τῶν αἰσθήσεων προσιτέον· ἐπακολουθοῦσι
γὰρ ταῖς ἀπάταις μάλιστα τῶν ψυχῶν αἱ
ζημίαι.

Cod. Rup. f. 45, ἐκ τῶν ἐν ἐξόδῳ ζητουμένων.

The following passages are from the lost book of Questions on *Levi-
ticus.*

Μείζονα καὶ σπουδαιοτέραν τὴν ἐπι-
μέλειαν ποιοῦ εἰς τοὺς δι' ἀρετὴν ἢ θεο-
σέβειαν πτωχεύσαντας ἢ πενομένους· ἀλλ'
ὡς εἰς τοὺς ἐκ νόσων ἢ συμπτωμάτων
ἀποροῦντας παρὰ τοὺς ἐκ κακοπραγίας καὶ
ἀσωτίας πτωχεύσαντας.

Mai, *Script. Vet.* VII. 104 (Cod. Vat.
1553), Φίλωνος· ἐκ τῶν ἐν τῷ Λευϊτικῷ
ζητημάτων.

Maximus (II. 568), reading ἄλλως τε

ὁμοίως καὶ, νόσων καὶ, κακοπραγμονίας ἤ.

On the other hand it should be noted
that Cod. Reg. 923 f, 120, gives the same
passage to Didymus, reading ἄλλως, ἢ
ἀσωτίας.

Ὡς δεινὸν παρὰ τὸ δέον παθεῖν καὶ ἁρ-
πάζειν τι παραδοθέν.

Mai, *Script. Vet.* VII. 109 (Cod. Vat.
1553). Φίλωνος· ἐκ τῶν ἐν τῷ νόμῳ ζητημάτων.

Fragments from the lost books of Philo, De Providentia.

These fragments are printed by Mangey from Eusebius: they corre-
spond to the following sections and pages in Aucher's Latin.

Mangey, II. 634.	Aucher, § 3. I. 45.
...... II. 634—642.	...... § 15—33. I. 54—72.
...... II. 626.	...... § 50. I. 81.
...... II. 643—647.	...... § 99—§ 112. I. 107—120.

The only additional notes that I have to make on these books are that the sentence

$$\text{'}\Omega\mu\hat{\eta}\varsigma\ \gamma\grave{\alpha}\rho\ \delta\acute{\iota}\chi\alpha\ \psi\upsilon\chi\hat{\eta}\varsigma\ o\grave{\upsilon}\ \kappa\alpha\theta\alpha\acute{\iota}\rho\epsilon\tau\alpha\iota\ \kappa\alpha\kappa\acute{\iota}\alpha,$$

which is quoted from Philo by Anton Melissa (*Patr. Gr.* 36, col. 1101), is *De Providentia*, II. § 31. Also without author's name in Georg. Monach. (*Patr. Gr.* 117, col. 1160).

Ἀεὶ πρὸς τὰ ὁμοιότροπα ἀδικοῦσιν ἀπολογία τὰ τῶν κρειττόνων.

From Cod. Rup. f. 27, τοῦ αὐτοῦ περὶ προνοίας.

Βασιλεῖ δὲ οὐκ ἔστι πρόσρησις οἰκειότερα πατρός.

From Cod. Rup. f. 113, ἐκ τοῦ περὶ προνοίας.

This is *De Provid.* II. 15 (Mang. II. 635, Aucher I. 53).

Fragments from the lost book of Philo, entitled Hypothetica[1].

The fragments of this book have been published by Mangey (II. 626—628, 628—631, 631—634). It will be seen that I include under this head the fragment on the Essenes. For Philo is affirmed to have written the *Hypothetica* against the accusers of the Jews (ὡς πρὸς κατηγόρους αὐτῶν ποιούμενος λόγον). And the commencement of the fragment on the Essenes in Eusebius is as follows: Τούτων δὲ ἀπὸ τῆς ὑπὲρ Ἰουδαίων ἀπολογίας λαβὼν σύγε ἀνάγνωθι ταῦτα. This last fragment contains the sentence quoted by Anton Melissa (*Patr. Gr.* 136, col. 1089), Φίλαυτον γυνὴ καὶ ζηλότυπον οὐ μετρίως καὶ δεινὸν ἤθη ἀνδρὸς παραλῦσαι, where Mangey reads παρασαλεῦσαι.

Cf. ad Gaium § 6 (II. 551)

Observe also that this sentiment with additional matter is quoted directly from Eusebius in Dam. Par. 777 (Cod. Rupef.) as follows:

Φίλαυτον γυνὴ καὶ ζηλότυπον οὐ μετρίως καὶ δεινὸν ἀνδρὸς ἤθη παραλῦσαι, καὶ συνέχεσι γοητείαις ὑπάγεσθαι· μελετήσασα γὰρ θωπείας λόγους καὶ τὴν ἄλλην ὑπόκρισιν, ὥσπερ ἐπὶ σκηνῆς, ὄψεις καὶ ἀκοὰς ὅταν δελεάσῃ διηπατημένων, ὡς ὑπήκοον τὸν ἡγεμόνα νοῦν φενακίζει. Παῖδες δὲ εἰ γένοιντο, φρονήματος ἀποπλησθεῖσα καὶ παρρησίας, ὅσα κατ᾽ εἰρωνείαν πρότερον ὑπούλως ὑπηνίττετο, ταῦτα ἀπ᾽ εὐτολμητοτέρου θράσους ἐκλαλεῖ, καὶ ἀναισχυντοῦσα βιάζεται πράττειν.

It is to this treatise that I think must also be referred the following

---

[1] For a discussion of the character of this book and of the meaning of the term Hypothetica, see a very interesting tract in Bernays, *Gesammelte Abhandlungen*, I. 269.

passage from Cod. Reg. 923, fol. 332 b, which is exactly in line with the succinct account given in the second fragment of the ethics of the Jews.

Οὐκ ἐπὶ φιλίας ἐν ψυχῇ τὸ βέβαιον συμβόλων φιλικῶν ἀμελητέον· ταῦτα δέ ἐστι· προσαγορεῦσαι· δεξιώσασθαι προσ-ιόντας· ὑπαναστῆναι· τὸ ἱμάτιον ἀφελέσ-

θαι τῆς κεφαλῆς· ἄχρι τῆς οἰκίας παρα-πέμψαι· δεομένῳ παραστῆναι· σχήματα μὲν ταῦτα τιμῆς, σύμβολα δὲ καὶ πρόξενα ἀγάπης καὶ χάριτος.

Edited fragments of Philo not previously identified, nor referred to in the preceding pages.

The preceding collection and identification has much reduced the formidable lists of fragments found in Mangey, Mai, Pitra, &c., &c. Of those which remain we may also identify a number: suppose we begin with the unidentified Parallels and remove those quotations which can be dealt with.

Dam. Par. 341. This is not Philo, but Nilus according to Reg. 923. Certainly it is there numbered ΓΛΙΓ after the manner of the quotations from Nilus, and the title Φίλωνος evidently belongs to the previous sentence from the *Quaest. in Gen.* It is referred to Philo again in Rup. f. 237 b.

Εἰ βούλει ὑπὸ τοῦ θεοῦ βασιλεύεσθαι, μὴ βούλῃ ἀμαρτάνειν· εἰ δὲ ἁμαρτάνεις, πῶς βασιλεύῃ ὑπὸ τοῦ θεοῦ;

In Dam. Par. 341 it is given to Clement; in 751 (= Cod. Rup.) it is Clem. VIII. *Strom.*, but in Cod. Reg. 923 it is Philo, and so in Cod. Barocc. 143 (Mang. II. 674). It is given to Clement in Maximus (II. 610). Zahn makes the identification in *Suppl. Clem.* p. 29, viz. Clem. *Eclog.* 11 (Dind. III. 459).

Φοβηθῶμεν, οὐχὶ νόσον τὴν ἔξωθεν, ἀλλὰ ἁμαρτήματα, δι᾽ ἃ ἡ νόσος· καὶ νόσον ψυχῆς οὐ σώματος.

Dam. Par. 343 following a quotation from *Quaest. in Exod.* but wanting in Cod. Reg. 923. In Dam. Par. 597 it is however expressly given to *Eusebius*, and so in Reg. 923, and should therefore probably be removed.

Ὅταν ἄνθρωπος κατορθώσῃ βίον ἐνάρετον δι᾽ ἀσκήσεως καὶ ἀγαθῆς πολιτείας, καὶ ἔστιν ὑπὸ πάντων ἐγνωσμένος, ὅτι ἔστιν εὐσεβὴς καὶ φοβούμενος τὸν θεόν, καὶ ἐκπέσῃ εἰς ἁμαρτίαν· τοῦτό ἐστι παράπτωμα. Ἀνῆλ-θεν γὰρ εἰς τὸ ὕψος τοῦ οὐρανοῦ, καὶ πέπτω-κεν εἰς τὸν πυθμένα τοῦ ᾅδου.

Dam. Par. 349.
This is *De Posteritate Caini*, § 17 (I. 237).
Also Cod. Rup. f. 80 b.

Ὁ νοῦς ἑκάστῳ μάρτυς ἐστὶν ὧν ἐν ἀφανεῖ ἐβουλεύσαντο, καὶ τὸ συνειδὸς ἔλεγχος ἀδέκαστος καὶ πάντων ἀψευδέστατος.

Dam. Par. 356.
Cod. Reg. f. 104. Also Anton Melissa (*Patr. Gr.* 136, col. 861).
De Justitia, § 13 (II. 372).

Εἰρήνη κἂν ᾖ σφόδρα ἐπιζήμιος, λυσιτελεστέρα πολέμου.

Dam. Par. 359.
Cod. Reg. 923 reading λεώσις for δηώσεις, and ἀπαγωγή; and gives the reference πρὸς Γάϊον, also in Cod. Rup. f. 32 omitting δηώσεις χωρίων, ἀπαγωγή.
It is *Ad Gaium* § 3 (II. 548).

Ὦ πόσα καὶ ἡλίκα κακὰ ἐξ ἀναρχίας φύεται! λιμός, πόλεμος, δηώσεις χωρίων, στέρησις χρημάτων, ἀπαγωγαί, οἱ περὶ δουλείας καὶ θανάτου φόβοι!

Dam. Par. 367 (Anonymi).
Cod. Reg. 923 (Philonis).
Ad Gaium § 46 (II. 600).

Ἃ πρέσβεις ὑπομένουσι ἐπὶ τοὺς πέμψαντας λαμβάνει τὴν ἀναφοράν.

Dam. Par. 363.
Cod. Reg. 923 refers to ἐκ τοῦ περὶ μέθης. Much more at length in Rup. f. 73 b.
It is *De Ebrietate* § 3 (I. 359).

Νόσου καὶ φθορᾶς αἴτιον ἀπαιδευσία.

Dam. Par. 397 and Cod. Reg. 923, f. 97 b.
Also in Anton Melissa, *Patr. Gr.* 136, col. 801.
From III. *Leg. Alleg.* § 53 (I. 118).

Τὰ μὴ σὺν λόγῳ πάντα αἰσχρά, ὥσπερ τὰ σὺν λόγῳ κόσμια.

A pretty specimen of confusion is found in Georg. Monach. (Migne, *Patr. Gr.* 117, col. 1142) where the passage is given τὰ μὴ συλλόγων πάντα αἰσχρά, ὥσπερ τὰ συλλόγων κόσμια. Upon which the Editor (Boissonade) notes: Codex ταμι, ac duplici scriptura, αἰσχρά et αἰσχρῶν. Sensum vix perspicio.

Ascribed to Nilus in Dam. Par. 397 but to Philo in Cod. Reg.
Also in Anton Melissa, *Patr. Gr.* 136, col. 797, 1055.
Also Georg. Monach. (Migne 117, 1153) referring to Cyril and adding ἐπι-

Χωρὶς θεωρίας ἐπιστημονικῆς οὐδὲν τῶν πραττομένων καλόν.

στήμη γὰρ ἔγγονον εὐβουλίας· ἀβουλία δὲ
οὐ καλόν.

It is found in *De Praemiis et Poenis*,
§ 8 (II. 416).

Philo in Dam. Par. 405 and Cod. Reg.
Without the last sentence in Anton
Melissa, *Patr. Gr.* 136, col. 1128. Excepting this sentence the passage is *De
Sacrificiis Abelis et Caini* § 26 (I. 180).
Antony continues the quotation, as opposite.

Ascribed to Philo in Dam. Par. 438,
but wrongly through the omission of the
title *Nili* which is given in Cod. Reg. 923.

Dam. Par. 520 and Cod. Reg.
In Flaccum § 2 (II. 518).

Wrongly ascribed to Philo in Dam.
Par. 563. It is ascribed to Evagrius
in Cod. Reg. and in Maximus II. 647.
It is found in Evagrius (*Patr. Gr.* 40,
col. 1268), *Sententiae ad Virgines.*

Dam. Par. 563 and Cod. Reg.
Also Tischendorf, *Philonea*, p. 152,
e Cod. Cahirino.
This is *De Vit. Contemp.* § 2 (II. 474).

Dam. Par. 564 ascribed to Clem. Alex.
but in 715 as Philo.
Cod. Reg. 923, f. 20, reading ἕτερον by
itacism and αἱ κολακείαι; and Cod. Rup.
f. 275.
It is III. *Leg. Alleg.* 64 (I. 123).

Dam. Par. 564 immediately following
the preceding and ascribed to Philo, *Ad
Gaium*, but in Cod. Reg. this is given to

Ἡ συνεχὴς ἄσκησις ἐπιστήμην παγίαν
ἐργάζεται, ὡς ἀμαθίαν ἀμελετησία· καὶ
πάλιν αὔξει τὴν πεῖραν ἡ περὶ αὐτὴν τριβή.

Μυρίοι γοῦν ἀθλήσεως ὄκνῳ καὶ τὴν ἐκ
φύσεως ἰσχὺν ἐξέλυσαν.

Εἴ τις πάσας τὰς ἀρετὰς διὰ σπουδῆς καὶ
νήψεως ἐγκεκόλπισται, οὗτος βασιλεὺς χρη
ματίζει, καὶ ἂν ἰδιώτης τυγχάνοι.

Τῷ μὲν ἀγνοίᾳ τοῦ κρείττονος διαμαρτά
νοντι συγγνώμη δίδοται· ὁ δὲ ἐξ ἐπιστήμης
ἀδικῶν ἀπολογίαν οὐκ ἔχει, προεαλωκὼς ἐν
τῷ τοῦ συνειδότος δικαστηρίῳ.

Λάλει ἃ δεῖ καὶ ὅτε δεῖ, καὶ οὐκ ἀκούσεις
ἃ μὴ δεῖ.

Χρόνου φείδεσθαι καλόν.

Οὐκ ἂν εἴποι τις ἑταῖρον κόλακα· νόσος
γὰρ φιλίας ἡ κολακεία.

Τὰς τῶν ἀρχόντων εὐπραγίας μᾶλλον ἢ
τοὺς ἄρχοντας αὐτοὺς εἰώθασι θεραπεύειν οἱ
πλεῖστοι.

Clement, and the ascription Philo, *Ad Gaium*, is carried on to the next sentence which is edited as Nilus. It is *Ad Gaium* § 21 (II. 566); om. οἱ πλεῖστοι.

This is a very good specimen of the way the Titles in Collections of Parallels get misplaced. Almost all the confusions are between Philo and Clement or Evagrius or Nilus. See Zahn, *Supplementum Clementinum* 62.

Dam. Par. 594, headed *Nili:* but Cod. Reg. 923, f. 386, *Evagrii:* both wrongly, the title *Philonis* having dropped.

It is *Leg. Alleg.* III. § 34 (I. 108).

Also Pitra, *Anal. Sac.* II. 306 from Cod. Coislin. 276, f. 258, reading ἐπέξεισιν and referring to III. *Alleg. Sac. Leg.*

Τοῖς ἁμαρτάνουσιν οὐκ εὐθὺς ἐπέξεισιν (Cod. Reg. ἐπεξέρχεται) ὁ θεός, ἀλλὰ δίδωσιν χρόνον εἰς μετάνοιαν καὶ τὴν τοῦ σφάλματος ἴασίν τε καὶ ἐπανόρθωσιν.

The passage occurs again (and as Philo) in Dam. Par. 710 and Cod. Reg. fol. 360, also in Georg. Monach. (col. 1104), with the sentence opposite prefixed, which may be found in the same section of the Allegories.

Θεοῦ ἴδιον τὰ μὲν ἀγαθὰ προτείνειν καὶ φθάνειν δωρούμενον, τὰ δὲ κακὰ μὴ ῥᾳδίως ἐπάγειν.

Dam. Par. 693 referring to *De Abrahamo*.

It is *De Abrahamo* § 46 (II. 39).

Τῷ ἄντι πρῶτος ὁ σοφὸς ἀνθρώπων γένους, ὡς κυβερνήτης μὲν ἐν νηΐ, ἄρχων δὲ ἐν πόλει, στρατηγὸς δὲ ἐν πολέμῳ, ψυχὴ μὲν ἐν σώματι, νοῦς δ' ἐν ψυχῇ, καὶ πάλιν οὐρανὸς μὲν ἐν κόσμῳ, θεὸς δ' ἐν οὐρανῷ..... πρεσβύτερος μὲν οὖν ἔστι τε καὶ λεγέσθω ὁ ἀστεῖος, νεώτερος δὲ καὶ ἔσχατος πᾶς ἄφρων, τὰ νεωτεροποιὰ ἐν ἐσχατίαις ταττόμενα μετιών.

Dam. Par. 683 reading καὶ ἁμαρ. and Cod. Reg. f. 324 b.

The passage is *Ad Gaium* § 1 (II. 546).

Ἡ κόλασις νουθετεῖ καὶ σωφρονίζει πολλάκις μὲν καὶ τοὺς ἁμαρτάνοντας· εἰ δὲ μή, πάντως γοῦν τοὺς πλησιάζοντας. Αἱ γὰρ ἑτέρων τιμωρίαι, βελτιοῦσι τοὺς πολλούς, φόβῳ τοῦ μὴ παραπλήσια παθεῖν.

Wrongly ascribed to Philo in Dam. Par. 613. It is Didymus in Cod. Reg. and also in Maximus (II. 583).

Τὸ εἰδέναι τινὰ ὅτι ἀγνοεῖ, σοφίας ἐστίν, ὡς καὶ τὸ εἰδέναι ὅτι ἠδίκησε, δικαιοσύνης.

In Pitra, *Anal. Sac.* II. 348, it is given from Cod. Barber. 16, f. 117, as Clem. Alex., although Barber. I. 158, f. 135, says Didymus.

Dam. Par. 692 and Cod. Reg. f. 331. Also Anton Melissa (*Patr. Gr.* 136, col. 1096) with some variations, such as ἀκούουσα for ἄκουσα. Cod. Rup. f. 261. Also Georg. Monach. (Migne, *Patr. Gr.* 117, col. 1073) reading ἀπομάττει. It is *De Profugis* § 3 (I. 548).

Βλαβεραὶ αἱ τῶν ἀνοήτων συνουσίαι· καὶ ἄκουσα πολλάκις ἡ ψυχὴ τῆς ἐκείνων φρενοβλαβείας ἀπομάττεται τὰ εἴδωλα.

Dam. Par. 704 and Cod. Reg. Also John Monach. II. 668 = Rup. f. 267. From I. *Alleg. Sac. Leg.* § 15 (I. 53).

Οἴησις ἀκάθαρτον φύσει.

Dam. Par. 711 ascribed to Chrysostom. Cod. Reg. to Philo. *De Sacrificiis Abelis et Caini* § 34 (I. 185). Cod. Rup. f. 274 with preceding and following matter.

Χαλεπὸν ἐναντιοῦσθαι φύσει.

John Monach. II. 668 = Rup. f. 274, as Philo, but in Dam. Par. 713 referred to *Evagrius*, and in Cod. Reg. to Clem. Alex. *Quis Dives*, which belongs to a previous sentence. In Maximus II. 621 it is given to *Evagrius*.

Ἄτοπόν ἐστι διώκοντα τὰς τιμάς, φεύγειν τοὺς πόνους δι᾽ ὧν αἱ τιμαὶ [πεφύκασι γίνεσθαι, Dam. Par.].

Dam. Par. 776 (Cod. Rupef. f. 115 b). Anton Melissa, *Patr. Gr.* 136, col. 1061. *Ad Gaium* § 29 (II. 374).

Νεότης μετ᾽ ἐξουσίας αὐτοκράτους ὁρμαῖς ἀκαθέκτοις χρωμένη κακὸν δύσμαχον γίνεται.

Dam. Par. 777 (Cod. Rupef.). *Ad Gaium* § 40 (II. 592).

Ἀσθενέστεραί τέ πώς εἰσιν αἱ γνῶμαι τῶν γυναικῶν ἔξω τῶν αἰσθητῶν μηδὲν ἰσχύουσαι νοητὸν καταλαβεῖν.

Joh. Monach. (II. 661). *De Mundi Opificio* § 19 (I. 13).

Οὐ πάντα τῷ θνητῷ γένει γνώριμα.

H.

11

Joh. Monach. (II. 661), and Cod.
Reg. 923 (f. 358).
De Vitâ Mosis, I. § 52.

Βέλτιον τῶν μὴ καθ᾿ ἡδονὴν λόγων ἡ
ἀκίνδυνος ἡσυχία.

Of the seven unidentified fragments published by Mangey from Cod.
Barocc. 143, three have been already discussed. The following passage is
also known :

Cod. Barocc. (Mang. II. 674) Cod.
Reg. 923 f. 310 b as *in Decalogo.*
Tischendorf, *Philonea* p. 152 e Cod.
Cahirino and Maximus II. 674 and in
Cod. Rupef. f. 255. It is *De Decem
Oraculis* § 27 (II. 203). Cod. Reg. and
Tisch. read συναυξάνοντα.

Ἐγχρόνιζον ἔθος φύσεως κραταιότερόν
ἐστι, καὶ τὰ μικρὰ μὴ κωλυόμενα [ἁμαρτή-
ματα Cod. Reg.] φύεται καὶ ἐπιδίδοται
πρὸς μέγεθος αὐξάνοντα.

The following are identified from Mai, *Script. Vet.* VII. (Cod. Vat. 1553).

p. 96. Φίλωνος· ἐκ τοῦ ζ΄ καὶ η΄ τῶν νόμων
ἱερῶν ἀλληγορίας.

Κυρίως οὔτε ἐπὶ χρημάτων ἢ κτημάτων
περιουσίᾳ οὔτε ἐπὶ δόξης λαμπρότητι, οὐδὲ
συνόλως ἐπί τινι τῶν ἐκτὸς ψυχρῶν τε
ὄντων καὶ ἀβεβαίων καὶ ἐξ ἑαυτῶν τὰς

This is *Quod Det. Pot.* § 37 (II. 217).
Also in Dam. Par. 326 and Cod. Reg. 923 f. 55 all against the printed text in
reading ψυχρῶν and in adding the last five words.

φθορὰς δεχομένων χαίρειν ἔνεστι καὶ μὴν
οὐδὲ ἐπὶ ῥώμῃ καὶ εὐτονίᾳ καὶ τοῖς ἄλλοις
σώματος πλεονεκτήμασιν, ἃ καὶ τῶν φαυ-
λοτάτων ἐστὶ κοινὰ καὶ τοῖς ἔχουσι πολλάκις
ὄλεθρον ἀπαραίτητον ἤνεγκεν διὰ τὸ ἀσύστα-
τον καὶ ἀβέβαιον.

p. 99. Φίλωνος· ἐκ τῶν η΄ καὶ θ΄ νόμων
ἱερῶν ἀλληγορίας.

Παιδείας σύμβολον ἡ ῥάβδος· ἄνευ γὰρ

This is *De Posteritate Caini* § 28 (I. 243).
Also in Dam. Par. 435 reading δυσωπηθῆναι and Cod. Reg. fol. 116 b referring
to Clem. Alex. *Strom.* α΄, reading as above, also ὧν for ἐνίων.

δυσωπῆναι (l. δυσωπηθῆναι) καὶ περὶ ἐνίων
ἐπιπληχθῆναι, νουθεσίαν ἐκδέξασθαι καὶ
σωφρονισμόν, ἀμήχανον.

p. 99. Εὐηθεῖς ὅσοι τῶν διδασκάλων μὴ
πρὸς τὴν τῶν γνωρίμων δύναμιν, ἀλλὰ πρὸς
τὴν ἑαυτῶν ὑπερβάλλουσαν ἕξιν ἐπιχειροῦσι
ποιεῖσθαι τὰς ὑφηγήσεις· οὐκ εἰδότες ὡς
διδασκαλίας ἐπίδειξις μακρῷ διενήνοχεν· ὁ
μὲν γὰρ ἐπιδεικνύμενος τῇ τῆς παρούσης

ἕξεως εὐφορίᾳ καταχρώμενος ἀνεμποδίστως
τὰ ἐν μακρῷ χρόνῳ πονηθέντα οἰκεῖα (cod.
οἰκεῖ·) καθάπερ γραφέων ἔργα πλαστῶν εἰς
τοὐμφανὲς προφέρει, τὸν παρὰ τῶν πολλῶν
θηρώμενος ἔπαινον· οὐδὲ διδάσκειν ἐπιχειρῶν
οἷά τις ἰατρὸς ἀγαθὸς οὐ πρὸς [τὸ τῆς

τέχνης μέγεθος, ἀλλὰ πρὸς] τὴν τοῦ θεραπευομένου δύναμιν ἀφορῶν οὐχ ὅσα ἐκ τῆς τέχνης πεπόρικεν, ἀμύθητα ταῦτά γε, ἀλλ'

ὅσον τῷ κάμνοντι δεῖ στοχαζόμενος (l. στοχαζόμενον) τοῦ μέτρου προφέρων δίδωσιν.

This is *De Posteritate Caini*, § 42 (I. 252). The passage in brackets is omitted by ὅμοιοτ. For the rest compare the printed text.

p. 103. Φίλωνος· ἐκ τῶν περὶ τοῦ ἱεροῦ.

Μεταδοτέον οὐ πᾶσι πάντων, ἀλλὰ τῶν ἐφαρμοζόντων τοῖς ληψομένοις. εἰ δὲ μή, τὸ κάλλιστον καὶ λυσιτελέστατον τῶν ἐν τῷ

βίῳ τάξις ἀναιρεθήσεται ὑπὸ τῆς βλαβερωτάτης παρευημερηθεῖσα συγχύσεως......τὰ ὅμοια τοῖς ἀναξίοις ἀπονέμειν ἄνισον· τὸ δὲ ἄνισον πηγὴ κακῶν.

De Monarchia II. 13 (II. 231), also found in Cod. Reg. 923 fol. 334 with slight variation, and adding from the same passage as follows:

Εἰ γὰρ ἴσον...οἴσονται ναῦται κυβερνήταις, ἴσον δὲ ἐν ταῖς μακραῖς τριήρεσι καὶ ναυάρχαις ἐρέται καὶ τὸ ἐπιβατικόν, ἔν τε στρατοπέδοις ἴσον ἱππεῖς μὲν χιλιάρχοις ὁπλῖται δὲ ταξιάρχαις, λοχαγοὶ δὲ στρατηγοῖς, ἐν δὲ πόλεσι δικασταῖς κρινόμενοι καὶ

βουλευταὶ προβούλοις καὶ συνόλως ἄρχουσιν ἰδιῶται, ταραχαὶ καὶ στάσεις γενήσονται, καὶ ἡ λόγῳ ἰσότης τὴν δι' ἔργων ἀνισότητα γεννήσει· τὸ γὰρ τὰς (add ὁμοίας) ἀξίας ἀνομοίοις ἀπονέμειν ἄνισον· τὸ δὲ ἄνισον πηγὴ κακῶν.

p. 107. Φίλωνος ἐκ τοῦ ζ καὶ ή τῆς νόμων ἱερῶν ἀλληγορίας.

Ἐν ᾗ μὲν ψυχῇ τὸ ἐκτὸς αἰσθητὸν ὡς μέγιστον ἀγαθῶν τετίμηται, ἐν ταύτῃ [add λόγος] ἀστεῖος οὐχ εὑρίσκεται· εἰ δὲ ἐκπεριπατεῖ (l. ἐμπεριπατεῖ) ὁ θεός, τὸ ἐκτὸς αἰσθητὸν ἀγαθὸν οὐχ ὑπείληπται.
Quod Det. Pot. § 2 (I. 192).

III. *Alleg. Sac. Leg.* § 25 (I. 103) much more at length in Cod. Rupef. f. 112 b.

p. 107. Φίλωνος· ἐκ τοῦ ζ καὶ η' τῆς νόμων ἱερῶν ἀλληγορίας.

Πάνυ εὐήθεις οἱ πρὸς τὸ πέρας ἧς τινος οὖν ἐπιστήμης ἀφικέσθαι διενοήθησαν· τὸ γὰρ ἐγγὺς εἶναι δόξαν μακρὰν ἄγαν τοῦ τέλους ἀφέστηκεν· ἐπεὶ τέλειος τῶν γεγονότων οὐδεὶς πρὸς οὐδὲν μάθημα, ἀλλὰ τοσοῦτον ἐνδεῖ ὅσον κομιδῇ νήπιος παῖς ἄρτι τὸ μανθάνειν ἀρχόμενος πρὸς πολιὸν ἤδη τὴν ἡλικίαν ἅμα καὶ τέχνης ὑφηγητήν.
De Posteritate Caini, § 44 (I. 255).

p. 107. Φίλωνος· ἐκ τῶν γ' τῆς νόμων ἱερῶν ἀλληγορίας.

Βασιλεὺς ἐχθρὸν τυράννῳ· ὅτι ὁ μὲν νόμων, ὁ δὲ ἀνομίας ἐστὶν εἰσηγητής.

The following are from Pitra, *Anal. Sac.* II.

p. xxiii. From Reg. 77 f. 660. Ἐσχάρα ἄνθραξι, καὶ ξύλα πυρί, ἀνὴρ δὲ λοίδορος εἰς ταραχὴν μάχης.
This is Prov. xxvi. 21.

p. xxiii. From the same. Τοῦ πυρὸς ἡ δύναμις, ἀπουσίᾳ μὲν ὕλης, ἡσυχάζει, παρουσίᾳ δέ, ἀνακαίεται.
Philo, *De Sobrietate* § 9.

p. 305. From Cod. Coislin. 276 f. 259 b. Ἐκ τῆς κατὰ Μωσέα κοσμοποιίας.

Οὐχ ὡς πέφυκεν ὁ θεὸς εὖ ποιεῖν οὕτω καὶ τὸ γενόμενον εὖ πάσχειν· ἐπεὶ τοῦ μὲν αἱ δυνάμεις ὑπερβάλλουσιν, τὸ δὲ ἀσθενέστερόν ἐστι δέξασθαι τὸ μέγεθος αὐτῶν.
It is *De Mundi Opificio*, § 6 (I. 5), also in Cod. Rupef. f. 277.

p. 305. From Cod. Coislin. 276 f. 138 et 151.

Ἴδιον θεοῦ· τὰ ἀδύνατα παντὶ γενητῷ μόνῳ δυνατὰ καὶ κατὰ χειρός [add εἶναι].
Vit. Mosis, I. § 31 (II. 108).

p. 306. From Cod. Coislin. 276 f. 258. Θεοῦ ἴδιον, τὰ μὲν ἀγαθὰ προτείνειν καὶ φθάνειν δωρούμενον· τὰ δὲ κακὰ μὴ ῥᾳδίως ἐπάγειν.

III. *Alleg. Sac. Leg.* § 34 (I. 108). Also in Dam. Par. 710 and Cod. Reg. 923 f. 361.

p. 306. From Cod. Coislin. 276 f. 258. Ἐκ τοῦ ἡ΄ καὶ θ΄ τῆς νόμων ἱερῶν ἀλληγορίας
(also in Rupef. 178 b.)

Ἀναζητοῦσιν τοῖς φιλοθέοις τὸ ὄν, κἂν μηδέποτε εὕρωσιν, συγχαίρομεν· ἱκανὴ γὰρ ἐξ ἑαυτῆς προσευφραίνειν ἡ τοῦ καλοῦ ζήτησις κἂν ἀπέχῃ τὸ τέλος αὐτῆς.
De Posteritate Caini, § 6 (I. 230).

p. 306. From Cod. Coislin. 276. Ibid. Ἐκ τῶν αὐτῶν.

Τὸ σὺν θεῷ πανεπαίνετον· τὸ δὲ ἄνευ θεοῦ, φευκτόν.
De Cherubim § 7 (I. 143), the text reading ψεκτόν.

p. 306. From Cod. Coislin. 276 f. 259. ἐκ τοῦ ἡ΄ καὶ θ΄ τῆς νόμων ἀλληγορίας.

Οὐ πάντα πᾶσιν χαριστέον, ἀλλὰ τὰ οἰκεῖα τῇ τῶν δεομένων χρείᾳ·...ἀλλὰ μηδὲ ὅσα δύνασαι, χαρίζου, φησὶν ὁ ἱερὸς λόγος, ἀλλ' ὡς ἱκανός ἐστιν ὁ δεχόμενος δέξασθαι· ἢ οὐχ ὁρᾷς ὅτι καὶ ὁ θεός, οὐκ ἀναλογοῦντας ἡμᾶς τῷ μεγέθει τῆς αὐτοῦ τελειότητος, χρησμοὺς ἀναφθέγγεται πρὸς τὴν τῶν ὠφεληθησομένων δύναμιν; ἐπεὶ καὶ τίς ἂν ἐχώρησεν θεοῦ λόγων ἰσχύν, τῶν ἁπάσης κρειττόνων ἀκοῆς;......τὸ γὰρ γεννητὸν οὐδέποτε μὲν ἀμοιρεῖ τῶν τοῦ θεοῦ χαρισμάτων, ἐπεὶ πάντως ἂν διέφθαρτο, φέρειν δὲ τὴν πολλὴν καὶ ἄφθονον αὐτῶν ῥώμην ἀδυνατεῖ· διὸ βουλόμενος ὄνησιν ἡμᾶς ἔχειν ὧν ἐπιδίδωσιν, πρὸς τὴν τῶν λαμβανόντων ἰσχὺν τὰ διδόμενα σταθμᾶται.

De Posteritate Caini, § 43 (I. 253 sq.), also Cod. Rupef. f. 276 b.

p. 307. Οὐκ ἐν χρόνῳ τὸ αἴτιον οὐδὲ συνόλως ἐν τόπῳ, ἀλλ' ὑπεράνω καὶ τόπου καὶ χρόνου.

De Posteritate Caini, § 5 (I. 229), from Cod. Coislin. 276 fol. 30 (ἐκ τῆς νόμ. ἀλληγ.) and fol. 44 (*De profugis*), also given in Cod. Rupef. f. 20, ἐκ τῆς νόμων ἀλληγορίας, reading οὖν ὅλως.

p. 308. From Cod. Coislin. 276 f. 47. Ἐκ τοῦ περὶ γενέσεως Ἄβελ.

Ἄγευστον παθῶν ἢ κακιῶν ψυχὴν εὑρεῖν, σπανιώτατον.
De Sacrificiis Abelis et Caini, § 34 (I. 185), and Cod. Rupef. f. 67 b.

Ἀδύνατον ἀπ' ἀρχῆς ἀνθρώπων γενέσεως ἄχρι τοῦ παρόντος βίου κατὰ τὸ παντελὲς ἀνυπαίτιον εὑρεῖν θνητῷ σώματι ἐνδεδεμένον.

De Mutatione Nominum, § 4 (I. 583), also Cod. Rupef. f. 24, headed περὶ γενέσεως Ἄβελ, and reading συνδεδεμένον, om. γενέσεως.

p. 309. From Cod. Coislin. 276 f. 245.
Φίλωνος, ἐκ τοῦ περὶ μέθης.

Οὐ δύναται τῶν φαινομένων ἀγαθῶν κατεξανίστασθαι ἡ τεθηλυμμένη ψυχή, πλούτου καὶ δόξης τυχόν, ἢ ἀρχῆς ἢ τιμῆς· ἀλλ' ἕως μὲν οὐδὲν τούτων πάρεστιν, ὑψηγοροῦμεν, ὡς ὀλιγοδείας ἑταῖροι, τὸν αὐταρκέστατον καὶ ἐλευθέροις καὶ εὐγενέσιν ἁρμόττοντα περιποιούσης βίον· ἐπειδὰν δὲ τῶν εἰρημένων ἐλπὶς αὐτῷ μόνον ἢ ἐλπίδος αὔρα βραχεῖα καταπνεύσῃ διελεγχόμεθα· ὑπείκοντες γὰρ εὐθὺς ἐνδιδόαμεν καὶ ἀντιβῆναι καὶ ἀντισχεῖν οὐ δυνάμεθα. Προδοθέντες δὲ ὑπὸ τῶν φίλων αἰσθήσεων ὅλην τὴν τῆς ψυχῆς συμμαχίαν ἐκλείπομεν καὶ οὐκέτι λανθάνοντες, ἀλλ' ἤδη φανερῶς αὐτομολοῦμεν.
This is *de Ebrietate,* § 14 (I. 365).

p. 309. From Cod. Coislin. 276 f. 138 and 259, ἐκ τοῦ περὶ τῶν μετονομαζομένων.

Οὐχ ἃ δοῦναι θεόν, ταῦτα καὶ ἀνθρώπῳ λαμβάνειν δυνατόν, ἐπειδὴ τῷ μὲν πλεῖστα καὶ μέγιστα χαρίσασθαι ῥᾴδιον, ἡμῖν δὲ οὐκ εὐμαρὲς τὰς προτεινομένας δέξασθαι δωρεάς.
De Mutatione Nominum § 39 (I. 611) and in Cod. Rup. f. 277.

p. 309. From Cod. Coislin. 276 f. 223.

Οὐ λήψῃ, φησίν, τὸ ὄνομα τοῦ θεοῦ σου ἐπὶ ματαίῳ· τὰ μὲν οὖν τῆς τάξεως γνώριμα τοῖς διανοίᾳ ὀξυδορκοῦσιν· ὄνομα γὰρ ἀεὶ δεύτερον ὑποκειμένου πράγματος, σκιᾷ παραπλήσιον, ἢ παρέπεται σώματι. Προειπὼν οὖν πρὸ τῆς ὑπάρξεως καὶ τιμῆς τοῦ ὑπάρχοντος, ἑπομένως τῷ τῆς ἀκολουθίας εἱρμῷ τὰ πρέποντα καὶ περὶ τῆς κλήσεως εὐθὺς παρήγγειλεν.
De Decem Oraculis, § 17 (II. 194).

p. 310. From Cod. Coislin. 276 f. 34, Ἐκ τῶν δι' ἐπῶν κεφαλαίων.
Αὐτὸς πάντα οἶδεν, ὁ ποιήσας τάδε ἀπ' ἀρχῆς μόνος.

Pitra remarks on this: "sub ambiguo titulo brevis locus caeteris miscetur Philoni jure ascriptis. Nec puto ibi senarios latere." The ascription of passages in Florilegia is generally uncertain and the titles which are often written in after the body of the text have a tendency to slip from their proper positions. But in this case the ascription ought to be correct, since according to Pitra the surrounding sentences are genuine Philonea. It is also found without title in Cod. Rupef. f. 51, following a passage from Philo and preceding one from the Clementine Homilies.

As to there being any latent iambics in the passage, it is clearly on the contrary a fragment of a hexameter verse (ἔπος) capable of immediate restoration. But now the interesting feature of the verse is that it is found in one of the Sibylline fragments (l. 16 of the second fragment as published by Friedlieb):

$$τίς\ γὰρ\ σάρξ\ δύναται\ θνητῶν\ γνῶναι\ τάδ'\ ἄπαντα ;$$
$$ἀλλ'\ αὐτὸς\ μόνος\ οἶδεν\ ὁ\ ποιήσας\ τάδ'\ ἀπ'\ ἀρχῆς.$$

It is universally agreed that this fragment is the work of an Alexandrian, this conclusion being suggested at once by the ridicule heaped on the worship of cat, crocodile and serpent. The time, however, of its production is not so generally agreed on: for while some hold it to be as old as the earliest parts of the third book of the Sibylline oracles, others depress it to the time of Trajan. Between the limits intimated we may safely take it to lie, and it will be remembered that the fragment is printed from Theophilus, *ad Autolycum*, II. 36, and that reference is also made thereto by Clem. Alex. and Lactantius. We may be sure, therefore, of the antiquity of the Preface quoted. Nor is it without interest that Gfrörer in his *Philo*, II. 123, has taken especial pains to point out the similarity of language and ideas between Philo and the author of the Preface, with the view of proving the indebtedness of Philo to writers who have gone before him! and certainly the parallels can be made very close. We shall simply say that we do not see any reason why this Proemium may not be referred very nearly to Philo in time, place, language, and range of ideas[1].

For the meaning of the term κεφάλαια we may compare Suidas, s. v. *Phocylides*, ἔγραψεν ἔπη καὶ ἐλεγείας, παραινέσεις ἤτοι γνώμας. ἅς τινες κεφάλαια ἐπιγράφουσιν.

---

[1] Friedlieb, *Orac. Sibyll.* c. IX. has made a mistake in saying that Philo has spoken of a Chaldean Sibyl: referring to Cramer. *Anecd. Paris.* I. 332. What Cramer has quoted is as follows: ὅτι ἡ Ἰουδαία Σίβυλλα καὶ Χάλδις ἐκαλεῖτο· καὶ γὰρ ὁ Φίλων τὸν Μωσέως βίον ἀναγράφων Χαλδαῖον εἶναι αὐτὸν λέγει κτλ.

p. 311.   Cod. Urbin. 125 f. 304.   Φίλωνος.

Λέγω δὲ μὴ καθαρούς, ὅσοι ἢ παιδείας εἰσάπαν ἄγευστοι διετέλεσαν, ἢ πλαγίως, ἀλλὰ μὴ ἐπ' εὐθεῖαν, αὐτὴν ἐδέξαντο, κάλλος τὸ σοφίας εἰς τὸ σοφιστείας αἶσχος μεταχαράξαντες· οὗτοι νοητὸν φῶς ἰδεῖν οὐ δυνάμενοι, δι' ἀσθένειαν τοῦ κατὰ ψυχὴν ὄμματος, ὃ ταῖς μαρμαρυγαῖς πέφυκεν ἐπισκιάζεσθαι, καθάπερ ἐν νυκτὶ διάγοντες ἀπιστοῦσι τοῖς ἐν ἡμέρᾳ ζῶσιν.

Quod omnis probus, § 1 (II. 445).

p. 311.   From the same.

Οὐ παντός ἐστι κτῆμα σωφροσύνη ἀλλὰ μόνου τοῦ θεοφιλοῦς.

II. *Alleg. Sac. Leg.* § 20 (I. 80).

p. 311.   From the same.

Ἡδονῇ ἐναντίον σωφροσύνη· ποικίλῳ πάθει, ποικίλη ἀρετή.

II. *Alleg. Sac. Leg.* § 20 (I. 80).

p. 311.   From the same.

Ὄντως ὑπὸ θεοῦ σώζεται, ὁ ἀποπίπτων τῶν παθῶν, καὶ στερίζων τῆς ἐνεργείας αὐτῶν. Μὴ πέσοι τοιοῦτον πτῶμά μου ἡ ψυχὴ καὶ μηδέποτε ἀνασταίη ἐπὶ τὸ ἵππειον καὶ σκιρτητικὸν πάθος ἵνα θεοῦ σωτηρίαν περιμείνασα εὐδαιμονήσῃ......ἐὰν ἀπαθεία κατάσχῃ τὴν ψυχήν, τέλειον εὐδαιμονήσει.

II. *Alleg. Sac. Leg.* § 25 (I. 85).   Μὴ πέσοι is an evident error for πέσοι.

p. 313.   From Cod. Vat. 1611 f. 232.   Φίλωνος.

Ἔτι ἐν τῷ νόμῳ τῆς λέπρας ὁ μέγας τὰ πάντα Μωσῆς, τὴν μὲν κίνησιν καὶ ἐπίπλειον αὐτῆς φορὰν καὶ χύσιν ἀκάθαρτον, τὴν δὲ ἠρεμίαν καθαρὰν ἀναγράφει· φησὶ γὰρ ὅτι ἐὰν διαχέηται ἐν τῷ δέρματι, μιανεῖ ὁ ἱερεύς· ἐὰν δὲ κατὰ χώραν μείνῃ τὸ τηλαύγημα καὶ μὴ διαχέηται, καθαριεῖ· ὥστε τὴν μὲν ἡσυχίαν καὶ μονὴν κακίας καὶ παθῶν κατὰ ψυχήν, ταῦτα γὰρ αἰνίττεται διὰ λέπρας, οὐχ ὑπαίτιον εἶναι· τὴν δὲ κίνησιν καὶ φορὰν ὑπαίτιον δὴ ὄντως· τὸ παραπλήσιον καὶ ἐν τοῖς πρὸς τὸν Κάϊν λόγοις περιέχεται σημειωδέστερον· λέγεται γὰρ πρὸς αὐτόν· Ἥμαρτες, ἡσύχασον τοῦ μὲν ἁμαρτεῖν, ὅτι κινεῖσθαι καὶ ἐνεργεῖν κατὰ τὴν κακίαν ἦν καὶ ὄντως ἐνόχου· τὸ δὲ ἡσυχάζειν, ὅτι ἴσχεσθαι καὶ ἤρεμον, ἀνυπαίτιον καὶ σωτήριον.

De Sobrietate, § 10 (I. 400).

Observe also that the whole of this passage is quoted in Corderius, *Catena in Lucam,* c. XVII. 12.

p. 348.   From Cod. Barber. I. 6 f. 92.   Ascribed to Clem. Alex.

Ἀμήχανον τὰ μεγάλα πρὸ τῶν μικρῶν παιδευθῆναι.

This passage is *not* Clement, but Philo, *Vit. Mosis,* I. § 11 (II. 90).

It is also found in Dam. Par. 363 and Cod. Reg. 923 f. 76 as *De Vit. Mosis,* and in Anton Melissa (*Patr. Gr.* 136, col. 938), all reading παιδευθῆναι for the τελεσθῆναι of the text.

p. 349. Ὅσον δοκεῖ μᾶλλον εἶναι (καλὸν γὰρ ἀεὶ) τῶν κρειττόνων ἢ τῶν χειρόνων ἀκολουθεῖν διὰ βελτιώσεως ἐλπίδα.

So Pitra prints from Cod. Barber. v. 11, f. 97 as a fragment of Clem. Alex.

Now Grabe, *Spicilegium* I. 269, claims this passage for Philo, following Cotelerius *ad* I *Ep. Clem.* § 48, who gives his authority in the Codex Claromontanus of the Eclogues of John Damascene: i.e. our Codex Rupefucaldi.

Anton Melissa (*Patr. Gr.* 136, col. 1093) also gives the reference to Philo.

The passage itself may be found in *De Decem Oraculis,* § 23 (II. 200), not however as given by Pitra, but as in Grabe and Anton Melissa.

Καλὸν γὰρ ἀεὶ τῷ κρείττονι τὸ χεῖρον ἀκολουθεῖν διὰ βελτιώσεως ἐλπίδα.

p. 349. Almost immediately following the preceding passage and either from the same codex or from Barber. I. 6, f. 119, Pitra gives as a passage of Clem. Alex.:

Μηδαμῶς τὴν φύσιν αἰτιώμεθα· πάντα γὰρ βίον ἡδὺν ἢ ἀηδῆ ἡ συνήθεια ποιεῖ.

In Maximus (II. 674) this passage is referred to Philo; and although I have not yet identified the extract, I incline to believe that Maximus is right.

In Cod. Reg. 923, f. 310 b. it is referred to Clem. Rom.: the preceding passage being from the Clem. Hom., and the following one from Philo.

The following are identified from Tischendorf, *Philonea.* 152 sqq.   From Cod. Vat. 746, f. 11.

Διατί τὸν ἐν τῷ σαββάτῳ συλλέξαντα ξύλα καταλευσθῆναι προσέταξεν; Ἀποφαίνεται ὁ θεὸς ὅτι θνήσκειν ὀφείλει καὶ οὐχ ἑτέρως ἢ καταλευσθείς, ἐπειδήπερ ὁ νοῦς εἰς κωφὴν λίθον μετέβαλεν εἰργασμένῳ τελεώτατον παρανόμημα.

De Vitâ Mosis, III. § 28 (Mang. II. 168).

From a Cairo MS.

Αἱ ἐκ χρημάτων καὶ κτημάτων ἐπιθυμίαι τοὺς χρόνους ἀναλίσκουσι· χρόνου δὲ φείδεσθαι καλον.

Tischendorf identifies this as *De Vit. Contemp.* § 2 (II. 474).   The last sentence has been already given from Dam. Par. 563.   The printed text omits ἐκ and reads ἐπιμέλειαι.   Also Maxim. II. 568.

From the same.

Τὰ καλὰ κἂν φθόνῳ πρὸς ὀλίγον ἐπισκιασθῇ χρόνον, ἐπὶ καιρῷ λυθέντα αὖθις ἀναλάμπει. *De Vitâ Mosis* II. § 5 (II. 138). Also in Cod. Reg. f. 354 b. Maxim. II. 658.

p. 154. Κακίας ἔξοδος ἀρετῆς εἴσοδον ἐργάζεται, ὡς καὶ τοὐναντίον ὑπεκστάντος ἀγαθοῦ τὸ ἐφεδρεῦον κακὸν εἰσέρχεται.

De Sacrif. Abelis et Caini § 39 (I. 190).

The passage is also found in Dam. Par. 438 (reading ἀποστάντος, also ἐπεισέρχεται with the printed text). Also Maxim. (II. 530) r. ἐπεισέρχεται.

Ἄτοπον γὰρ ἁμαρτήμασιν ἐνόχους εἶναι τοὺς τοῖς ἄλλοις τὰ δίκαια βραβεύειν ἀξιοῦντας...καὶ τὸ μὲν δωροδοκεῖν ἐπ᾽ ἀδίκοις παμπονήρων ἐστὶν ἀνθρώπων ἔργον, τὸ

δ᾽ ἐπὶ δικαίοις ἐφ᾽ ἡμισείᾳ πονηρευομένων, (also with some extension, the first sentence in Rupef. 175 b).

De Judice, §§ 1, 3 (II. 345, 346).

p. 155. Ἐγκρατείας μὲν ἴδιον ὑγίεια καὶ ἰσχύς· ἀκρασίας δὲ ἀσθένεια καὶ νόσος γειτνιῶσα θανάτῳ.

Identified by Tischendorf as *Ad Gaium*, § 2 (II. 548). Also Rupef. f. 217.

p. 155. Πέφυκεν ὁ ἄφρων ἀεὶ ἐπὶ τὸν ὀρθὸν λόγον κινούμενος ἠρεμίᾳ καὶ ἀναπαύσει δυσμενὴς εἶναι.

Also in Cod. Rupef. f. 138 b. *De Posteritate Caini* § 8 (I. 230).

The following are the identified but not previously mentioned passages from the Cod. Reg. 923. For convenience we will take them in the order of the printed editions of Philo, observing that in the nature of the case there are repeated not a few passages which are given in the printed Parallels of Lequien and which (because they were identified by Mangey and used by him in his text) do not appear amongst the published fragments.

De Mundi Opificio.

Fol. 334 b § 7 (Mangey I. 6). Καλὸν οὐδὲν ἐν ἀταξίᾳ. τάξις δὲ ἀκολουθία καὶ εἱρμός ἐστι προηγουμένων τινῶν καὶ ἐπο-μένων, εἰ μὴ ἄρα καὶ τοῖς ἀποτελέσμασιν, ἀλλά τοι ταῖς τῶν τεκταινομένων ἐπινοίαις.

Fol. 106 b § 41 (I. 29). Ἐκ τοῦ κατὰ Μωσέα. Τὰ κατὰ γαστρὸς βρέφη μησὶν ἑπτὰ ζωογονεῖσθαι πέφυκεν, ὡς παραδοξό-τατόν τι συμβαίνειν· γίνεται γὰρ ἑπτάμηνα γόνιμα, τῶν ὀκταμήνων ἐπίπαν ζωογονεῖσ-θαι μὴ δυναμένων.

Also Dam. Par. 407.

Fol. 375 b § 46 (I. 32). Τοῦ τεχνίτου χοῦν λαβόντος καὶ μορφὴν ἀνθρωπίνην ἐξ αὐτοῦ διαπλάσαντος τὴν ψυχὴν ὑπ' οὐδενὸς εἴληφε γεννητοῦ τὸ παράπαν, ἀλλ' ἐκ τοῦ πατρὸς καὶ ἡγεμόνος τῶν ἁπάντων. Τὸ γὰρ "ἐνεφύσησεν" οὐδὲν ἦν ἕτερον ἢ πνεῦμα θεῖον ἀπὸ τῆς μακαρίας καὶ εὐδαίμονος φύσεως ἐκείνης ἀποικίαν τὴν ἐνθάδε στειλάμενον ἐπ' ὠφελείᾳ τοῦ γένους ἡμῶν.

Fol. 376 § 47 (I. 33). Ὁ δημιουργὸς ἀγαθὸς

ἦν τά τε ἄλλα καὶ τὴν ἐπιστήμην,......ὅτι δὲ καὶ περὶ τὴν ψυχὴν ἄριστος ἦν, φανερόν. Οὐδενὶ γὰρ ἑτέρῳ πράγματι τῶν ἐν γενέσει πρὸς τὴν κατασκευὴν αὐτῆς ἔοικε χρήσασθαι, μόνον δέ, ὡς εἶπον, τῷ ἑαυτοῦ λόγῳ. Διὸ φησιν ἀπεικόνισμα καὶ μίμημα γεγενῆσθαι τούτου τὸν ἄνθρωπον ἐμπνευσθέντα εἰς τὸ πρόσωπον, ἔνθα τῶν αἰσθήσεων ὁ τόπος... Ἀνάγκη δὲ παγκάλου παραδείγματος πάγκαλον εἶναι τὸ μίμημα.

Alleg. Sac. Leg. I.

Fol. 376 § 29 (I. 62). Ὁ νοῦς ἐν ἑκάστῳ ἡμῶν τὰ μὲν ἄλλα δύναται καταλαβεῖν, ἑαυτὸν δὲ γνωρίσαι ἀδυνάτως ἔχει· ὥσπερ γὰρ ὁ ὀφθαλμὸς τὰ μὲν ἄλλα ὁρᾷ, ἑαυτὸν δὲ οὐχ ὁρᾷ· οὕτω καὶ ὁ νοῦς [τὰ μὲν ἄλλα

νοεῖ], ἑαυτὸν δὲ (Cod. μὲν) οὐ καταλαμβάνει. εἰπάτω γάρ τις, τί ἐστιν καὶ ποταπός, πνεῦμα ἢ πῦρ ἢ αἷμα ἢ ἀὴρ ἢ ἕτερόν τι· ἢ τοσοῦτόν γε, ὅτι σῶμά ἐστιν ἢ πάλιν ἀσώματον.

Referred to *Vita Mosis*, and in Cod. Rupef. f. 279 b, ἐκ τοῦ περὶ Μωυσέως.

Fol. 268 § 32 (I. 64). Σπάνιον μέν ἐστι τὸ ἀγαθὸν τὸ δὲ κακὸν πολυχοῦν. διὰ τοῦτο

σοφὸν μὲν πιστὸν εὑρεῖν ἕνα ἔργον, φαύλων δὲ πλῆθος ἀναρίθμητον.

Ascribed to *Didymus*: but in Rupef. 230 b Φίλωνος.

Alleg. Sac. Leg. III.

Fol. 42 b § 2 (I. 88). Πάντα πεπλήρωκεν ὁ θεὸς καὶ διὰ πάντων διῆλθεν, καὶ κενὸν οὐδὲν οὐδὲ ἔρημον ἀπολέλοιπεν ἑαυτοῦ·

ποῖον γάρ τις τόπον ἐφέξει ἐν ᾧ οὐχ ὁ θεὸς ἔστι; πρὸ γὰρ παντὸς γενητοῦ ὁ θεὸς ἔστι καὶ εὑρίσκεται πανταχοῦ.

Also Dam. Par. 301, and Cod. Rupef. f. 51 with slight variations.

Fol. 129 § 3 (I. 89). Ἀξίως γὰρ οὐδεὶς τὸν θεὸν τιμᾷ ἀλλὰ δικαίως μόνον· ὁπότε γὰρ οὐδὲ τοῖς γονεῦσιν ἴσας ἀποδοῦναι χάριτας

ἐνδέχεται—ἀντιγεννῆσαι γὰρ οὐχ οἷόν τε τούτους...

Headed Philo. Dam. Par. 427 and Maximus (II. 605), also Rupef. f. 153 b.

Fol. 45 b § 15 (I. 96). Εἰ ζητεῖς θεόν, ὦ διάνοια, ἐξελθοῦσα ἀπὸ σαυτῆς ἀναζήτει.

Dam. Par. 304 and much more at length in Cod. Rupef. 55 a.

Fol. 369 b § 28 (I.104). Ἡ χαρὰ εὐπάθεια ψυχῆς ἐστίν· οὐ γὰρ ὅταν παροῦσα δραστηρίως ἐνεργῇ μόνον καὶ εὐφραίνει, ἀλλὰ καὶ ὅταν ἐλπίζηται, προγανοῖ—ἐξαίρετον

γὰρ καὶ τοῦτ' ἔχει—καὶ ἴδιον καὶ κοινὸν ἀγαθόν ἐστιν—ὥστε, κυρίως εἰπεῖν, μηδὲν εἶναι ἀγαθόν, ᾧ μὴ πρόσεστι χαρά.

Also in Cod. Rupef. f. 276 b, wrongly referred to *De Mut. Nom.*

De Posteritate Caini.

Fol. 331 b § 41 (ι. 252). Μόνος ὁ σοφὸς ἐλεύθερός τε καὶ ἄρχων, καὶ ἂν μυρίους τοῦ σώματος ἔχῃ δεσπότας.

De Ebrietate.

Fol. 16 b § 7 (ι. 361). Ἐσταλμένον καὶ σπάνιον τὸ ἀγαθόν.

Also Cod. Rupef. f. 39 which gives the preceding sentence in the text and the heading ἐκ τοῦ περὶ μέθης α΄.

Fol. 201 § 42 (ι. 384). Γίνεται θηρίον ὃ καλεῖται τάρανδος, μέγεθος μὲν βοός, ἐλάφῳ δὲ τὸν τοῦ προσώπου τύπον ἐμφερέστατον. Λόγος ἔχει τοῦτο μεταβάλλειν ἀεὶ τὰς τρίχας πρός τε τὰ χωρία καὶ τὰ δένδρα οἷς

Also Dam. Par. 531.

ἂν ἐγγὺς ἵσταται, ὡς διὰ τὴν τῆς χροίας ὁμοιότητα λανθάνειν τοὺς ἐντυγχάνοντας καὶ ταύτῃ μᾶλλον ἢ τῇ περὶ τὸ σῶμα ἀλκῇ δυσθήρατον εἶναι. (ἐκ τοῦ περὶ μέθης.)

Quis Rerum Div. Haeres.

Fol. 265 § 2 (ι. 473). Πότε ἄγει παρρησίαν οἰκέτης πρὸς δεσπότην; ἆρ᾽ οὐχ ὅταν ἠδικηκότι μὲν ἑαυτῷ μηδὲν συνειδῇ, πάντα δὲ ὑπὲρ τοῦ κεκτημένου καὶ λέγοντι καὶ πράττοντι; πότε οὖν ἄξιον καὶ τὸν τοῦ θεοῦ δοῦλον ἐλευθεροστομεῖν πρὸς τὸν ἑαυτοῦ τε καὶ τοῦ παντὸς δεσπότην καὶ ἡγεμόνα; ἢ ὅταν ἁμαρτημάτων καθαρεύοι (sic Cod.) καὶ τὸ φιλοδέσποτον ἐκ τοῦ συνειδότος κρίνῃ, πλείονι χαρᾷ χρώμενος ἐπὶ τῷ θεράπων γενέσθαι θεοῦ ἢ εἰ τοῦ παντὸς ἀνθρώπων γένους ἐβασίλευσε;

Fol. 376 § 11 (ι. 481). Φησὶν ὁ νομοθέτης ἀντικρύς, ψυχὴ πάσης σαρκὸς αἷμά ἐστιν, τὸ πρόσνεμον τῶν σαρκῶν ὄχλῳ τὴν αἵματος

ἐπιρροὴν οἰκεῖον οἰκείῳ· τοῦ δὲ νοῦ τὴν οὐσίαν ἐξ οὐδενὸς ἤρτησε γεννητοῦ, ἀλλ᾽ ὑπὸ θεοῦ καταπνευσθεῖσαν εἰσήγαγεν. ἐνεφύσησεν γάρ, φησίν, ὁ ποιητὴς τῶν ὅλων εἰς τὸ πρόσωπον αὐτοῦ πνοὴν ζωῆς καὶ ἐγένετο ὁ ἄνθρωπος εἰς σάρκα (sic) ζῶσαν. εἰ κατὰ τὴν εἰκόνα τοῦ ποιητοῦ θεοῦ λόγος ἔχει τυπωθῆναι τὸν ἄνθρωπον· διττὸν εἶδος ἀνθρώπων. τὸ μὲν θείῳ πνεύματι, λογισμῷ βιούντων· τοῦτο (l. τὸ) δὲ αἵματι καὶ σαρκὸς ἡδονῇ ζώντων· τοῦτο τὸ εἶδός ἐστι πλάσμα γῆς, ἐκεῖνο δὲ θείας εἰκόνος ἐμφερὲς ἐκμαγεῖον· χρεῖος δέ ἐστιν ὁ πεπλασμένος ἡμῶν χοὸς καὶ ἀναδεδυμένος αἵματι, βοηθείας τούτου.

The passage has the additional interest that it preserves the old title given by Eusebius, Τίς ὁ θείων ἐστὶ κληρονόμος καὶ [περὶ τῆς] εἰς τὰ ἴσα καὶ ἐναντία τομῆς.

Fol. 268 § 22 (ι. 487). Μύριοι ἔξαρνοι παρακαταθηκῶν ἐγένοντο, τοῖς ἀλλοτρίοις ὡς ἰδίοις ὑπ᾽ ἀμέτρου τῆς πλεονεξίας καταχρησάμενοι.

And in Cod. Rupef. f. 230 b.

Fol. 266 b § 60 (ι. 516).　Οἱ πιθανῶν σοφισμάτων εὑρέται ἐξ ἀπάτης πλανῆσαι φενακίσαι καὶ παρακρούσασθαι μόνον εἰδότες τοῦ ἀψευδεῖν οὐ πεφροντίκασιν....οἷς ὁ τῶν ἀγελαίων καὶ ἡμελημένων ἀνθρώπων ἀπατώμενος ὄχλος συνεπιγράφεται.

De Mutatione Nominum.

Fol. 130 § 3 (ι. 581).　Κύριος γεννητὸς πρὸς ἀλήθειαν οὐδείς, καὶ ἂν ἀπὸ περάτων εἰς πέρατα εὑρύνας τὴν ἡγεμονίαν ἀνάψηται· μόνος δὲ ὁ ἀγέννητος ἀψευδῶς ἡγεμών.

Referred to *De Mut. Nom.*　Also Dam. Par. 434 and Anton Melissa (*Patr. Gr.* 136, col. 1064).

Fol. 305 b § 5 (ι. 584).　Τῷ Ἀβραὰμ εἴρηται ἐκ προσώπου τοῦ θεοῦ· εὐαρεστεῖν ἐνωπίον ἐμοῦ, τουτέστι μὴ ἐμοὶ μόνῳ ἀλλὰ καὶ τοῖς ἐμοῖς ἔργοις παρ' ἐμοὶ κριτῇ ὡς (Cod. ᾧ) ἐφόρῳ καὶ ἐπισκόπῳ. Τιμῶν γὰρ γονεῖς ἢ πένητας ἢ φίλους εὐεργετῶν ἢ πατρίδος ὑπερασπίζων, ἢ τῶν κοινῶν πρὸς πάντας ἀνθρώπους δικαίων ἐπιμελούμενος (Cod. ἐπιμελώμενος), εὐαρεστήσεις μὲν πάντως τοῖς χρωμένοις, θεοῦ δὲ ἐνώπιον εὐαρεστήσεις· ἀκοιμήτῳ γὰρ ὀφθαλμῷ βλέπει πάντα...τοιαῦτα οὖν πράττε, ἃ γενήσεται ἐπάξια τοῦ φανῆναι θεῷ καὶ ἅπερ ἰδὼν ἀποδέξεται......τὸ γὰρ καθ' ἑκατέραν τάξιν (Cod. ἑτέραν ἄξιαν) εὐδοκιμῆσαι καὶ τὴν πρὸς [τὸ ἀγέννητον καὶ Cod. om.] τὴν πρὸς τὸ γεννώμενον (Cod. γενόμενον) οὐ μικρᾶς ἐστὶ διανοίας, ἀλλά, εἰ δεῖ τὸ ἀληθὲς εἰπεῖν, κόσμου καὶ θεοῦ μεθόριον. Συνόλως τε προσήκει τὸν ἀστεῖον ὀπαδὸν εἶναι (Cod. ἐστιν) θεοῦ, μέλει γὰρ τῷ πάντων ἡγεμόνι καὶ πατρὶ τοῦ γενομένου.

The latter part from τὸ καθ' ἑτέραν ἀξίαν is also in Cod. Rupef. f. 24 with many variations : e.g. γεγεννημένον, om. θεοῦ, καὶ καθόλου προσήκει, σπουδαῖον εἶναι, Cod. Rupef. also continues the passage a little further than Reg. The whole passage again in Rupef. f. 253 b.

Fol. 255 b § 38 (ι. 611).　Τοῦ κατ' ἀρετὴν βίου, ὅς ἐστιν ἀψευδεστάτη ζωή, μετέχουσιν ὀλίγοι, οὐχὶ τῶν ἀγελαίων φημί, τούτων γὰρ οὐδὲ εἷς τῆς ἀληθοῦς ζωῆς κεκοινώνηκεν, ἀλλ' εἴ τισιν ἐξεγένετο τὰς ἀνθρώπων φυγεῖν βλάβας καὶ θεῷ μόνῳ ζῆσαι.　τροπὴν ψυχῆς ῥέουσαν ἀκατασχέτως· ἀμύθητα γὰρ ἐνθύμια, ἄλλα ἐπ' ἄλλοις τρικυμίας τρόπον ἐπιτρέχει, κυκῶντα καὶ πᾶσαν αὐτὴν βιαίως ἀνατρέποντα (cod. ἐπιτρέποντα)· τὸ μὲν οὖν ἄριστον τῆς καθάρσεως καὶ τελειότατον τοῦτό ἐστι, μὴ ἐνθυμεῖσθαι τῶν ἀτόπων......Βαρὺ δὲ τὸ διὰ λόγου τὰ πονηρὰ προφέρειν ὅ ἐστιν ἄδικος πρᾶξις· λόγος γὰρ ἔργου, φασίν, σκιά· σκιᾶς δὲ βλαπτούσης πῶς οὐ τὸ ἔργον βλαβερώτερον;

Fol. 358 b § 41 (ι. 615).　Χαλεπὸν ψυχῆς τροπὴν [εἰς om. Cod.] ἠρεμίαν ἀγαγεῖν καὶ θᾶττον ἄν τις χειμάρρου φορὰν ἐπίσχοι, ἢ

Referred to *De Mut. Nom.*

De Somniis I.

Fol. 105 § 2 (ι. 622).　Ἀνθεῖ πρὸς ἐπιστήμην ψυχὴ ὁπότε τοῦ σώματος ἀκμαὶ μήκει (add χρόνου) μαραίνονται.

Ascribed to Evagrius and so in Dam. Par. 404 reading ἀνθεῖται.

De Abrahamo.

Fol. 105 § 46 (II. 39). Ὁ ἀληθείᾳ πρεσβύτερος οὐκ ἐν μήκει χρόνου, ἀλλ' ἐπαινετῷ καὶ τελείῳ βίῳ θεωρεῖται. τοὺς μὲν οὖν αἰῶνα πολὺν τρίψαντας ἐν τῇ μετὰ σώματος ζωῇ δίχα καλοκἀγαθίας πολυχρονίους παῖδας λεκτέον, μαθήματα πολιᾶς ἄξια μηδέποτε παιδευθέντας.

Also Dam. Par. 404 referring expressly

to *De Abrahamo* and reading χρόνων, ἐν ἐπαινετῷ.

The second sentence occurs again on f. 36 b, reading τοὺς χρόνον πολὺν. Observe also that Anton Melissa (*Patr. Gr.* 136 col. 1056) gives the first sentence reading ἐν ἐπαινετῷ.

De Josepho.

Fol. 180 and 186 b § 24 (II. 61). Πλούτου τὸ κάλλος οὐκ ἐν βαλαντίοις ἀλλ' ἐν τῇ τῶν χρῃζόντων ἐπικουρίᾳ.

Also Dam. Par. 481, 502, Anton Melissa, col. 884.

Vita Mosis, I.

Fol. 246 § 7 (II. 86). Οἱ ξένοι παρ' ἐμοὶ κριτῇ τῶν ὑποδεξαμένων ἱκέται γραφέσθωσαν.

Also in Cod. Rupef. f. 217 b.

Fol. 57 b § 41 (II. 117). Ὀλισθηραὶ γὰρ αἱ πρῶται φῆμαι, χρόνῳ μόλις ἐμφραγιζόμεναι (l. ἐνσφραγιζόμεναι).

De Decem Oraculis.

Fol. 332 § 2 (II. 181). Τιμὴ τίς ἂν γένοιτο, μὴ προσούσης ἀληθείας, ἢ καὶ ὄνομα καὶ ἔργον ἔχει τίμιον;

Fol. 266 b § 12 (II. 189). Πλάνος τις οὐ μικρὸς τὸ πρῶτον τῶν ἀνθρώπων γένος κατέσχηκε...ἐντεθεάκασι (l. ἐκτεθείκασι) γὰρ οἱ μὲν τέσσαρας ἀρχάς, γῆν καὶ ὕδωρ καὶ ἀέρα καὶ πῦρ, οἱ δὲ ἥλιον καὶ σελήνην καὶ τοὺς πλανήτας καὶ ἀπλανεῖς ἀστέρας, οἱ δὲ μόνον τὸν οὐρανόν, οἱ δὲ συμπάντα τὸν κόσμον. τὸν δὲ ἀνωτάτω καὶ πρεσβύτατον καὶ γεννητήν, τὸν ἄρχοντα τῆς μεγαλοπόλεως, τὸν στρατιάρχην τῆς ἀνωτάτω στρατιᾶς, τὸν κυβερνήτην ὃς οἰκονομεῖ σωτηριώδως ἀεὶ τὰ σύμπαντα, παρεκαλύψαντο.

Fol. 313 § 17 (II. 195). Ὁ ἑκάστῃ ψυχῇ

συμβεβηκὼς ἔλεγχος οὐδὲν εἰωθὼς παραδέχεσθαι τῶν ὑπαιτίων, μισοπονήρῳ καὶ φιλαρέτῳ χρώμενος (Cod. adds δεῖ) τῇ φύσει, καὶ κατήγορος ὁμοῦ καὶ δικαστὴς αὐτὸς ὤν, διακινηθεὶς ὡς μὲν κατήγορος αἰτιᾶται καὶ κατηγορεῖ ἡμῶν καὶ δυσωπεῖ, πάλιν δὲ ὡς δικαστὴς διδάσκει, νουθετεῖ μεταβάλλεσθαι· κἂν μὲν ἰσχύσῃ (Cod. ἰσχύσει) πεῖσαι, γεγηθὼς καταλλάττεται, μὴ δυνηθεὶς δὲ ἀσπονδεὶ πολεμεῖ, μήτε μεθ' ἡμέραν μήτε νύκτωρ ἀφιστάμενος, κεντῶν καὶ τιτρώσκων ἀνίατα (Cod. ἀνιᾶται) μέχρι τὴν ἀθλίαν ζωὴν ἀπορρήξῃ (Cod. ἀπορριξει).

Fol. 358 § 19 (ΙΙ. 196). Οἶδά τινας ἀδυναμίᾳ ἡσυχίας ἐν βεβήλοις καὶ ἀκαθάρτοις χωρίοις ἐν οἷς οὔτε πατρὸς οὔτε μητρός, ἀλλ' οὐδὲ τῶν ὀθνείων πρεσβύτου τινὸς εὖ βεβιωκότος (? Cod. εὐσεβιωκότος) ἄξιον μεμνῆσθαι, διομινμένους καὶ ὅλας ῥήσεις ὅρκων συνείροντας, τῷ τοῦ θεοῦ πολυωνύμῳ καταχρωμένους ὀνόματι ἔνθα μὴ δεῖ πρὸς ἀσέβειαν.

Also in Rup. f. 219 more at length.

Followed in Reg. by an unidentified sentence, for which vide infra.

De Fortitudine.

Fol. 87 § 3 (ΙΙ. 377). Ὁ φαῦλος ἀεὶ πολυδεής, ἀεὶ διψῶν τῶν ἀπόντων, ἀπλήστου καὶ ἀκορέστου χάριν ἐπιθυμίας ἣν πυρὸς τρόπον (Cod. τρόπος) ἀναρριπίζων ἐπὶ πάντα μικρά τε καὶ μεγάλα τείνει.

Referred ἐκ τοῦ περὶ ἀρετῶν.

Also in Dam. Par. 378, and Rup. f. 46.

Fol. 238 § 3 (ΙΙ. 337). Ὁ σπουδαῖος ὀλιγοδεής, ἀθανάτου καὶ θνητῆς φύσεως μεθόριος, τὸ μὲν ἐπιδεὲς ἔχων διὰ σῶμα θνητόν, τὸ δὲ μὴ πολυδεὲς διὰ ψυχὴν ἐφιεμένην ἀθανασίας.

Also Dam. Par. 365 but referred to Evagrius; and Maximus (ΙΙ. 574).

De Praemiis et Poenis.

Fol. 97 b § 8 (ΙΙ. 416). Χωρὶς θεωρίας ἐπιστημονικῆς οὐδὲν τῶν πραττομένων καλόν.
Ascribed to Nilus in Dam. Par. 397 and to Cyril in Georg. Monach. col. 1153.
Vide supra, p. 78, et infra, p. 96.

Fol. 376 b § 11 (ΙΙ. 418). Παντὸς ἀνθρώπου κατ' ἀρχὰς ἅμα τῇ γενέσει κυοφορεῖ δίδυμα ἡ ψυχή, κακόν, καὶ ἀγαθόν, ἑκάτερον φαντασιούμενον.

Fol. 368 b § 17 (ΙΙ. 425). Οἷς ὁ ἀληθινὸς πλοῦτος ἐν οὐρανοῖς ἀπόκειται διὰ σοφίας καὶ ὁσιότητος, τούτοις καὶ ὁ τῶν χρημάτων ἐπὶ γῆς περιουσιάζει, προνοίᾳ καὶ ἐπιμελείᾳ θεοῦ τῶν ταμείων πληρουμένων, ἐκ τοῦ τὰς ὁρμὰς τῆς διανοίας καὶ τῶν χειρῶν τὰς ἐπιβολὰς μὴ ἐμποδίζεσθαι πρὸς τὴν τῶν ἀεὶ σπουδαζομένων καλῶν κατόρθωσιν. Οἷς δὲ ὁ κλῆρος οὐκ ἔστιν οὐράνιος δι' ἀσέβειαν καὶ ἀδικίαν καὶ γηΐνας μερίμνας ἀπρεπεῖς, οὐδὲ τῶν ἐπὶ γῆς ἀγαθῶν εὐοδεῖν πέφυκεν ἡ κτῆσις. Also in Cod. Rupef. f. 276.

In Flaccum.

Fol. 157 § 2 (ΙΙ. 518). Τῷ μὲν ἀγνοίᾳ τοῦ κρείττονος διαμαρτάνοντι συγγνώμη δίδοται· ὁ δὲ ἐξ ἐπιστήμης ἀδικῶν ἀπολογίαν οὐκ ἔχει, προεαλωκὼς ἐν τῷ τοῦ συνειδότος δικαστηρίῳ. Also Dam. Par. 520, Maximus (ΙΙ. 610). Vide supra, p. 79.

Ad Gaium.

Fol. 140 § 32 (ΙΙ. 580). Οὐδεὶς οὕτω μέμηνεν, ὡς δοῦλος ὢν ἐναντιοῦσθαι δεσπότῃ.
Also Dam. Par. 448 and Anton Melissa, col. 1068.
In Cod. Rupef. fol. 59 b a sentence is added: οὐκ ἀσφαλὲς τοῖς βουλομένοις ἐπὶ τῶν πάντων ἡγεμόνα καὶ δεσπότην θεὸν ἐκβαλεῖσθαι τὰ πράγματα.

De Mundo.

Fol. 376 b § 5 (II. 607). Τῆς ψυχῆς τὸ εἶδος οὐκ ἐκ τῶν αὐτῶν στοιχείων, ἐξ ὧν τὰ ἄλλα ἀπετελεῖτο, διεπλάσθη, καθαρωτέρας δὲ καὶ ἀμείνονος ἔλαχε τῆς οὐσίας ἐξ ἧς καὶ αἱ θεῖαι φύσεις ἐδημιουργοῦντο. Παρ' ὃ καὶ μόνον τῶν ἐν ἡμῖν εἰκότως ἄφθαρτον ἔδοξεν εἶναι διάνοια· μόνην γὰρ αὐτὴν ὁ γεννήσας πατὴρ ἐλευθερίας ἠξίωσε καὶ τὰ τῆς ἀνάγκης ἀνεὶς δεσμὰ ἄφετον εἴασε, δωρησάμενος αὐτῇ τοῦ πρεπωδεστάτου καὶ οἰκειοτάτου κτήματος αὐτῶν (Cod. αὐτῷ) τοῦ ἑκουσίου μοῖραν, ἣν ἠδύνατο δέξασθαι.

Referred to *de Gigantibus,* vide supra, p. 9.

The following passage, in addition to two previously referred to, is identified from the extracts given by Cramer.

Anecd. Oxon. IV. 254 from Cod. Bodl. Clark, 11 b.

᾿Αναισχυντία μὲν ἴδιον φαύλου. αἰδὼς δὲ σπουδαίου, τὸ δὲ μὴ αἰσχύνεσθαι μήτε ἀναισχυντεῖν, τοῦ ἀκαταλήπτως ἔχοντος καὶ ἀσυγκαταθέτως.

This is II. *Leg. Alleg.* § 17 (I. 78), and in Maximus II. 633.

The following should also be reckoned as verified in Anton Melissa.

Col. 793. ῾Η θεωρία τῆς ἀρετῆς παγκάλη καὶ ἡ πρᾶξις καὶ ἡ χρῆσις περιμάχητος.

Also in Cod. Rupef. f. 148.

From I. *Leg. Alleg.* § 17 (I. 54).

Col. 812. Δεσμὸς οἴκων ὀθνείων αἱ ἐπιγαμίαι, τὴν ἀλλοτριότητα εἰς οἰκειότητα μετάγουσαι.

Ad Gaium § 10 (II. 556).

Col. 832. Τὸ μὲν μηδὲν συνόλως ἁμαρτάνειν ἴδιον θεοῦ, τάχα δὲ καὶ θείου ἀνδρός. τὸ δὲ ἁμαρτάνοντα μεταβάλλειν πρὸς ἀνυπαίτιον ζωὴν φρόνιμον καὶ τὸ συμφέρον ἅπαν εἰς ἀπάθειαν ἔρχεται.

De Poenitentia § 1 (II. 405).

Col. 933. ῞Ωσπερ γὰρ ὁ ἥλιος ἁπάντων ἐστὶ φῶς τῶν ὄψεις ἐχόντων, οὕτω καὶ ὁ σοφὸς τούτων οἳ λογικῆς κεκοινήκασι φύσεως.

De Somniis I § 28 (I. 647).

Col. 1004. Βασιλεῦ δικαιότατε, παραπεμφθεὶς ὑπὸ τῆς φύσεως ἐπὶ πρύμναν ἀνωτάτω καὶ τοὺς οἴακας ἐγχειρισθεὶς πηδαλιούχει τὸ κοινὸν ἀνθρώπων σκάφος σωτηρίως, ἐπὶ μηδενὶ μᾶλλον χαίρων καὶ τερπόμενος ἢ ἐν τῷ τοὺς ὑπηκόους εὐεργετεῖν.

Ad Gaium § 7 (II. 553).

The same passage more at length in Cod. Rupef. f. 113.

Col. 1033. ῞Οταν ἄρχων ἀπογνῷ τὸ δύνασθαι κρατεῖν ἀνάγκη τοὺς ὑπηκόους εὐθὺς ἀφηνιάζειν, καὶ μάλιστα τοὺς ἐκ μικρῶν καὶ τῶν τυχόντων πεφυκότας ἀνερεθίζεσθαι.

In Flaccum § 4 (II. 519), also in Cod. Rupef. f. 29 b.

Col. 1044. ῞Οπερ, οἶμαι, θεὸς πρὸς κόσμον, τοῦτο πρὸς τέκνα γονεῖς, ἐπειδὴ ὡς ἐκεῖνος τῷ μὴ ὑπάρχοντι ὕπαρξιν κατειργάσατο, καὶ οὗτοι μιμούμενοι καθ' ὅσον οἷόν τε τὴν ἐκείνου δύναμιν, τὸ γένος ἀθανατίζουσιν.

De Parentibus Colendis (Mai p. 9).

Col. 1049. Οἱ γονέων ἀλογοῦντες ἑκατέρας μερίδος εἰσὶν ἐχθροί, καὶ τῆς πρὸς θεὸν καὶ τῆς πρὸς ἀνθρώπους.

De Decem Oraculis § 22 (II. 199).

Col. 1056. Μετὰ τὸν ἐν νεότητι πρακτικὸν βίον ὁ ἐν γήρᾳ θεωρητικὸς βίος ἄριστος καὶ ἱερώτατος, ὃν οἷα κυβερνήτην παραπέμψας ὁ θεός, ἐνεχείρισε τοὺς οἴακας, ὡς ἱκανὸν πηδαλιουχεῖν τὰ ἐπίγεια· χωρὶς γὰρ θεωρίας ἐπιστημονικῆς οὐδὲν τῶν πραττομένων καλόν.

De Praem. et Poen. § 8 (II. 416).
Also in Rup. f. 131.

Col. 1065. Μέγιστον ἐγκώμιον οἰκέτου, μηδενὸς ὧν ἂν ὁ οἰκοδεσπότης προστάξει ὀλιγωρεῖν, ἀόκνως δὲ καὶ φιλοπόνως ὑπὲρ δύναμιν πάντα σπουδάζειν αἰσίᾳ γνώμῃ κατορθοῦν.

Also in Cod. Rupef. f. 159.
Quis Rer. Div. § 2 (I. 474).

Col. 1084. Τῶν φαύλων οὐδενὶ χαίρειν ἐφίεται καθάπερ ἐν προφητικαῖς ᾄδεται ῥήσεσι· χαίρειν οὐκ ἔστι τοῖς ἀσεβέσιν, εἶπεν ὁ θεός. Λόγος γὰρ ὄντως καὶ χρήσιμός ἐστι θεῖος· σκυθρωπὸν καὶ ἐπίλυπον καὶ μεστὸν βαρυδαιμονίας εἶναι τὸν παντὸς μοχθηροῦ βίον.

De Mut. Nom. § 31 (I. 604).
Also Cod. Rupef. f. 237 b.

Col. 1105. Ἐγὼ οὖν ὅταν τινὰ τῶν σπουδαίων διαιτώμενον κατ' οἰκίαν ἢ πόλιν θεάσωμαι, τὴν οἰκίαν ἢ τὴν πόλιν ἐκείνην εὐδαιμονίζω, καὶ οἶμαι τήν τε τῶν παρόντων ἀγαθῶν ἀπόλαυσιν βέβαιον καὶ τὴν τῶν ἀπόντων προσδοκίαν τελεσφορουμένην σχήσειν, τοῦ θεοῦ τὸν ἀπεριόριστον καὶ ἀπερίγραφον πλοῦτον αὐτοῦ διὰ τοὺς ἀξίους καὶ τοὺς ἀναξίους δωρούμενον.

De Sacrificiis Abelis et Caini § 37 (I. 187).

This passage is also in Cod. Rupef. f. 33 b (τοῦ αὐτοῦ εἰς τὸν Ἄβελ), reading γοῦν, ἀπάντων, ἔχειν, ἀπερίγραπτον wrongly; and τοῖς ἀναξίοις rightly.

Col. 1089. Δεινὸν γυνὴ γνώμην ἀνδρὸς παραλῦσαι καὶ παραγαγεῖν καὶ μάλιστα μάχλος. Ἕνεκα γὰρ τοῦ συνειδότος κολακικωτέρα γίνεται [Cod. μαλακικωτέρα].

Ad Gaium § 6 (II. 551) and Rup. f. 136.

Col. 1116. Ἀνώμαλον φύσει ἡ ἄσκησις, ποτὲ μὲν ἐς ὕψος ἰοῦσα, ποτὲ δὲ ὑποστρέφουσα πρὸς τοὐναντίον, καὶ ποτὲ μέν, καθάπερ ναῦς, εὐπλοίᾳ τῇ τοῦ βίου, ποτὲ δὲ δυσπλοίᾳ χρωμένη. Ἐτερήμερος, ὡς ἔφη τις, τῶν ἀσκητῶν ὁ βίος, ἄλλοτε μὲν ζῶν καὶ ἐγρηγορώς, ἄλλοτε δὲ τεθνηκὼς ἢ κοιμώμενος. Καὶ τάδε οὐκ ἀπὸ σκοποῦ λέγεται· σοφοὶ μὲν γὰρ τὸν ἀνθρώπινον χῶρον ἔλαχον οἰκεῖν, ἄνω φοιτᾶν ἀεὶ μεμαθηκότες, κακοὶ δὲ τοὺς ἐν ᾅδῃ μυχούς, ἐξ ἀρχῆς ἄχρι τέλους ἀποθνῄσκειν μεμαθηκότες, καὶ εἰς γῆρας ἐκ σπαργάνων φθορᾶς ἐθάδες ὄντες· οἱ δ' ἀσκηταὶ μεθόριοι τῶν ἄκρων εἰσὶν (add καὶ) ἄνω καὶ κάτω πολλάκις ὡς ἐπὶ κλίμακος βαδίζουσιν, ἢ ὑπὸ τῆς χείρονος ἀντισπώμενοι, μέχρις ἂν ὁ τῆς ἁμίλλης καὶ διαμάχης ταύτης βραβευτὴς θεὸς ἀναδῷ τὰ βραβεῖα τάξει τῇ βελτίονι, τὴν ἐναντίαν εἰς ἅπαν καθελών.

De Somniis I. § 23 (I. 643).

Col. 1124. Ἀρχήν, εἰ δεῖ τἀληθὲς εἰπεῖν, παντὸς ἀγαθοῦ καὶ ἀρετῆς ἁπάσης ὁ θεὸς ἐνέδειξεν ἀνθρώποις πόνον, οὗ χωρὶς τῶν ἀγαθῶν οὐδέν ἐστι παρὰ τῷ θνητῷ γένει συνιστάμενον.......θνητῷ γὰρ οὐδενὶ κτῆσιν ἀγαθοῦ δίχα πόνων ἡ φύσις δεδώρηται.

De Sacrificiis Abelis et Caini § 7 (I. 168), and Cod. Rupef. f. 274.

Col. 1124. Ὁ μὲν τὸν πόνον φεύγων φεύγει τὰ ἀγαθά· ὁ δὲ τλητικῶς καὶ ἀνδρείως ὑπομένων τὰ δυσκαρτέρητα σπεύδει πρὸς μακαριότητα.

Vit. Mos. III. § 22 (II. 163), and more at length in Cod. Rupef. f. 274.

Col. 1156. Ὅρκος ἐστὶ μαρτυρία θεοῦ περὶ πράγματος ἀμφισβητουμένου.

III. Leg. Alleg. (I. 127).

Col. 1157. Ἐκ πολυορκίας ψευδορκία φύεται.

De Decem Oraculis, § 19 (II. 196), and in Georg. Monach. (col. 1092) reading πολυλογίας.

Col. 1157. Φασί τινες τὸ εὐορκεῖν οὐκ ἀπόβλητον, ἀλλ᾽ ἤδη ὅ γε ὀμνὺς εἰς ἀπιστίαν ὑπονοεῖται.

De Decem Oraculis, § 17 (II. 195).

Col. 1157. Μαρτυρία θεοῦ ἐστι περὶ πραγμάτων ἀμφισβητουμένων ὁ ὅρκος· μάρτυρα δὲ καλεῖν ἐπὶ ψεύδει τὸν θεὸν ἀνοσιώτατον.

De Decem Oraculis, § 17 (II. 195).

Col. 1157. Τὸν ὀμνύντα μάτην ἐπ᾽ ἀδίκῳ θεὸς ὁ τὴν φύσιν ἵλεως οὔποτε τῆς αἰτίας ἀπαλλάξει, δυσκάθαρτον καὶ μιαρὸν ὄντα, κἂν διαφύγῃ τῆς ἀπ᾽ ἀνθρώπων τιμωρίας.

De Parentibus Colendis (Mai 29).

Col. 1193. Δυσεύρετον ἢ καὶ παντελῶς ἀνεύρετον ἐν πεφυρμένῳ βίῳ τὸ καλόν.

De Profugis, § 26 (Mang. I. 568).

Also in Georg. Monach. (col. 1084).

Col. 1209. Ἐπειδήπερ ἀοράτως εἰς τὸν τῆς ψυχῆς χῶρον εἰσδύεται ὁ θεός, παρασκευάζωμεν τὸν τόπον ἐκεῖνον ὡς ἔνεστι κάλλιστον ἀξιόχρεων ἐνδιαίτημα θεοῦ γενησόμενον· εἰ δὲ μή, λήσεται μεταναστὰς εἰς ἕτερον οἶκον ὁ θεός.

De Cherubim, § 28 (I. 157).

Col. 1209. Οἶκος θεοῦ σοφοῦ διάνοια· τούτου καλεῖται θεὸς ἰδίως ὁ τῶν συμπάντων· ὥς φησιν ὁ προφήτης, ὡς θεὸς ἐμπεριπατεῖ οἷα βασιλείῳ.

The same quotation with slight extension in Rupef. f. 137 and f. 195 b.

De Praem. et Poen. § 20 (II. 428).

Col. 1209. Ὀφθαλμοῖς μὲν τὰ ἐν φανερῷ καὶ τὰ ἐν χερσὶ καταλαμβάνεται· λογισμὸς δὲ ἀκέραιος φθάνει καὶ πρὸς τὰ ἀόρατα καὶ μέλλοντα.

Also in Rup. 195 b.

Ad Gaium, § 1 (II. 545).

The fragments left over from the printed Parallels are as follows: in which it is to be understood that every other passage of Philo in the texts of Lequien and Mangey is either a known quotation, or has been referred to its probable origin in the preceding pages.

The passages from the Vatican Parallels are fourteen in number.

Dam. Par. 372 and 675.
Also Cod. Reg. 923 fol. 38 b omitting τῶν...εὐαρεστοῦσα by ὅμοιοτ. And in Georg. Mon. (col. 1116) omitting τῶν... παράπαν and reading εὐχαριστοῦσα.

Μακαρία φύσις ἡ ἐπὶ παντὶ χαίρουσα καὶ μηδενὶ δυσαρεστοῦσα τῶν ἐν τῷ κόσμῳ τὸ παράπαν, ἀλλ᾽ εὐαρεστοῦσα τοῖς γινομένοις ὡς καλῶς καὶ συμφερόντως γινομένοις.

Dam. Par. 404 and Cod. Reg. f. 105.

Ἀκύμαντος λιμὴν πολιά.
Σώματος παρακμὴ καταστολὴ παθῶν.

Dam. Par. 435.
Mai, *Script. Vet.* VII. 100 (Cod. Vat. 1553) omits σεαυτῷ and σοφίας.
Cod. Reg. f. 116 b.

Ἐπίστησον, ὁ διδάσκων, ἐξέτασον ἀκριβῶς ἀκοὴν τοῦ μανθάνοντος. Εὐήθης γὰρ ὁ κωφῷ διαλεγόμενος καὶ μάταιος ὁ λίθον νουθετῶν. Καὶ σὺ ἔνοχος ἁμαρτίας σεαυτῷ ἔσῃ, ὁ μὴ ἐπισκεψάμενος ὅπως καὶ πηνίκα καὶ πότε δεῖ λόγον προέσθαι σοφίας.

Dam. Par. 436 and Cod. Reg. f. 118, which refers εἰς τὸν Ἰωσήφ, but I cannot find the passage in *De Josepho*.

Διάβολοι καὶ θείας ἀπόπεμπτοι χάριτος οἱ τὴν αὐτὴν ἐκείνῳ διαβολικὴν νοσοῦντες κακοτεχνίαν, θεοστυγεῖς τε καὶ θεομισεῖς πάντῃ καὶ πάσης εὐδαιμονίας ἀλλότριοι.

Τί ἂν γένοιτο διαβολῆς χεῖρον; κηλεῖ γὰρ τὰ ὦτα καὶ ἐκπλήττει τὴν διάνοιαν τῶν ἀκροατῶν, ἐκθηριοῖ δὲ αὐτοὺς οἷόν τι θήραμα τοῖς κακοῖς ἀεὶ ἐφεδρεύοντας. Οἱ δὲ τῷ σώφρονι λογισμῷ μάλα ἑρματισμένοι καὶ ἀναχαιτιζόμενοι τῷ διαβάλλοντι ἀπεχθαίνουσι μάλιστα ἢ τῷ διαβεβλημένῳ, ἐπιτιμήσαντες καὶ ἐπιστομίσαντες ταῖς πρὸς μέμψιν ὁρμαῖς, ἄχρις ἂν ἐναργὴς μαρτυρίῳ ἡ ἀπόδειξις γένηται.

Dam. Par. 551.
Referred to the treatise against Gaius in Cod. Reg. 923 f.
Also Rup. 190 b (φίλωνος).

Ἄξιον θαυμάσαι θάλασσαν, δι' ἧς τὰς ἀντιδόσεις τῶν ἀγαθῶν αἱ χῶραι ἀλλήλαις ἀντεκτείνουσιν καὶ τὰ μὲν ἐνδέοντα λαμβάνουσιν ὧν δὲ ἄγουσι[1] περιουσίαν ἀναπέμπουσι.

Dam. Par. 630.
The first part of the sentence is very nearly as in Isocrates *ad Demon.* § 29, and is so given in Georg. Monach. col. 1117.

Μηδενὶ συμφορὰν ὀνειδίσῃς—κοινὴ γὰρ ἡ φύσις, καὶ τὰ ἐπιόντα ἄδηλα—μήποτε τοῖς αὐτοῖς ἁλοὺς αὐτοκατάκριτος ἐν τῷ συνειδότι εὑρεθῇς.

Dam. Par. 681.

Αἱ πάντων ἀθρόως πρὸς τὰ ἐναντία μεταβολαὶ σκληρόταται, καὶ μάλιστα ὅταν μήκει χρόνου αἱ ὑποῦσαι στηριχθῶσι δυνάμεις.

Dam. Par. 683 and Rup. f. 259; also Cod. Reg. with addition of the words in brackets.

Χρήσιμον [καὶ τοῖς ἑτέρων πάθεσιν διδάσκοντας σωφρονεῖν] καὶ ταῖς ἑτέρων ἀτυχίαις σωφρονίζεσθαι.

[1] The printed text gives ἀργοῦσι. For the expression cf. *de Fortitudine* II. 383.

Dam. Par. 688, without a name, but following Greg. Naz.

Cod. Reg. f. 327 b, *Philonis.*

Τῷ στρατιώτῃ οὐδὲν δεῖ ἔξω τῶν κατὰ τὴν στρατείαν περιεργάζεσθαι, ἀλλὰ μεμνῆσθαι ἀεὶ ὅτι τέτακται τὴν εἰρήνην φυλάττειν.

Dam. Par. 693.

Πᾶς σοφὸς θεοῦ φίλος.

Dam. Par. 704.

Note that on p. 629 this is given to Cyril, and so in Cod. Reg. 923 f. 36 b.

Οἴησις, ὡς ὁ τῶν ἀρχαίων λόγος, ἐστὶν ἐκκοπὴ προκοπῆς· ὁ γὰρ κατοιόμενος βελτίωσιν οὐκ ἀνέχεται.

Dam. Par. 711.

Ὥσπερ τὸ παρὰ φύσιν ἐγκεντρίσαι καὶ εἰσοικίσαι τι τῇ φύσει δύσεργον, οὕτω καὶ αὖ πάλιν τὰ φύσει πεφυκότα μεταθεῖναι καὶ ἀναχαιτίσαι. Εἴρηται γὰρ εὖ· Φύσεως ἀντιπραττούσης κενὰ πάντα.

The following passages remain unrecognized or unnoticed in the Parallels from the Cod. Rupefucaldi, as printed by Lequien.

Dam. Par. 754 and Maxim. II. 599.

Ὁ σοφὸς μέτοικος καὶ μετανάστης ἐστὶν ἐκ τοῦ περιπεφυρμένου βίου πρὸς εἰρηναίοις καὶ μακαρίοις πρέπουσαν ζωήν.

Dam. Par. 782, = Rup. f. 189.

Ἄτοπον ἐν μὲν ταῖς πόλεσιν νόμον εἶναι, τοῦ μυστικὰ μυστήρια μὴ ἐξαγγεῖλαι τοῖς ἀμυήτοις, τὰς δὲ ἀληθεῖς τελετάς, αἳ πρὸς εὐσέβειαν ἄγουσιν καὶ ὁσιότητα, εἰς ὦτα μεστὰ φλυαρίας ἐκρίπτειν.

The following belong to the fragments which Mangey could not identify in the so-called Parallels of John Monachus.

Σοὶ λέγεται, ὦ γενναῖε καὶ τῶν θείων ὑπήκοε· παντὶ σθένει πειρῶ μὴ μόνον ἀσινῆ καὶ ἀκιβδήλευτα φυλάττειν ἃ ἔλαβες, ἀλλὰ καὶ πάσης ἐπιμελείας ἀξιοῦν, ὡς αὐτεξούσιος καὶ δυνατός, ἵνα ὁ παρακαταθέμενος μηδὲν ἔχῃ τῆς παραφυλακῆς αἰτιάσασθαι. Παρακατέθετο δὲ τῇ σῇ προαιρέσει ψυχήν, λόγον, αἴσθησιν ὁ ζωοπλάστης. Οἱ μὲν οὖν ταῦτα καλῶς δεξάμενοι, καὶ φυλάξαντες τῷ δεδωκότι, τὴν μὲν διάνοιαν ἐτήρησαν, ἵνα μηδὲν ἄλλο ἢ περὶ θεοῦ καὶ τῶν ἀρετῶν αὐτοῦ διανοῆται· τὸν δὲ λόγον, ἵνα ἀχαλίνῳ στόματι ἐγκωμίοις καὶ ὕμνοις γεραίρῃ τὸν τῶν ὅλων πατέρα· τὴν δὲ αἴσθησιν, ἵνα φαντασιουμένη τὸν αἰσθητὸν ἅπαντα κόσμον, οὐρανὸν καὶ γῆν καὶ τὰς μεταξὺ φύσεις, ἀδόλως καὶ καθαρῶς τῇ ψυχῇ διαγγέλλῃ.

I see now that this is from *Quis Rer.*

Div. § 22 (I. 487). It should therefore
be added to the identified passages.

Τόπος τῶν κατὰ γῆν ἱερώτερος σοφοῦ
διανοίας οὐδὲ εἷς ἐστίν, ἣν τρόπον ἀστέρων
ἀρεταὶ περιπολοῦσιν. Rup. f. 33 b.

Ἡ τῶν μελλόντων κατάληψις ἀνοίκειος
ἀνθρώπῳ. Τὸ τέλος τῶν ἀποβησομένων
θεὸς οἶδε μόνος. Rup. f. 36.

Deut. xii. 8.　"Οὐ ποιήσετέ," φησιν ὁ νομοθέτης,
"πάντα ὅσα ἡμεῖς ποιοῦμεν ὧδε σήμερον,
ἕκαστος τὸ ἀρεστὸν ἐναντίον αὐτοῦ,"
μονονουχὶ βοῶν ὅτι πάντα τὰ κακὰ ἡ
φιλαυτία καὶ αὐταρεσκία δημιουργεῖ, ἣν ὡς
ἀνίερον ἐκθυτέον τῆς διανοίας. Μηδεὶς οὖν
τὸ ἀρεστὸν ἑαυτῷ μᾶλλον ἢ τῇ φύσει δεξιω-
σάσθω· τὸ μὲν γὰρ βλάβης, τὸ δὲ ὠφελείας
εὑρίσκεται αἴτιον. Rup. f. 40 b. and
again on f. 185.

Ἀκερδὴς ὁ βραδὺς λογισμός, καὶ ἀνωφε-
λὴς ὁ ἐν ἐσχάτοις μετάμελος. Rup. f.
125 b. and Anton Melissa (col. 801).

Ὁ καλὸς καὶ ἀγαθὸς τοῦ διδασκάλου τρόπος, καὶ ἂν ἐν ἀρχῇ σκληραύχενας ἴδῃ φύσει,
οὐκ ἀπογινώσκει τὴν ἀμείνω μεταβολήν·
ἀλλ᾽ ὥσπερ ἀγαθὸς ἰατρὸς οὐκ εὐθὺς ἐπιφέρει τὴν θεραπείαν ἅμα τῷ κατασκῆψαι τὴν
νόσον, ἀλλ᾽ ἀναχώρησιν τῇ φύσει δούς, ἵνα
προανατέμνῃ τὴν εἰς σωτηρίαν ὁδόν, τηνι-
καῦτα χρῆται τοῖς ὑγιεινοῖς καὶ σωτηρίοις
φαρμάκοις, οὕτω καὶ σπουδαῖος λόγοις κατὰ
φιλοσοφίαν καὶ δόγμασιν. Rup. f. 137.

Ἡ τυχοῦσα τῆς κακίας γένεσις δουλοῖ
τὸν λογισμόν, καὶ ἂν μήπω τέλειον αὐτῆς
ἐκφυτήσῃ (l. ἐκφύσῃ) τὸ γέννημα. Rup.
f. 138, referring to *De Mut. Nom.*

Οἱ ἄνανδροι ὑπὸ τῆς ἐμφύτου μαλακίας,
πρὶν ἢ δυνατώτερον ἀντιβιάσονται προκατα-
πίπτοντες, αἰσχύνη καὶ γέλως ἑαυτῶν γίνονται. Rup. f. 138 b.

Τοῦ φαύλου ἕτερα μὲν τὰ ἐνθύμια, ἕτερα
δὲ τὰ ῥήματα, πολλαὶ δὲ αἱ πράξεις, διάφορα
δὲ καὶ μαχόμενα πάντα πᾶσι λέγει γὰρ οὐχ
ἃ φρονεῖ, καὶ βεβούλευται τὰ ἐναντία οἷς
διέξεισι, καὶ πράττει τὰ τούτοις μὴ συνᾳ-
δοντα· ὥστε κυρίως εἰπεῖν, ὅτι τοῦ φαύλου ὁ
βίος πολέμιος. Rup. f. 138 b.
Also as far as μαχόμενα in Tischendorf,
Philonea, p. 153 from Cod. Cahir.,
Maximus (I. 530), Anton Melissa (col.
1084) and Cod. Lips. Tischendorf. VIII.,
all reading ἄλλαι for πολλαί.

Ἀνελεύθερον τὸ ἀδιάκριτον, ἀπονοίας καὶ
ὑπεροψίας αἴσχιστον βλάστημα. Ὡς γὰρ
συνέσεως καὶ φρονήσεως ἅμα ἡ ἐφ᾽ ἑκάστου
τῶν πρακτέων διάκρισις, τιμητικόν τε καὶ
ἐπαινετόν, οὕτω γε ἀφροσύνης καὶ ἀτιμίας
τὸ ἀνερυθρίαστον. Ὅθεν ἐν ἀσεβέσιν ὁ
ἕτερος λόγος συντάττει τὸν τοιόνδε νοσοῦντα
πάθος, φάσκων· "Ἀσεβὴς ὁ μὴ εἰδὼς τι-
μῆσαι πρόσωπον ἐντίμου, μηδὲ ἐξανίστασθαι
ἀπὸ προσώπου πρεσβυτέρου, μηδὲ κατευθύ-
νειν αὐτὸν πρὸς τὸ εὖ ἔχον." Rup. f. 141 a.

Οἱ ὑπηρέται τῶν σπουδαίων τὴν πρὸς τὸν
θεὸν ἑκούσιον ἀναδέχονται λατρείαν· οὐ γὰρ
ἀνθρώποις ἀνθρωπίνοις δουλεύουσιν, ἀλλὰ
σοφοῖς· ὁ δὲ σοφίας δοῦλος θεραπευτὴς
λέγοιτο ἂν δικαίως εἶναι θεοῦ. Rup. f.
143 b.

Ἄσπονδος καὶ ἀκήρυκτος πόλεμός ἐστι
ἀθέοις πρὸς τοὺς φιλοθέους, οὕτως ὥστε καὶ
δεσποτείαν ἀπειλεῖν. Rup. f. 145 b.

Σωτήριον ἐν τοῖς μάλιστα δικαιοσύνη, καὶ ἀνθρώπων καὶ τῶν τοῦ κόσμου μερῶν, γῆς καὶ οὐρανοῦ. Rup. f. 148.

Καλόν ἐστιν ἀρξαμένους καθ᾽ ἑκάστην ἡμέραν ἀπὸ τῶν θείων καὶ ἁγίων ἔργων ἐπὶ τὰς κατηναγκασμένας ὑπηρεσίας τοῦ βίου χωρεῖν. Διὰ τοῦτο καὶ τὴν τῶν προσταγμάτων μελέτην προσέταξεν ἀεί, μάλιστα δὲ εὐθὺς περιαναστάντας ἅμα τῇ ἕω ποιεῖσθαι, ἵνα πάσης ἀνθρωπίνης πράξεως αἱ ἅγιαι σπονδαὶ προηγῶνται, χορηγὸν ἔχουσαι τὴν περὶ θεοῦ μνήμην.

Ψυχὴ πᾶσα ἣν εὐσέβεια λιπαίνει τοῖς ἰδίοις ὀργίοις, ἀκοιμήτως ἔχει πρὸς τὰ θεῖα καὶ διανίσταται πρὸς τὴν θέαν τῶν θέας ἀξίων. Τοῦτο γὰρ τὸ πάθος τῆς ψυχῆς ἐν ἑορτῇ μεγίστῃ καὶ καιρὸς ἀψευδὴς εὐφροσύνης. Rup. f. 153 b.

Μακρὰν τὰ τῆς γενέσεως τοῦ ἀγεννήτου, καὶ ἂν σφόδρα συνεγγίζῃ, ταῖς ὁλκαῖς χάρισι τοῦ σωτῆρος ἐπακολουθοῦντα. Rup. f. 154 b.

Ὥσπερ τῶν τελειοτάτων ἀγαθῶν τὸ ἰσόμετρον αἴτιον, οὕτω τῶν μεγίστων κακῶν ἡ ἀμετρία, τὸν ὠφελιμώτατον λύουσα δεσμὸν ἰσότητος. Rup. f. 191 and f. 220 reading σύμμετρον, θεσμόν.

Τὸ ἄνισον λυπηρὸν καὶ διαστατικόν, ὥσπερ καὶ τὸ ἴσον ἄλυπον καὶ συνδετικόν εἰς ὠφέλειαν. Rup. f. 191.

Τὸ ἔννομον καὶ τὸ ἴσον εἰρήνης σπέρμα, καὶ σωτηρίας αἴτιον καὶ τῆς εἰς ἅπαν διαμονῆς. Ἀνισότης δὲ καὶ πλεονεξία ὁρμητήρια πολέμου καὶ λυτικὰ τῶν ὄντων. Rup. f. 191.

Referred to *De Ebrietate*, perhaps the lost book on this subject which may have preceded our present one.

Τὰ τῶν προτέρων κολαστήρια τῶν δευτέρων εἰσίν, εἰ σωφρονοῖεν, φυλακτήρια καὶ σωτήρια. Rup. f. 197.

Ἐὰν πολὺς ῥέῃ πλοῦτος, μὴ συγκατασυρῇς τῇ φορᾷ, πειρῶ δὲ ἀντιλαμβάνεσθαί τινος ξηροῦ πρὸς ἵδρυσιν τῆς γνώμης βεβαιοτάτην· τοῦτο δὲ ἦν ἡ μετὰ δικαιοσύνης καὶ χρηστότητος ἐπιδέξιος χρῆσις. Καὶ ἂν τὰ ποιητικὰ (l. κινητικὰ) τῶν μετὰ γαστέρα ἐπιθυμιῶν ἀφθόνως χορηγῆται, μὴ συναρπασθῇς αὐτῶν τῇ περιουσίᾳ, τὴν σωτήριον εὐκολίαν ἀντιθείς, οἷα ξηρὸν ἔδαφος εἰς πορείαν ἀντὶ βαραθρώδους τέλματος.

Ἡ αὐτάρκεια, πηγὴν ἔχουσα σωφροσύνης, μέτρον ἐστὶ τῶν ἀναγκαίων καὶ χρησίμων εἰς τὸν βίον· ταύτης ἀδελφὰς συμβέβηκεν ὀλιγοδείαν, εὐκολίαν, ἀπερίττους ἄρτους— πάντα ὅσα τῦφος διαίρει εἰς ὕψος, ἐπιχειροῦσα καθαιρεῖν. Rup. f. 220. Anton Melissa as far as βίον in *Patr. Gr.* 136 col. 881.

Ἀσκητέον ὀλίγων δεηθῆναι· τοῦτο γὰρ ἐγγυτάτω θεῷ, τὸ δὲ ἐναντίον μακροτάτω. Rup. f. 220. Also Anton Melissa (*Patr. Gr.* 136 col. 881).

Ἡ ἀληθὴς ἱερουργία τίς ἂν εἴη πλὴν ψυχῆς θεοφιλοῦς εὐσέβεια, ἧς τὸ εὐχάριστον ἀθανατίζεται παρὰ τῷ θεῷ, συνδιαιωνίζουσα ἡλίῳ καὶ σελήνῃ καὶ τῷ παντὶ κόσμῳ; Rup. f. 233 b. Also Anton Melissa (*Patr. Gr.* 136 col. 773) reading ἱεραρχία, συνδιαιώνιζον.

Ἀβέβαιοι αἱ πονηρῶν ἀνθρώπων ἐλπίδες, εἰκαζόντων μὲν τὰ χρηστότερα, τὰ δὲ παλίμφημα, καὶ ὧν ἄξιοί εἰσι, πάσχοντες (l. πασχόντων). Rup. f. 237 b. Also in Anton Melissa col. 1084.

Τίς ἐξαμαρτὼν οὐχί, ὥσπερ ἐν δικαστηρίῳ, ὑπὸ τοῦ συνειδότος κατηγορεῖται κἂν μηδεὶς ἕτερος ἐλέγχῃ; Rup. f. 256.

Also in Cod. Reg. f. 314 b.

῟Ωι μὴ ἐφεδρεύει αἰδὼς ἢ φόβος, ἀχάλινον τὸ στόμα καὶ ἀνειμένη γλῶττα λέλυται. Rup. f. 262.

Φυσικώτατα ταῦτα δέδεικται· κατάβασιν μὲν ψυχῆς τὴν δι' οἰήσεως ἀνάβασιν, ἄνοδον δὲ καὶ ὕψος τὴν ἀλαζονείας ὑπονόστησιν. Rup. f. 264.

Τὸν καρτερίας καὶ φρονήσεως καὶ δικαιοσύνης ἐραστὴν οἴησιν χρὴ καὶ τὸ μεγάλαυχον καθαιρεῖν· τοῦ γὰρ ἐπιτηδεύειν ἀνόθως ἀρετὴν δεῖγμα οὐ μικρὸν ἄσκησις ἀτυφίας. Rup. f. 264 and Anton Melissa (col. 1180).

Ἐὰν δόξαις καὶ ἀρχαῖς μέγα φυσώσαις ἐφίεσαι, καθάπερ νηὸς ἀγαθῆς κυβερνήτης τὴν πολλὴν τῶν ἱστίων χύσιν στεῖλον, ἵνα μὴ εἰς ἀτόπους πράξεις ἐκτραχηλισθῇς. Rup. f. 264 and Anton Melissa (col. 1180).

Βουληθεὶς οὖν ὁ θεὸς τῆς θείας ἀρετῆς ἀπ' οὐρανοῦ ἐπὶ γῆς τὴν εἰκόνα καταπέμψαι, δι' ἔλεον τοῦ γένους ἡμῶν, ἵνα μὴ ἀτυχήσῃ τῆς μείζονος μοίρας συμβολικῶς τὴν ἱερὰν σκηνὴν καὶ τὰ ἐν αὐτῇ κατασκευάζει, σοφίας ἀπεικονίσματα καὶ μιμήματα· τῆς γὰρ ἀκαθαρσίας ἡμῶν ἐν μέσῳ φησὶ τὸ λόγιον τὴν σκηνὴν ἱδρῶσθαι (sic), ἵνα ἔχωμεν ᾧ καθαρθησόμεθα, ἐκνιψάμενοι καὶ ἀπολουσάμενοι τὰ (cod. πρὸς τὸν) καταρρυπαίνοντα ἡμῶν τὸν ἄθλιον καὶ δυσκλείας γέμοντα βίον. Rup. 162 b, but I see now that this is from *Quis Rer. Div.* § 23 (i. 488).

A comparison of the last passage with its form as edited by Mangey will shew that the whole of his transcripts need to be revised with the recovered Codex Rupefucaldi by some scholar of sufficient means. Besides these there are between thirty and forty other passages from Philo in the MS. for which I can find no reference in Mangey, nor am I able as yet to furnish an identification.

The three following passages remain unrecognised among the fragments printed by Mangey from Cod. Barocc. 143.

Mang. ii. 674.

Ἡ πρὸς τοὺς φίλους βεβαιότης τῆς ὅλης ἐστὶ τῶν ἠθῶν εὐσταθείας σημεῖον. Διὸ χρὴ πρότερον δοκιμάσαντα οὕτως συναινεῖν εἰς φιλίαν. Μετὰ γὰρ τὸ κτήσασθαι φίλον ἅμα χρὴ φέρειν τὰ βάρη ὅσα ψυχὴν καθέλκοι, καὶ μὴ διΐστασθαι τῆς συναφείας. Ἀγνοούμενος γὰρ τοῖς πολλοῖς ὁ τῆς δια-

Also in Cod. Reg. 923 fol. 338 b, and referred to περὶ ἄθλων, but I cannot find it in *De Praemiis et Poenis.*

Cf. Teaching of Apostles, c. xii.

στάσεως αἴτιος κοινὴν κατηγορίαν ἀμφοῖν, πολλάκις δὲ καὶ ἀναιτίου μᾶλλον ἢ αἰτίου, εἴωθε ποιεῖσθαι.

Τῶν ἀπορρήτων ἃ μὲν τὴν σὴν ἀρετὴν αὐξάνει, κοινώνει τοῖς φίλοις· ἃ δὲ τὴν γνώμην φαυλίζει, μήτε αὐτὸς μετέρχου, μήτε τοῖς φίλοις ἀνατίθη.

Τὴν εὐταξίαν μητέρα τῆς κατὰ σῶμα εὐεξίας ἰατρῶν παῖδες ἐδογμάτισαν, τῆς κατὰ ψυχὴν ὑγιείας ἥκιστα φροντίσαντες. Ἡμεῖς

δὲ οὐ τὴν τῶν σωματικῶν περιττωμάτων
ἀναιρετικὴν τιθέμεθα μόνην εὐταξίαν, πολλῷ
δὲ μᾶλλον τὴν τῶν ψυχοφθόρων παθῶν
καθαιρετικὴν ὑγιείαν ἀληθεστάτην γνωρίζο-
μεν.

We come next to the fragment remaining from the fifty-six published by Mai.

Καθάπερ τὰ ἐκ προνοίας ἀμείνω τῶν
ἀκουσίων [τὰ] κατορθώματα, τὸν αὐτὸν
τρόπον ἐν τοῖς ἁμαρτήμασι κουφότερα τῶν
ἑκουσίων τὰ ἀκούσια.

Mai, *Script. Vet.* VII. 102 (Cod. Vat. 1553).

Φίλωνος· ἐκ τοῦ ζ´ καὶ ιγ´ τῆς νόμων ἱερῶν ἀλληγορίας.

What this numeration means I do not understand. It ought to be ζ´ καὶ η´, one would suppose, which is the number by which the MS. denotes the treatise *Quod Det. Pot.*, but I cannot find the passage there.

Those extracts which follow are the unidentified passages published by Pitra.

Pitra, *Anal. Sac.* II. p. xxiii. from Reg. 77, f. 660.

Τὴν εὐκατάπρηστον ὕλην ἐπιμελὲς ἡμῖν
ὅτι πορρωτάτω τοῦ πυρὸς ἀποτίθεσθαι.

p. 310. From Vat. Reg. 40, f. 224, headed Φίλωνος. The passage is certainly Philo, however much the first words suggest the New Testament; and the last part is very like I. *Alleg. Sac. Leg.* § 14.

Ζητοῦσιν βρῶσιν ψυχαί, αἱ ὄξιον θεοῦ
λόγον ἔχουσαι, ἐκ τοῦ διανεστηκέναι τῷ
φρονήματι, καὶ τὸ πολίτευμα ἔχειν ἐν
οὐρανοῖς· ὥσπερ γὰρ ἀνατείλας ὁ ἥλιος τὸν
ζόφον τοῦ ἀέρος φωτὸς ἐνέπλησεν, οὕτως
καὶ ἀρετὴ ἀνατείλασα ἐν ψυχῇ τὴν ἀχλὺν
αὐτῆς αὐγάζεται καὶ τὸ σκότος σκεδάννυσιν,
καὶ τὰ τῶν παθῶν θηρία κοιμίζει.

Phil. iii. 20.

p. 312. From Palat. 203 f. 261 and Vat. 1553 f. 129; Cat. Lips. I. col. 823 and Cat. Burney f. 140.

[1] Burney, χωρίς τινων.

Πρὸς τούτοις, εἴποι τις ἄν, οὐκ ἐβούλετο
αὐτοὺς καταπεσεῖν εἰς τὸ ῥάθυμον, καὶ τῆς
ἐπαγγελίας κατακληρονομῆσαι τὴν γῆν
ἀγώνων χωρὶς[1]· τὰ γὰρ πόνῳ κτηθέντα παρὰ
τοῖς ἔχουσι τίμια· τὰ δ᾽ ἀπόνως κτηθέντα
καταφρονεῖται ῥᾳδίως· ὅθεν βουλόμενος
αὐτοὺς νήφειν καὶ ἐγρηγορέναι, καὶ ὡς
ἔχοντας ἐχθροὺς πρός τε τὸν θεὸν ἐπι-
στρέφειν καὶ τῆς παρ᾽ αὐτοῦ ἐπικουρίας

² Burney, πορεῖν ἐπαγγείλεται.

³ Burney, γυμνάζων which seems the proper form.

⁴ Sirach xii. 10 : Cat. Burney adds ἑπτὰ γὰρ πονηρίαι εἰσὶν ἐν αὐτῷ (Prov. xxvi. 25).

The previous passage is found attached to an extract from II. Quaest. *in Exod.* XXV. A reference to Procopius *in Exod.* XXIII. 29 (ed. Gesner, p. 209) will shew that the same passage is the basis of his commentary.

δεῖσθαι, τοῦτο ποιεῖν ἐπαγγέλλεται², ὁμοῦ καὶ γυμνίζων³ αὐτοὺς πρὸς ἀντίστασιν ἐχθρῶν. τοῦτο δὲ καὶ νοητῶς ὁρῶμεν γινόμενον· ψυχὴ γὰρ διὰ τῆς θείας συνεργείας ἀπαλλαγεῖσα παθῶν, εἰ πρὸς τὸ ῥᾴθυμον ὀλισθήσει, ὡς μηκέτι παθεῖν ὑποπτεύουσα, ὑπὸ τῶν ἀοράτων καὶ πονηρῶν πνευμάτων περιστοιχίζεται, δίκην (add θηρίων) αὐτῇ ἐπιθρωσκόντων, καὶ σφοδρότερον πολεμούντων· ὅθεν καὶ λόγιον ἡμᾶς διδάσκει μὴ πιστεύειν ἐχθρῷ⁴.

The following three passages remain unidentified amongst those published by Tischendorf from the Cairo MS.

Philonea p. 153. Also Cod. Barocc. 143 and Maximus II. 554.

Τοιοῦτος γίνου περὶ τοὺς σοὺς οἰκέτας οἷον εὔχῃ σοὶ τὸν θεὸν γενέσθαι· ὡς γὰρ ἀκούομεν, ἀκουσθησόμεθα, καὶ ὡς ὁρῶμεν, ὀραθησόμεθα ὑπ' αὐτοῦ· προενέγκωμεν οὖν τοῦ ἐλέου τὸν ἔλεον ἵνα τῷ ὁμοίῳ τὸ ὅμοιον ἀντιλάβωμεν. Matt. vii. [1]

Philonea p. 155.

Δοκεῖ γάρ μοι μηδὲν οὕτως ὁ θεὸς ἐμφανὲς ἀπεργάσασθαι μίμημα ὡς ὄψιν λογισμοῦ.

Philonea p. 156 and Maximus II. 559. If this is really Philo it is based on an earlier gnomic saying: for Curt Wachsmuth in restoring the primitive Byzantine Gnomologium from Democritus, Isocrates and Epictetus, quotes the sentence θεὸς δεῖται οὐδενός· σοφὸς δὲ δεῖται μόνου θεοῦ. I believe it is found in this form also in

Ὁ μὲν θεὸς οὐδενὸς δεῖται, ὁ βασιλεὺς δὲ μόνου θεοῦ· μιμοῦ τοίνυν τὸν οὐδενὸς δεόμενον καὶ δαψιλεύου τοῖς αἰτοῦσι τὸ ἔλεος, μὴ ἀκριβολογούμενος περὶ τοὺς σοὺς ἱκέτας ἀλλὰ πᾶσι παρέχων τὰς πρὸς τὸ ζῆν αἰτήσεις· πολὺ γὰρ κρεῖττόν ἐστι διὰ τοὺς ἀξίους ἐλεεῖν καὶ τοὺς ἀναξίους, καὶ μὴ τοὺς ἀξίους ἀποστερῆσαι διὰ τοὺς ἀναξίους.

Philo. For further references to Hippocrates, Sextus Pythagoreus, &c., see Boissonade, *Anecdota,* Vol. I. p. 45.

Philonea p. 155 and Maximus II. 556.

Πλέον ἀγάπα, βασιλεῦ, τοὺς λαμβάνειν παρὰ σοῦ χάριτας ἱκετεύοντας ἤπερ τοὺς σπουδάζοντας δωρεάς σοι προσφέρειν· τοῖς μὲν γὰρ ὀφειλέτης ἀμοιβῆς καθίστασαι, οἱ δὲ σοὶ τὸν ὀφειλέτην ποιήσουσιν τὸν οἰκειούμενον τὰ εἰς αὐτοὺς γινόμενα καὶ ἀμειβόμενον ἀγαθαῖς ἀντιδόσεσιν τὸν φιλάνθρωπόν σου σκοπόν.

The following remain from the Cod. Reg. 923.

Fol. 179 b ascribed to Evagrius in Dam. Par. 481 but to Philo in Cod. Reg. I do not think it is Philo.

In Cod. Barocc. it follows a passage given above from Tisch. *Philonea,* p. 153.

Λεία ὁδὸς ὑπὸ ἐλεημοσύνης γίνεται.

Fol. 305 b referred to *De Mut. Nom.*

Κοινωνικὸν καὶ οὐ μονωτικὸν ζῷον ὁ ἄνθρωπος.

Fol. 310 b *vide supra,* p. 88.

Μηδαμῶς τὴν φύσιν αἰτιώμεθα. πάντα γὰρ βίον ἡδὺν ἢ ἀηδῆ ἡ συνήθεια ποιεῖ.

Fol. 310 b referred to *De Virtutibus :* perhaps a lost part of the treatise against Gaius. It is added by Cod. Barocc. 143 at the close of a quotation from *De Decem Oraculis,* § 26 (II. 203). In Georg. Monach. (Migne *Patr. Gr.* 117 col. 1084) it is apparently given as Isocrates.

Δυσεκρίζωτος ἡ πλάνη ὅταν διαδράμῃ πολλῷ χρόνῳ.

Fol. 357 b following a quotation from the *Vita Mosis.*

Φιλοῦσιν οἱ ἄνθρωποι λόγους πλάττειν· ἡνίκα δὲ προφάσεως ἐπιλάβωνται μείζονας περὶ ὧν βούλονται φήμας ἐξάπτουσιν.

Fol. 358 b following a quotation from *De Decem Oraculis,* § 19. Something seems wanting to the sense of the passage.

Τίς ἔχει σφόδρα ἐμπρεπὲς ἀπαρατηρήτως αὐτῷ καὶ ἀδιακρίτως οὕτω διακεῖσθαι γλωσσαλγίας;

H.

14

The two following fragments remain unidentified among those published by Cramer, *Anecd. Oxon.* Vol. IV.

p. 243 e Cod. Barocc. 30 f. 74. The extract cannot be a genuine passage of Philo?

Τὸ δὲ μάννα ὁ Φίλων ἑρμηνεύων ἔφη τοιαύτην αὐτοῦ εἶναι τὴν πιότητα, ὥστε κατὰ τὴν φαντασίαν τοῦ ἐσθίοντος μετα-κιρνᾶσθαι καὶ εἶναι μὲν καθ' ἑαυτὸν οἰονεὶ κέγχρον ἑψημένον ἐν μέλιτι· παρέχειν δὲ νῦν μὲν ἄρτου, νῦν δὲ κρέως καὶ κρέως τοιοῦδε ἢ πετεινοῦ ἢ χερσιαίου, νῦν δὲ λαχάνου, τοῦ κατὰ τὴν ἐπιθυμίαν ἑκάστου καὶ ἰχθύος, ὡς τὸ ἰδίωμα τῆς καθ' ἕκαστον γένος πιότητος, ἀκριβῶς δὲ καὶ τῇ γεύσει τοῦ ἐσθίοντος διασώζεσθαι.

p. 254 Cod. Bodl. Clark 11.

Τὸ μὴ αἰσχύνεσθαι κακὸν ὄντα κακίας ὑπερβολή.

The unidentified passages in Maximus and Anton Melissa I have not thought it worth while to print.

The following passages in the Burney Catena are unidentified.

Fol. 35 b. At the close of a passage from II. *Quaest. in Gen.* § 15 is added (not Philo but Procopius in the Leipsic Cat. I. 144):

Οὐκ ἐπειδὴ τῷ δημιουργῷ τὰ μὲν καθαρὰ τὰ δὲ ἀκάθαρτα· τὸ γὰρ ἄνω φησὶν ὅτε τὰ ζῶα παρήγαγεν ὁ θεὸς " καὶ εἶδεν ὁ θεὸς καὶ ἰδοὺ πάντα καλὰ λίαν·" ἀλλὰ παρ' ἡμῖν καὶ τοῖς τότε καθαρὰ ἢ ἀκάθαρτα καλούμενα καὶ νομιζόμενα· καὶ γὰρ καὶ θεοὺς τῶν ἐθνῶν ὀνομάζει τοὺς δαίμονας· οὐχ ὅτι εἰσίν· ἀλλ' ὅτι οὕτως προσαγορεύονται.

Fol. 36 b. Φίλωνος ἐπισκόπου.
Also in Cat. Lips. I. col. 151.

Ἑβδόμῃ καὶ εἰκάδι τοῦ μηνὸς ἐξηράνθη ἡ γῆ· ἑβδόμῃ καὶ εἰκάδι τοῦ μηνὸς τοῦ δευτέρου ὁ κατακλυσμὸς ἔρχεται· καὶ εἰκάδι ἑβδόμῃ τοῦ ἑβδόμου μηνὸς ἐκάθισεν ἡ

κιβωτὸς καὶ εἰκάδι ἑβδόμῃ τοῦ δευτέρου μηνὸς καθ' ἣν ἡμέραν ὁ κατακλυσμὸς γέγονεν ἔξεισι Νῶε......ὡς εἶναι τέλειον ἐνιαυτὸν ἀκριβῶς ἀριθμούμενον· τοὺς μέντοι προειρη-μένους καιροὺς προσετάχθησαν καὶ Ἰουδαῖοι ἑορτάζειν.

The passage need not be Philo Judaeus, and yet one becomes very sceptical as to the existence of another Philo, following closely on the lines of the former, and so often wrongly placed for him. Is it possible that Philo Episcopus is the name given to an expanded edition of the original writer, with perhaps a few Christian glosses?

Fol. 37 b τοῦ αὐτοῦ (sc. Φίλ. ἐπισκ.).

Τόξον μὲν τεταμένον ἀπειλὴν βέλους ἀφεθησομένου σημαίνει· τὸ δὲ ἐν τῇ νεφέλῃ τόξον ὑπερθέσεως μὲν καὶ διαθήκης σημεῖον τοῦ μὴ κατακλυσθῆναι τὴν γῆν τῆς δὲ μελλούσης ἐναργὲς κολάσεως· ὅτι πρὸς τὴν μέλλουσαν τιμωρίαν ἀφορῶν ὁ θεός φησι, τὴν παροῦσαν ὑπερθήσομαι.

The passage, as in the Leipsic Cat. (I. 160), is attributed to the same author as the preceding quotation in the Cat., who is certainly Philo : but the reference to the "wrath to come" makes it pretty

clear that this second fragment is by a Christian hand.

Fol. 222. A passage is also added at the close of a long quotation from III. *Vit. Mos.* § 31 which does not however seem to be Philo, and I have accordingly omitted it, as no doubt might have been done with the preceding.

There are a few similar passages in the Leipsic Catena, e.g.

I. col. 105. Φίλωνος ἐπισκόπου· Διδύμους αὐτοὺς εἶναι ἀπὸ μιᾶς συλλήψεως, διό φησι πρόσκειται τῷ 'ἔτεκε Κάϊν' 'καὶ προσέθηκε τεκεῖν τὸν ἀδελφὸν αὐτοῦ.'

τὸν τοιοῦτον θάνατον· ἐπεὶ γὰρ ἐπλήσθη φησὶν ἡ γῆ ἀδικίας ἀπ' αὐτῶν· ὥστε οὐκ ἂν ἐνειστήκει εἰ μὴ ἡμάρτανον.

I. col. 137. Φίλ. Ἑβρ. Δῆλον δὲ καὶ ἐκ τούτου, ὡς οὐχ εἱμαρμένη αὐτοῖς ἐπήνεγκε

I. 141. Φίλ. Ἑβρ. Ἰδοὺ τοῦτό ἐστιν ὃ εἶπεν ἄνω· οὐ μὴ μείνῃ τὸ πνεῦμα ἐν τοῖς ἀνθρώποις τούτοις.

None of these passages seem to me to be Philo: they are ordinary glosses and nothing more.

The following passage is also referred to Philo Hebraeus in Cat. Lips. I. 397 :

Ἄγγελος ἦν ὁ παλαίσας μετὰ Ἰακὼβ καὶ οὐ θεὸς ὡς ἐνόμισεν ὁ Ἰακώβ· λέγει γὰρ τελευτῶν, ὁ ἄγγελος ὁ ῥυσάμενός με ἐκ νεότητός μου· καὶ αὐτὸς ᾔδει ὅτι ἄγγελος μὲν ἦν, θεὸς δὲ δι' ἀγγέλου εἰργάζετο· καὶ

εἶπεν, ἀπόστειλόν με· ὁ δὲ εἶπεν, οὐ μή σε ἀποστείλω καὶ τὰ ἑξῆς· ἆρα γὰρ ἀναχωρεῖν οὐκ ἠδύνατο; ἀλλὰ διδοὺς χώραν αὐτῷ εἰπεῖν· πάντως γὰρ ἤθελεν εἰπεῖν, ὤκνει δέ· λαβὼν δὲ παρρησίαν, φησίν, οὐ μή σε ἀποστείλω.

The remaining passages in the Catena, more than three hundred and fifty in number, are, with the most trifling exceptions, identified. The results, however, are not worth the space which they would take to record.

The following (Latin) passages in the Catena of Zephyrus I have not yet succeeded in identifying.

Fol. 110. Quis constituit te principem et iudicem super nos ?

Cervicosum hunc hominem fuisse autumant quem Moses pridie defenderat ab opprimente.

Fol. 187. *Num.* VIII. Quoniam dono dati sunt mihi a filiis Israel.

Nullius rei indigus atque adeo nihil accipiens, aliquid accepisse fatetur ut pietatem studiumque religionis imprimat

14—2

in animis nostris. Damus igitur ut accipiamus vicissim a Deo, sed ut illud improprie dictum est, ita hoc ex ipsa re verum arguitur.

Fol. 206.   *Num.* xxxv.   Ut fugiat ad ea qui fuderit sanguinem.

Non in templis sacrisque aperuit asyla, ne ab immundis inficerentur: neque rursus effugium dedit in loca quae deserta forent aut parum tuta, ne caedis invitae reus facile caperetur, tradereturve consanguineis defuncti, sed iubet ut ad sacras urbes Levitarum confugiat, ubi non modo se quisque facile credere poterat sed non parum quoque solatii percipere, videns apud eos confugisse qui praemium caedis a Deo ornatissimas urbes accepissent. Eos enim qui vitulum pro deo conflaverant, etiam consanguineos Levitae suis manibus volentes interemerant.

The following passages are referred to Philo in Georgidius Monachus (Migne, *Patr. Gr.* 117) but not previously quoted in these pages.

Col. 1116.   Μή σε καταπληττέτω τὰ τῆς ψυχῆς φυσήματα· εἴδωλα γὰρ εἰδώλων τὰ τῶν ἀνθρώπων τετύχηκε πράγματα.

Col. 1136.   Σοφιστείας ἔργον εὑρεσιλογεῖν, σοφίας δὲ ἕκαστα διερευνᾶν τῶν ἐν τῇ φύσει μετ' αἰδοῦς καὶ τῆς ἁρμοττούσης ἀποδοχῆς.

We shall conclude this book by printing the passages from Cod. Rup. to which reference was made on p. 102, and express a strong hope that some one will be able to furnish the necessary identifications.

f. 27.   Ἐπειδὰν ἡγεμὼν ἄρξῃ καθηδυπαθεῖν καὶ πρὸς τὸν ἀβροδίαιτον ἀποκλίνειν βίον, σύμπαν ὀλεῖσθαι δεῖ τὸ ὑπήκοον, τῶν γαστρὸς καὶ τῶν μετὰ γαστέρα πρὸς ἀναρρήδοσιν (l. προσαναρρηγνυμένων) ἔξω τῶν ἀναγκαίων ἐπιθυμιῶν· εἰ μή τινες εὐμοιρίᾳ χρήσαιντο φύσεως, ψυχὴν οὐκ ἐπίβουλον ἀλλ' εὐμενῆ καὶ ἵλεω κτησάμενοι· ἐὰν δὲ αὐστηροτέραν καὶ σεμνοτέραν ἕληται προαίρεσιν, καὶ οἱ λίαν αὐτῶν ἀκράτορες μεταβάλλουσι πρὸς ἐγκράτειαν, ἢ φόβῳ ἢ αἰδοῖ σπουδάζοντες ὑπόληψιν ἐμποιεῖν ὅτι ζηλωταὶ τῶν ὁμοίων εἰσίν.

Referred to *De Vit. Mos.*

f. 30.   Τὸ λέγειν ἄνευ τοῦ πράττειν ἀτελές.

f. 38.   Τὸ περὶ θεὸν ἁμαρτάνειν τοῦ περὶ ἄνθρωπον ἀφορητότερον.

f. 71.   Τὸ μέγιστον ἀγαθὸν εἰρήνη ὃ μηδεὶς ἱκανὸς ἀνθρώπων παρασχεῖν, ἐπεὶ θεῖον τοῦτο δῶρον.

Also in Anton Melissa, col. 861.

f. 72 b. Ἐκ τοῦ περὶ μέθης δευτέρου κεφαλαίου.

Ἀλήθεια ἐστὶν ἡ τὰ τῶν συνεσκιασμένων πραγμάτων ἀνακαλυπτήρια ἄγουσα δύναμις. Ἐκ τοῦ αὐτοῦ. Ἀλήθεια αὐταρκέστατος ἔπαινος.

f. 113 a. Ἐκ τῆς αὐτῆς (sc. ad Gaium).

Ὁ τῆς εἰρήνης φύλαξ, ὁ διανομεὺς τῶν ἐπιβαλλόντων ἑκάστοις, ὁ τὰς χάριτας ἀταμιεύτους εἰς μέσον προθείς, ὁ μηδὲν ἀποκρυψάμενος ἀγαθὸν ἢ κακὸν ἐν παντὶ τῷ ἑαυτοῦ βίῳ.

Ἐκ τῆς αὐτῆς. Οὐκ ἀσφαλὲς τοῖς βουλομένοις ἐπὶ τὸν πάντων ἡγεμόνα καὶ δεσπότην ἐκκαλεῖσθαι τὰ πράγματα.

f. 125. Ἐκ τῶν περὶ τῶν μετονομαζομένων.

Ὁ μηδέποτε ἐν ταὐτῷ βεβαίως ἱδρυμένος, ἄλλοτε ἀλλοίας δεχόμενος μεταβολὰς καὶ ὑποσκελιζόμενος, δυστυχής ἐστιν· ὄλισθος γὰρ σύμπας ἐστὶν ὁ βίος αὐτῷ· κάλλιστα γοῦν εἴρηταί τινι

βέβαιος ἴσθι καὶ βεβαίοις χρῶ φίλοις.

f. 148. Νόμος οὗτος θεῖος· τὴν ἀρετὴν δι' ἑαυτὴν τιμᾶν.

Ἀρετὴ προηγούμενον φύσεως ἔργον ἀρχαῖον· Ἀρεταὶ μόναι τῶν ἀνθρώπων τὰ πράγματα ἐπίστανται.

f. 157 b. Ὅταν αἰτιᾶται δικαστὴς κρινομένου, ἀνάγκη σιωπᾶν.

f. 171. Φιλοῦσι τὰ ἁμαρτήματα ἀπὸ πλήθους ὄχλου (l. ὄλβου) καὶ εὐθηνίας τῶν ἀναγκαίων τίκτεσθαι.

f. 187 b. Τοῖς ἐντυγχάνουσι μὴ χείλεσιν ἄκροις οἱ θεῖοι νόμοι ἐλπίδας ἀγαθὰς δημιουργοῦσι.

f. 195 b. Ὦ διάνοια, δέξαι τύπον ἀκιβδήλευτον ἵνα περί τε ἀρχῆς τοῦ αἰτίου καὶ ἀγαθότητος ἀναδιδαχθεῖσα καρπώσῃ κλῆρον εὐδαίμονα, γνώσῃ δὲ εὐθὺς καὶ τὴν τῶν ἀκροτάτων δυνάμεων σύνοδόν τε καὶ κρᾶσιν· ἐν οἷς μὲν ὁ θεὸς ἀγαθός, ἐμφαινομένου τοῦ τῆς ἀρχῆς ἀξιώματος, ἐν οἷς δὲ ἄρχων, ἐμφαινομένης τῆς ἀγαθότητος· ἵνα τὰς τούτων ἀπογενομένας ἀρετάς, ἀγάπην καὶ εὐλάβειαν θεοῦ κτήσῃ, μήτε ἐν οἷς πάσχεις ὑψηγοροῦσα διὰ τὸ τῆς ἡγεμονίας τοῦ βασιλέως μέγεθος, μήτε ἐν οἷς ὑπομένεις τι τῶν ἀβουλήτων ἀπογινώσκουσα τὰς ἀμείνους ἐλπίδας δι' ἡμερότητα τοῦ μεγάλου καὶ φιλοδώρου θεοῦ.

f. 196 b. Τῷ ἔνδον οἰκείῳ δικαστηρίῳ πᾶς ἄφρων ἁλίσκεται.

Also Anton Melissa, col. 1213.

f. 200 b. Τοῖς ἀγαθοῖς ἀγαθὰς ὑπέχειν ἔοικε γνώμας ὁ θεὸς δι' ὧν ὠφελοῦντες ὠφεληθήσονται.

Also Anton Melissa, col. 1077.

f. 213 b.   Φίλωνος ἐκ τοῦ περὶ μετονομαζομένων.

Πόνος μὲν τοῖς συμφέρουσι, ῥαστώνη δὲ τοῖς βλαβεροῖς ἔπεται· πόνου δὲ ῥαστώνην προκρίναντος (l. προκρίνοντες) τοῖς τὰ συμφέροντα εἰσηγουμένοις ἀπεχθάνονται.

Again on f. 142, and Anton Melissa, col. 1128.

f. 218 *bis* b.   Ἐνέχυρον οὐ μικρὸν ἀψευδίας αἰδὼς ἡ πρὸς θεόν.

Ἔστω οὖν ὁ λόγος ἰσότιμος ὅρκῳ· οἷς δὲ ὀμνύναι τίς ἀναγκάζῃ (l. ἀνάγκη), μαθέτωσαν ὡς ἐστιν ὅρκος μαρτυρία θεοῦ περὶ πράγματος ἀμφισβητουμένου.

f. 244 b.   Φεύγετε πᾶν τὸ ἡδὺ ὅτι βιαίως παρακαλεῖ.

Also Anton Melissa, col. 824.

Οὐκ ἔστι τῶν ἱσταμένων καὶ ἠρεμούντων ἡ ἡδονὴ ἀλλὰ τῶν κινουμένων καὶ ταραχῆς γεμόντων· ὥσπερ γὰρ φλογμοὺς κινήσει, οὕτω φλογμοῦ τινὰ τρόπον τὸ πάθος ἐν ψυχῇ κινούμενον ἠρεμεῖν αὐτὴν οὐκ ἐᾷ.

f. 247.   Θυμῷ μάλιστα δεῖ κυβερνήτῃ χρῆσθαι· καταλειφθεὶς γὰρ ἀκυβερνήτης ἄνω καὶ κάτω κυκώμενος ὑπὸ σάλου καὶ κλύδωνος τὴν ψυχὴν ὅλην καθάπερ ἐνορμάτιστον (l. ἀνερμάτιστον) σκάφος ἀνατρέφει (l. ἀναστρέφει) συναναστρέψας καὶ τὸ σῶμα.

f. 249.   Γονέας τίμα· οὗτος γὰρ νόμος θεῖός τε καὶ φυσικός.

f. 257.   Οὐδενὶ τῶν φαύλων ἐπιστὰς ἔλεγχος δι' ἡδονῆς ἐστίν.

Also Anton Melissa, col. 1153.

f. 261 b.   Ἀπὸ ἑνὸς συνετοῦ συνοικισθήσεται πόλις.

Οὐκ ἔστιν ἀντάλλαγμα πεπαιδευμένης ψυχῆς.

f. 267.   Ἐκ τοῦ περὶ μέθης. Τίς τιμῆς ἢ ἀρχῆς καταπεφρόνηκε; σχεδὸν τῶν ἔτι πεφυρμένων ἐν κεναῖς δόξαις οὐδεὶς τὸ παράπαν.

Also Anton Melissa, col. 1184.

f. 274.   Αὕτη τρυφὴ ψυχῆς ἀσκητικῆς ἥδιστον ἀντὶ πικροῦ τὸ πονεῖν ὑπολαμβάνειν.

Also Anton Melissa, col. 1124.

NOTE. In *Quæst. in Genesim* XIX. 14 emend κρατούμενοι to καρπούμενοι and compare Plato, *Phædrus* 251 E; *Legg.* I. 636 D; *Rep.* VIII. 548 B, IX. 586 E; *Conviv.* 187 E.

CAMBRIDGE: PRINTED BY C. J. CLAY M.A. AND SONS, AT THE UNIVERSITY PRESS.

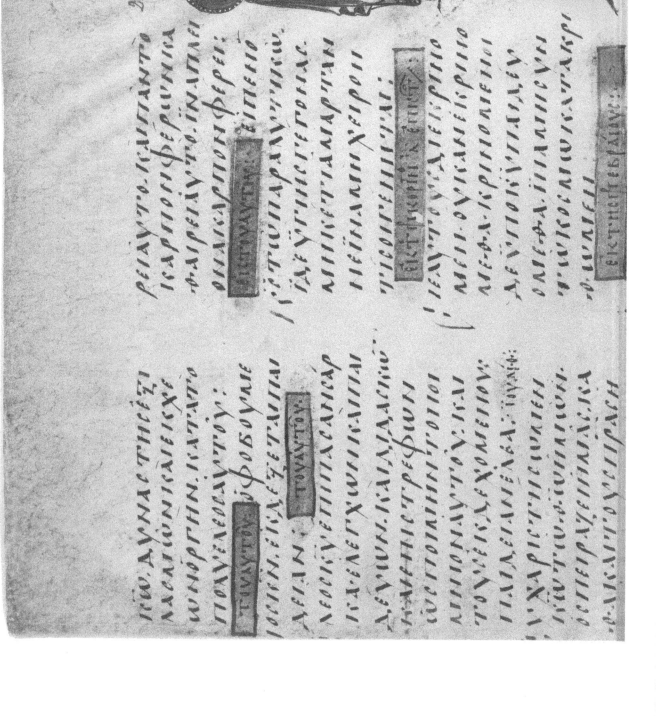

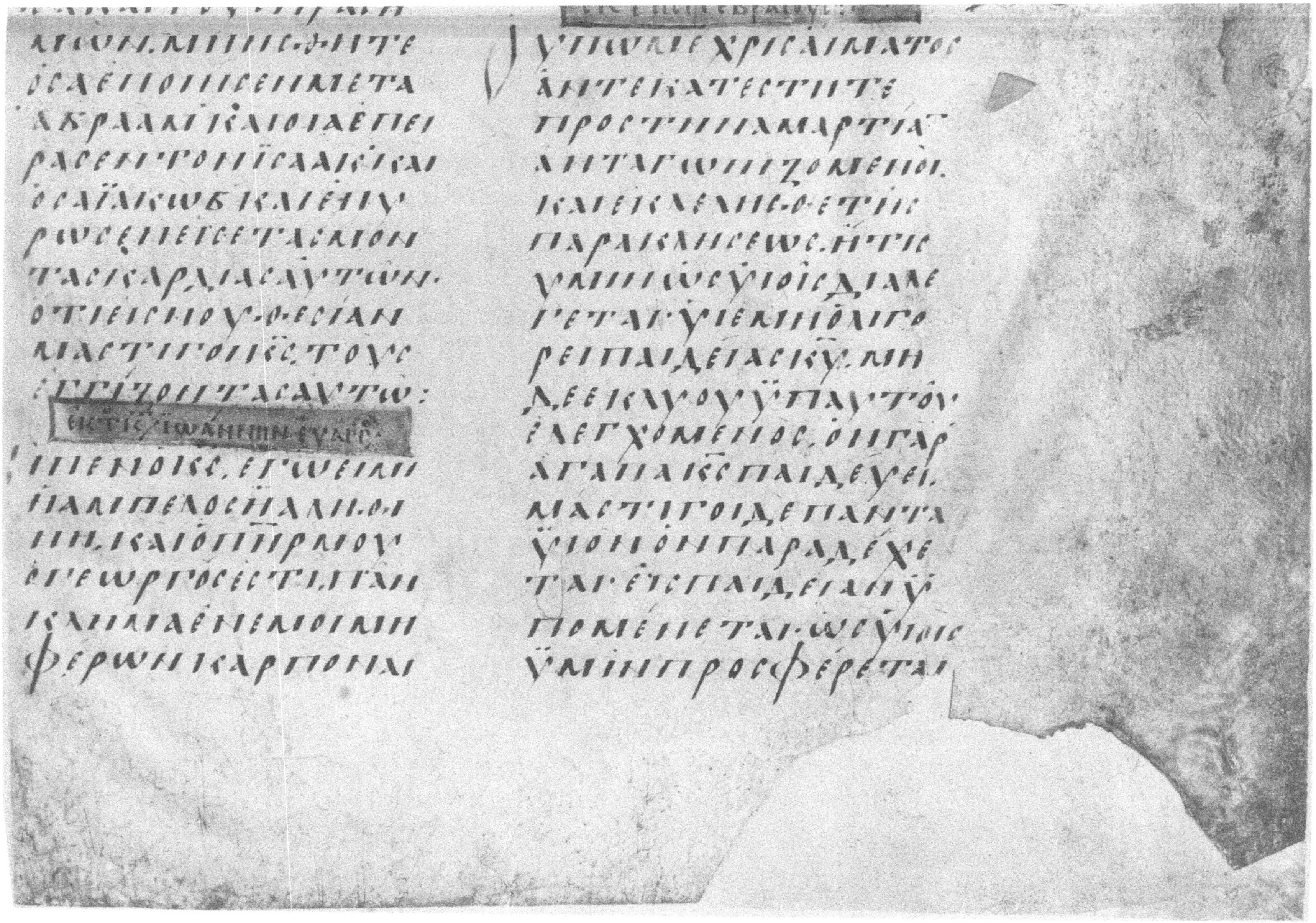

COD. REG. 923 fol. 260.

For EU product safety concerns, contact us at Calle de José Abascal, 56–1°,
28003 Madrid, Spain or eugpsr@cambridge.org.